Conversations with
Legends from the Disne
Theme Parks, Movies,
and Television

The
DISNEY
INTERVIEWS

Volume I

LOU MONGELLO

Published by Second Star Media, L.L.C.

13506 Summerport Village Pkwy. Suite 327, Windermere, FL 34786

Copyright © 2020 Lou Mongello and Second Star Media

All rights reserved. No part of this book may be reproduced in any form or by any means, electronic or mechanical, including photocopying, recording, or by an information storage and retrieval system, without written permission from the publisher or author, except in the case of a reviewer, who may quote brief passages embodied in critical articles or in a review. This ebook may not be reproduced or copied except for the use of the original purchaser.

Limit of Liability and Disclaimer of Warranty: The author and publisher have used their best efforts in preparing this book, and the information provided herein is provided "as is." Lou Mongello and Second Star Media, L.L.C. make no representation or warranties with respect to the accuracy or completeness of the contents of this book and specifically disclaims any implied warranties of merchantability or fitness for any particular purpose and shall in no event be liable for any loss of profit or any other commercial damage, including but not limited to special, incidental, consequential, or other damages.

Trademarks: This book identifies product names and services known to be trademarks, registered trademarks, or service marks of their respective holders. They are used throughout this book in an editorial fashion only. In addition, terms suspected of being trademarks, registered trademarks, or service marks have been appropriately capitalized. Use of a term in this book should not be regarded as affecting the validity of any trademark, registered trademark, or service mark. Neither the author nor the publisher makes any commercial claim to their use. Lou Mongello and Second Star Media, L.L.C. is not associated with The Walt Disney Company, or any other company, product or vendor mentioned in this book.

This book is unauthorized and unofficial. It has not been reviewed by The Walt Disney Company or any other company or individual referenced to herein, and is in no way authorized, endorsed or approved by the company, its sponsors, partners or affiliates.

TABLE OF CONTENTS

Dedication	v
About Lou Mongello	vii
Introduction	1
The Disney Interviews	3
Ralph Kent	5
George McGinnis	27
Alice Davis	49
Dave Smith	87
Julie Andrews	109
Richard M. Sherman	121
Charles Ridgway	161
Marty Sklar	191
Bill "Sully" Sullivan	209
Tom Nabbe	229
Al Konetzni	263
Lonnie Burr	281
Conclusion	306
There's More...	308
Get Even More!	318

WALT DISNEY

DEDICATION

First and foremost, This book is dedicated to YOU, my friend, the reader. Not only would this book not exist without you, but it is because of you that I am blessed with the incredible opportunity to do and share what I love every day.

It is thanks to you that I was able to leave my career as an attorney, completely shift my trajectory, and pursue my passion for something I truly love. I am so grateful for your love, support, and friendship. You might not realize it, but simply by virtue of you reading this book and listening to the WDW Radio show, you are an important, cherished, and valuable member of our community. Because of you, I was able to get to know everyone who I interviewed on the show and in this book. As a Disney fan, they are literal dreams come true, and I hope that you enjoy these conversations as much as I did. I say and believe this to be true, and hope you do as well... We are friends, whether we have met yet or not.

To the countless dreamers and doers at the Walt Disney Company, including the Imagineers and Cast Members who clearly love what they do, and bring the magic to so many people each and every day.

To my mom and dad... It is not an overstatement to say that I owe everything to you. From the moment I was born, through every. In my life, through every success or failure, you were there to guide, love, support, and teach me. I could fill every page of this book with the reasons why I need to thank you both... I am the person that I am today because of you. I only hope, as I always have, that I make you proud.

To my brother, Fred, who has shared with me so many good times and bad, (as well as monorail rides), is both my trusted friend and someone who I know will always be there for me. We'll always be kids at heart.

This book is for, and because of, my always oh-so-very-supportive wife, Deanna, and my incredible children, Marion and Nicolas. Everything I do, I do for you... And none of this would have been possible without you. From that very first conversation where I said, "I'm thinking about writing a book..." and through every difficult and wonderful step of the way, you have always been there to stand behind everything I do. All of you have always been so understanding of my often hectic and crazy schedule, "research trips," and ups and downs throughout this journey. The best part of it all, is that we have been on this adventure together... And I know the best is still yet to come. I hope you are proud, and that I have been a good example to and for you. Whatever you want to do, whatever you want to be, wherever you want to go, anything is possible with passion, patience, and persistence. You're all amazing. I love you, and this book is for you.

The opportunity and ability to share this book is a gift to me.

So from the bottom of my heart... Thank you.

ABOUT LOU MONGELLO

"When I get home, I shall write a book about this place..."

ALICE IN WONDERLAND

OK, so I never really said that. Actually, I never planned to write a book about Walt Disney World at all... let alone **four** books, seven Audio Tours, 600+ podcast episodes, countless live videos, events, lasting memories, and hopefully, having a positive impact on the lives of others.

My journey to this book has been a long and very circuitous one. The (very) condensed version of the story goes like this:

Everything I have done (and do) about Disney comes from a love and passion for a place that has meant so much to me throughout my life. At the age of three, my parents took me for the first (of many) times to Walt Disney World, in November, 1971, just a few weeks after the park opened. My father took a photo of me, bad hair and all, on the curb of Main Street, USA in a place which has come to be known affectionately to me as "The Spot", and from that moment on, I was hooked.

Fast forward to 2003, when I wrote my first book, the Walt Disney World Trivia Book Volume I, after setting a personal challenge for myself to see if I could write a book and get it published. I wrote the book I wanted to read, one that didn't exist, and would allow me to do something with all of the "useless knowledge" I had about Walt Disney World floating around in my head. I started a web site (DisneyWorldTrivia.com) and community in 2004, and in 2005, I started podcasting.

By 2007, I had left my law practice and the IT consulting company I had started in New Jersey, to pursue my passion, and share my love of Disney with others... full-time. Just a year or so later, I took a huge leap of faith, sold my house (at a huge loss), put all our stuff into storage (pro tip: sell it all before you move!), moved to Florida (to rent a house I hadn't even seen before), to take a chance and see if I could turn what I love into what I do.

Since that time, my life has changed in incredibly wonderful and profound ways... thanks to you.

My podcast, WDW Radio (WDWRadio.com), has been awarded Best Travel Podcast for 9 consecutive years, and in addition to a second Walt Disney World Trivia Book, I am also the author and publisher of another book, 102 Ways to Save Money for and at Walt Disney World book, free guide of 102 Things To Do at Walt Disney World at Least Once, as well as seven guided binaural audio walking tours of the secrets, history, stories, and details of Magic Kingdom in Walt Disney World. (Available at WDWRadio.com/Shop). But the most important part of what I do is, remains, and will always be our fun, friendly, and welcoming community, and it is thanks to you.

As an early adopter of many media platforms, I have been fortunate to be able to connect with our large, loyal and heavily engaged community via a variety of social networks and live events.

Recognized as an authority on Disney, podcasting, live video, community, and social media, I have been fortunate to have been featured in USA Today, The Wall Street Journal, The Associated Press, People Magazine, the BBC, Bloomberg Business, CBS News, Atlanta, Parenting Magazine, Readers' Digest, Fodors, and numerous others, and been named as one of the Top 40 Social Media Influencers, Top 100 Digital Marketing Experts, Top 50 Social Media Influencers, and Top 50 Social Media Experts.

I am also the founder of The Dream Team Project, which has raised more than $350,000.00 to send children with life-threatening illnesses to Walt Disney World through the Make-A-Wish Foundation of America. Learn more at DreamTeamProject.org, and find out how you can help, and have some fun as a member of the WDW Radio Running Team by visiting WDWRadio.com

I am also a keynote speaker, coach, and consultant who shares with businesses, associations and schools the magic of Disney and/or the power of new and social media, entrepreneurship, brand-building, storytelling, podcasting and more. In my desire to help others, I also provide mentoring and consulting to those looking to build their business and brand, and turn what they love into what they do, and host my Momentum Weekend Workshop and Retreat in Walt Disney World. To learn more and see how we can work together, please visit LouMongello.com

I never could have imagined when I came up with the idea for that first book down in my basement where this all would have led. I am truly blessed to be able to share my love of Disney and passionate entrepreneurship with you.

I hope you enjoy this book and the interviews in it as much as I enjoyed writing it.

Thank you.

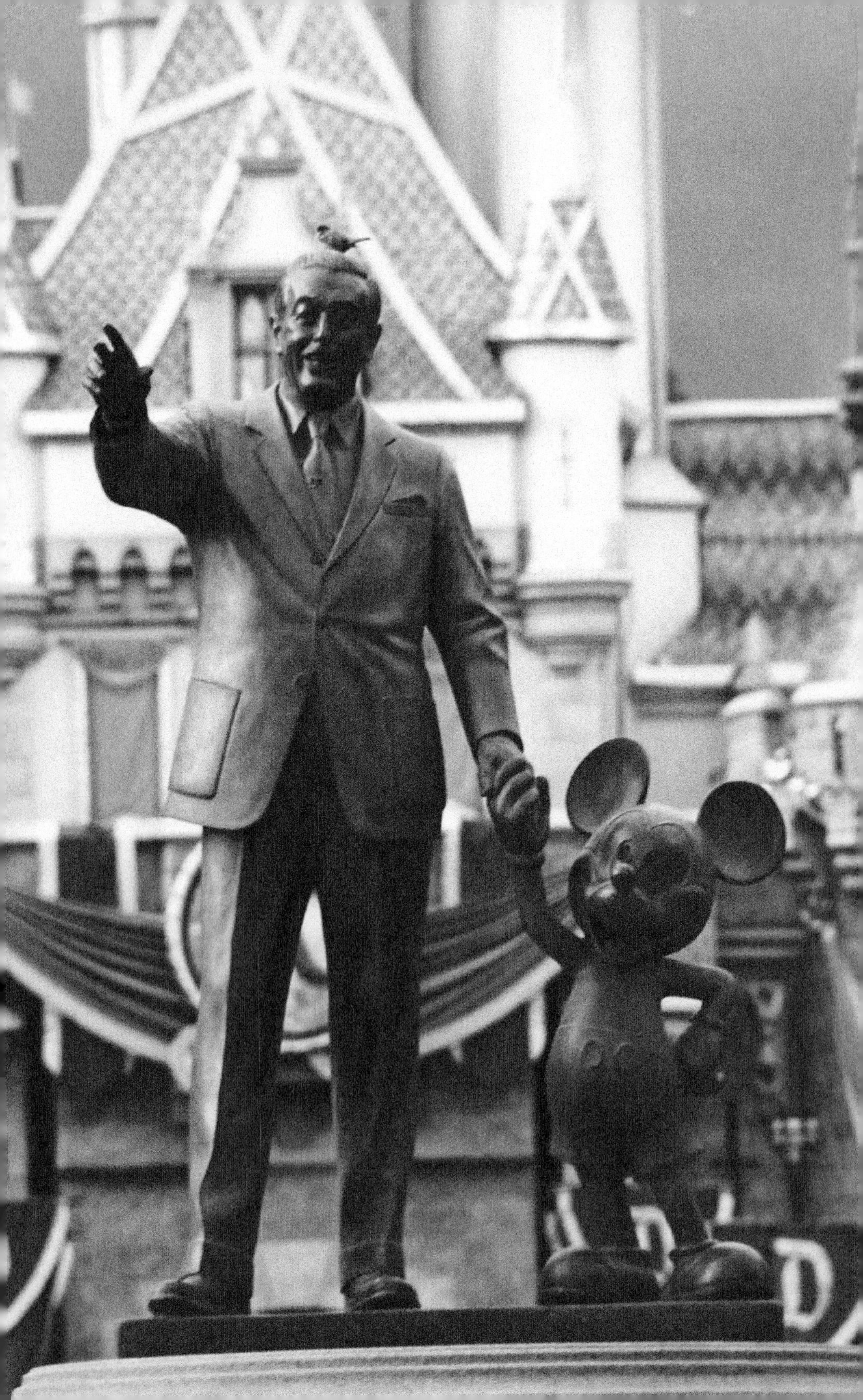

INTRODUCTION

*"You can design and create,
and build the most wonderful place
in the world. But it takes people to
make the dream a reality."*

WALT DISNEY

One of the greatest joys and blessings of being able to do what I do with my WDW Radio podcast has been able to meet, interview, and in some cases, even befriend some people whose work I have enjoyed and respected for so many years… In some cases, even going back to my childhood.

This book is a compilation of just some of the interviews I have conducted since I started podcasting in early 2005. I reach out to people I want to interview for the show out of a personal interest and desire to speak with people whose work has brought me such great joy. I always felt that it didn't matter if anyone else even listened… it was just such a personal honor and thrill to be able to speak with them.

In most cases, I simply sought them out, reached out, and explained what I wanted to do. In every case, everyone was so agreeable, friendly, and made me feel at ease, no matter how nervous I may have been on the inside (I cleared the house and had 3 recorders going simultaneously when I interviewed Julie Andrews! When the interview was over, and we were saying our goodbyes, I almost broke down in tears when she said, in her practically perfect Mary

Poppins accent, *"Oh, Lou... thank you so much."* I literally hung up, jumped up and screamed, *"MARY POPPINS JUST SAID MY NAME!!!"*)

I asked questions that I not only wanted to know the answers to, but asked ones I imagined you, a fellow Disney enthusiast, would want to know the answers to. I do these interviews standing in your place, and I hope you're happy with the job I did and the questions I asked. Believe it or not, I actually think it was my training as a trial attorney which hopefully helped me in terms of my preparation and lines of questioning and stories I hoped they would share.

I carefully select in these interviews to be included in this book, but also because each of them personally knew and worked for or with Walt Disney, or was instrumental in helping to preserve his legacy and history. They all share individual stories of how Walt influenced their lives and careers, many through his personal trust, guidance, and friendship. I hope that you, like me, can imagine those conversations taking place in your mind's eye, just as I did as they were recounting them to me.

In typical Disney fashion, every one of the individuals in this book completely over delivered, and far exceeded my expectations. I hope they do for you as well.

Their emotion, joy, and the passion truly comes through, and I hope that you enjoy reading these interviews as much as I did conducting them.

The DISNEY INTERVIEWS

Conversations with Legends from the Disney Theme Parks, Movies, and Television

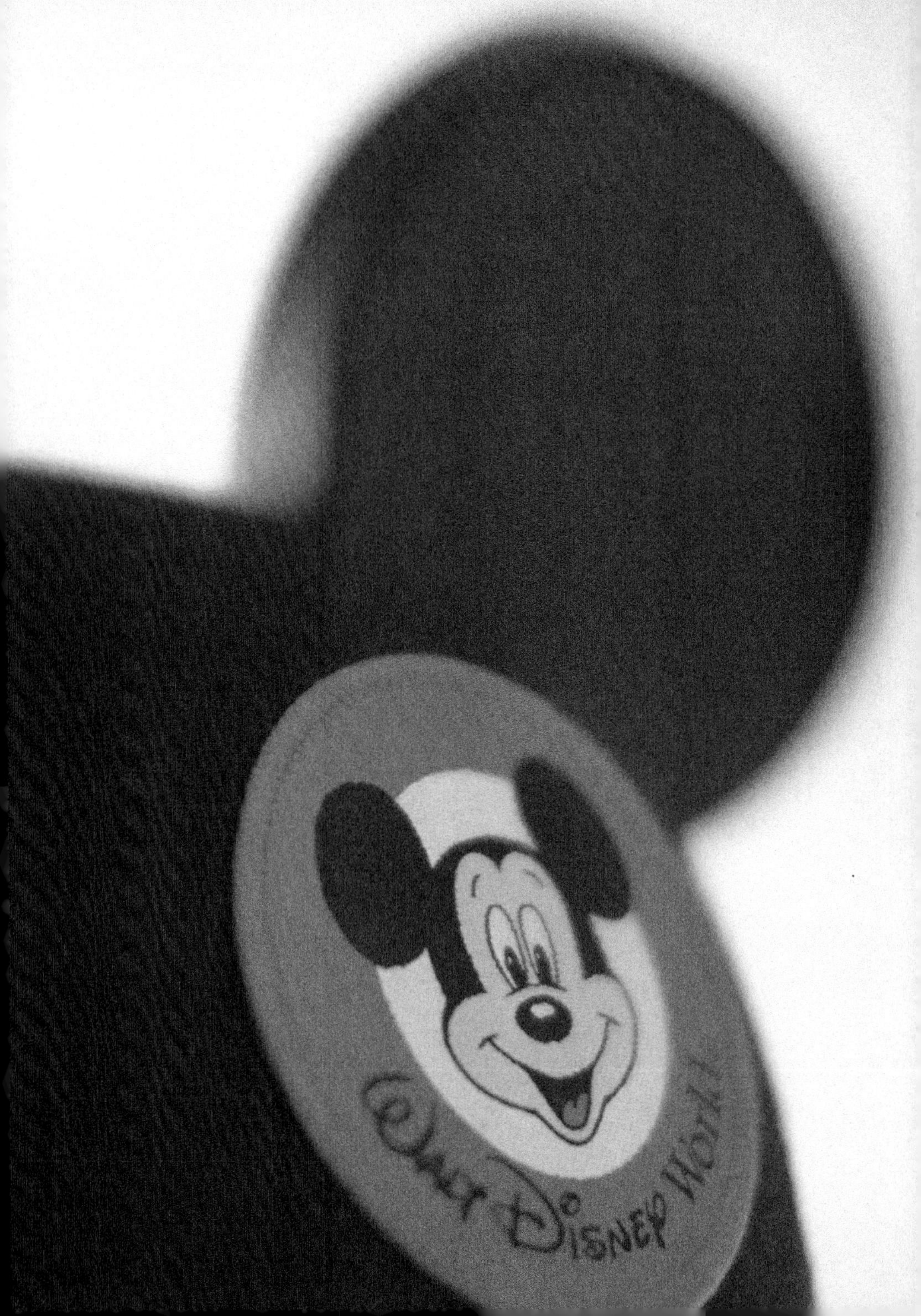
Walt Disney World

Ralph Kent

Born Ralph Kwiatkowski on January 28, 1939, Ralph Kent realized his childhood dream and met and worked for Walt Disney. Enamored with Disney animation after seeing "Pinocchio" while a child in New York, he instantly became attached to that character, including his innocent sense of wonder and awe. At 10 years of age, he painted the basement walls of his home with a mural of Disney characters, including Alice in Wonderland, Cinderella, and of course, Pinocchio.

His love of Disney and the films inspired him to write a letter to Walt Disney, and one to which Walt personally replied.

Ralph attended the University of Buffalo Albright Art School, and in 1960, joined the U.S. Army, illustrating military training aids and films.

In 1963, his greatest dream was finally realized when he was hired as a marketing production artist for Disneyland, in order to develop marketing materials for the Jungle Cruise, Enchanted Tiki Room and other classic attractions. When he finally had a chance to meet Walt Disney in person, he referred to the letter from the "kid from Buffalo." Walt not only recalled the letter, but asked Ralph why he hadn't approached him sooner, to which Ralph replied, "I was just in awe of you, and still am."

Ralph later went on to create training materials for attractions at the 1964–1965 New York World's Fair, and spent time as director of Walt Disney Imagineering East, overseeing Florida staff support for EPCOT Center and Tokyo Disneyland. He worked with fellow Legends Van Arsdale France and Dick Nunis, creators of Disney University, developing training materials for the Company's four attractions featured at the 1964–1965 New York World's Fair, including it's a small world. He also served as art director to Celebrity Sports Center in Denver, which Walt co-owned with celebrities including Art Linkletter and Jack Benny

One of Ralph's greatest personal achievements was the creation of the first limited-edition Mickey Mouse watch in 1965. Originally designed for 25 of Walt Disney's top executives, it sparked the creation of countless other watches being created for sale to Guests.

In 1971, Ralph moved on to creating souvenirs for Walt Disney World, and in 1979 became Director of Walt Disney Imagineering East. He later became Corporate Trainer for the Disney Design Group, teaching the new artists the finer points of character model drawing.

Ralph retired in May, 2004 after 41 years with the Company, and was named a Disney Legend that same year. He was awarded with one of Disney's highest honors—the dedication of a window on Main Street, USA in the Magic Kingdom. His window, which is over Casey's Corner and faces Cinderella Castle, and appropriately reads, "The Ralph Kent Collection: Fine Arts and Collectibles. Anaheim, Lake Buena Vista and Tokyo."

In 2005, I had a chance to meet Mr. Kent and visit with him at his home. In what was an amazing and memorable experience, I had the chance to sit and chat with someone whose work was worthy of his status as a Disney Legend. I also conducted an interview with him for my first podcast (the now-defunct MouseTunes), podcast where he shared wonderful stories about working with Walt Disney, as well as his accomplishments in Walt Disney World, including Epcot, and work at the Disney Design Group.

The late Marty Sklar, Disney Legend and former vice chairman and principal creative executive of Walt Disney Imagineering (WDI), called Kent, "A real pixie... a big guy with a soft manner and always warm smile."

I considered Ralph and his wife to be friends, and was saddened by his passing in 2007, and am honored to share my conversation with Ralph with you in this book.

Lou Mongello: For those of you who don't know, a Disney Legend is a program that was established back in 1987 and that basically is to acknowledge and award a lot of the people who work for Disney whose talents and dreams really created that magic. They give the awards out every year in a ceremony at the Walt Disney Studios; they are chosen by a selection committee led by Roy E. Disney, and they honor everyone from Animators to Imagineers to Songwriters, Actors, anyone who really has had an impact on the Disney Family. If you go out to the Walt Disney Studios you can see they now have a Disney Legends Plaza that has bronze sculptures and plaques and things like that. They give different Legends different kinds of awards and things like that.

I was able, thanks to some of our friends in the Disney community, to be introduced and welcomed into the home of a Disney Legend, and this Disney Legend is Ralph Kent. And, above and beyond just being a Legend, he has a window on Main Street. I know for me, and for anybody that works for Disney, that really is the highest honor that I think that you can get. In fact, not only does he have a window on Main Street, but I think he has one that's in a very special position in that it faces Cinderella Castle. For a long time, Walt Disney's was the only name; they did add another window on top of Casey's Corner that included Tony Baxter and some other Imagineers. Well, Ralph Kent has his own window right next to that on top of Casey's Corner facing Cinderella Castle.

I'm going to let Ralph really talk about his career, but he has done everything from develop marketing materials, he worked with Dick Nunis and Van Arsdale France at Disney University; he worked as an Art Director at the Celebrity Sports Center (you may recognize that as something that was co-owned by Walt with people like Art Linkletter and Jack Benny. That's where the original Walt Disney World cast members were trained.) He also worked at Walt Disney World; he designed tons of souvenirs. Chances are if you own a souvenir, Ralph Kent had a hand in it. He later became the Director of Walt Disney Imagineering East; he was a trainer at the Disney Design Group. The list goes on and on. He oversaw the staff for Epcot Center and Tokyo Disneyland; he has just an incredible resume. He worked with the company for 41 years and retired in May 2004 and received his window.

I am pleased and honored to be welcomed into the home of Disney Legend Ralph Kent. His career at Disney is so storied and so impressive that it is really hard to know where to begin. Mr. Kent, first I want to thank you very much for inviting me into your home and doing this interview with us.

Ralph Kent: My pleasure to be here, Lou.

Lou: Your career at Disney is so long I don't know where to begin so let's start at the beginning. (Ralph laughs.) Why don't you start by telling us about your early background — pre-Disney days?

Ralph: Pre-Disney — and this story has been told so many times, now — when I was a little boy, my grandmother used to take us to see the movies during the holidays. And I saw the Disney movies, I saw Pinocchio and Bambi and all of those. We'd go to lunch after a while, and here we were these little 4 or 5 year olds being treated like little adults. One day I turned to my grandmother and said "You know, someday I'm going to work for him," and she said "Who?" And I said "Mr. Disney." And she said "Mr. Disney?" And I said "Yeah." She said "Well, why don't you write him?" Now, I was 8 years old at that time, and I said "He's not going to take time to write to this little 8 year old from Buffalo, NY." She said "If you want to work for him, you write to him now." So I did, and, luckily, I got an answer back from Walt. He encouraged me to go to Art School and everything. First thing he said was "I don't have any openings for an 8 year old right now, but if you're serious..." and then he went on to tell me what I should do. And every time I wrote him he said "I promise I'll write you back."

Lou: Wow. So you actually received a letter from Walt on more than one occasion.

Ralph: Oh, yeah.

Lou: Do you still have those letters, do you save those?

Ralph: Yeah. (Laughs.)

Lou: That must be an incredible keepsake for a number of reasons.

Ralph: Yeah, yeah.

Lou: I read, and I had known, that you did have this fascination with Pinocchio; you kind of identified with the character himself and, from what I understand, always wanted to be Geppetto. And, judging from the room we are sitting in it seems that that may have come true at some point.

Ralph: Yeah, I have a workshop out back that I just restored and revamped. You know, it went through some hurricane damage, but now it's up and running. As soon as I'm up and running, I'll be out there making toys and games and things like that that I always wanted to do.

Lou: That's great. Let's go back to your childhood just a little bit, because one thing I did read was that, at age 10, you had done something to the basement in the home in which you had lived

Ralph: My cousin, who is a couple years older than I, had a boyfriend who was a commercial artist. And in her basement he had painted some oil paintings on the wall. As soon as I saw those, I looked in my basement and got out my little Tempera Colors — at that time they were called Poster Paint — and then I decorated our basement walls with Mickey Mouse and the Cinderella characters, because that was just about the time Cinderella came out, with Gus and Jacque. And Alice in Wonderland was out around that time, too, all in that early 50's time frame. I actually did take some Super 8 movies while I was back up home. Now the house is gone, but I do have that on film.

Lou: It's too bad that the mural was taken down by a subsequent owner.

Ralph: No, the whole house was demolished. The whole neighborhood was renovated.

Lou: Too bad, too bad. It sounds like that is where you got your start, maybe with your love...

Ralph: Yeah, about when I was 4 years old I saw a book with a little pencil drawing of a deer on it, and I was always fascinated by it so I took it and I copied it. And that's when I started drawing. And then some friends of mine used to draw out of comic books—and this is when I was real small—and so I got Disney Comic Books and I lay on the floor and I'd start doing the Disney Characters, and that was all part of the beginning of it.

Lou: Well, without jumping ahead, that definitely sounds like the dream of everybody that works for Disney. They start out by drawing it on the floor of their parent's bedroom somewhere and eventually have a window on Main Street. Tell us a little bit about your formal training in art.

Ralph: Then I had 4 years of Art School in High School. There are only 2 in the State of New York that has a 4 year course in the arts. And I had sculpting and three dimensional design and all that. Then from there I went on to the University of Buffalo Albright Art School, which was off campus. It was a gallery in its own right, and we had many famous paintings there. So I had another four years there. And while I was going to school I was working in an art department in a big printing house, a big lithographic house. And so I worked in that department for them; I started in paste-up and went through the whole works, doing the camera work and the stripping and all that. So I had a good basic knowledge of production and what it took to get a printed piece made.

Lou: Now, in the 60's, you joined up with the army and did some illustration of training aids, correct?

Ralph: Right. Training pamphlets and books and then also some films.

Lou: And you were discharged in '63?

Ralph: In '63, right.

Lou: How did you go from the U.S. Army to working for the Mouse?

Ralph: Drove directly across the country, packed up everything I had. I pulled up to, well, my wife's grandparents lived in Whittier, CA, and so we stayed with them for a couple weeks. Then I finally got on the Throughway and went up to Buena Vista Boulevard in Burbank—and my knees were rattling. But I did pull up to the Security Host and I said "Hi, my name is Ralph Kent, and Mr. Disney is expecting me." (Lou and Ralph laugh.) And he said "Sure he is." I said, "No, you don't understand. Just call him and he'll let me in." So, the Security Host said "Look, right now we are laying off in animation, and the whole industry is down," and he said "Why don't you come back in about 3 years and things will get better." So, my whole world collapsed around my feet. While I was in Burbank I hit all the other studios, too. The only one that I got into actually was Warner Brothers; and I was filling out the application and the young lady said, "By the way, do you belong to the Cartoonist's Union?" And I said, "No." And she said, "Hmm. Well, keep filling out the application. But, all these other people that are being laid off will have to be hired back before we can even consider bringing you on."

So, from that point on, everybody I met I asked them if they worked for Disney. And, if they didn't, do you have a relative that works for Disney? Do you have a neighbor that works for Disney? Do you know anybody that works for Disney? And, finally, I met a painter that worked at Disneyland and he painted the Shooting Galleries, and they would paint them every night. And he knew the guys in Marketing, and he said "they're looking for a part-time artist for about 3 weeks." I said, "Well, yeah, let me go interview... I just need a foot in the door." And so I met Jack Lindquist and Charlie Boyer, who was one of the guys that interviewed me, and worked for them for the three weeks. Then they said their goodbyes and they said if they had more work they'd call me back. And that Monday, they called me back: and that was 41 years ago.

Lou: And the rest, as they say, is history.

Ralph: Well, yeah, they finally put me on part-time, 'cause they kept bringing me in and laying me off, bringing me in and laying me off. And Van France finally went to Dick Nunis and said "Why don't we make this guy permanent, because we're spending more money wasting on the paperwork that it's taking to process him." So, we did, and I worked for Van and Nunis on the World's Fair. And for Marketing, my first job was marketing invitations and promos for the Tiki Room that just came out, and also the elephant wading pool (they put in a new addition to the Jungle Cruise). And then from there, I went on to doing the training materials because of my background with Disney—I had every piece and article that was ever written about the studio and Walt: I knew it inside and out. And so they said, well, you have such knowledge of the history of the company; this would be a good spot for you. Then we started what is known as the Traditions Program, which is now the University of Disney and Disneyland and Walt Disney World.

So I worked on the World's Fair, that was '64, '65. And then, when that was over with, they put me in the Merchandise Division. Nunis didn't have any need for an artist anymore; he thought we were too highly paid. (Laughs.)

Lou: I'm sure you thought otherwise...

Ralph: Yeah. It was $125 a week. So, Jack Olson in Merchandising was a friend of Van, so they put me in that department. We had two guys at that time. And then everything grew from there. Every time they needed anything, we were support to the whole park. Whenever they'd need artwork or anything, they'd come to the art department, of course. And we got into the display business because the guy who was doing our windows in the Emporium, they had so much work to do that they couldn't devote all their time, full time, to Disney windows. And Card Walker wanted to promote our films in the windows. And the first film that we had to do — and we had a couple months to do those windows in the Emporium — was the One and Only, Genuine, Original Family Band. Now, these were actors: Buddy Ebson, Leslie Ann Warren, John Davidson, and so we didn't have the sculpting facilities at the time. So we took plywood and we painted them realistically so they looked like the actors and actresses, which was another thing with getting permission to do that and paying royalties. Then we stuffed the clothes with cotton and we went out and bought little prints from all the material shops we could find so we could put everything in scale. From there on, we started to do all the animated windows.

And, back at Disneyland, they weren't meant to have those displays in them. And the temperatures got over 130 degrees, so we'd have to experiment with rubber flex for the skin and things like that. Actually, we worked it out here at Walt Disney World through the University, UCF. And we worked with them, and they developed a self-skinning urethane that we could put over our matures that would bend and not crack. So, we eventually ended up doing the, in the castle at Disneyland, we did the walkthrough diorama there with all the different scenes from the movie, and the big Maleficent and the Dragon. And, for the neck we had a great big vacuum hose that was pliable and we built the skin around that and it would shoot the fire out, the simulated fire. (Laughs). It was an experience; it was flying by the seat of our pants.

Lou: Well, it definitely worked and, like I said, the names that you mentioned and the products that you mentioned and the access to the information that you must have had is just incredible, especially to Disney fans like us.

Ralph: Oh, an anecdote to that Security Host story: A year to the day, I had access with Walt's approval to go to the Studio and talk to the head of any of the departments that I wanted, and so I rolled up to the gate and there was the same Security Host and I said "Hi, I'm Ralph Kent, and Mr. Disney's expecting me. (Laughter) And I never told him that I was there a year ago. And we became good friends, and I still never told him how he turned me away that one day, but that was very ironic.

Gosh, I had worked there for a year and a half, three years, and we had a sports complex in Denver, CO, and it was a gourmet restaurant and it had an Olympic size swimming pool, 80 bowling alleys, a big Rathskeller room, in which we took huge barrels, they had to be 12 feet in diameter and we cut the ends off and made booths out of them, and those lined the Rathskeller, and they served pizza and beer and all that stuff in there. Versus the gourmet restaurant which was on the other side. And it seems like a strange combination to have a bowling alley with a gourmet restaurant. The Olympic size pool was so big, we had publicity in there, and we had a water skier up there on skis being towed by a 16 foot outboard.

And it was all glass enclosed. And this is Denver, CO, so in winter time you had all the snow out there and things like that. And we had an underground garage that we turned into — Walt wanted — slot car tracks; they were big in the early 60's. So we designed three of the largest tracks in the country, and... I'm going blank as far as the company... Aurora built the tracks for us. And just as we got it finished — they were great, it was all family-oriented and each station that had the driver there, he could pull out this workstation and then you could repair your cars and all that stuff and you had all the tools to change your tires and do whatever. And, just as we finished and we put a shooting gallery downstairs, 'cause we owned McGloshen Guns, which manufactured our shooting galleries for us, and Walt was forced to get out of that business because of bad publicity: the Vietnam War was on, and people thought we were gun runners. (Lou and Nathan laugh). So, we ditched McGloshin. And one time, you know everything was metal, and that painter I told you about, they had to repaint the galleries because they had lead shot on metal targets. But, for this other gallery that we built the owner wanted a Plexiglas pirate ship. So we built it for him, and, needless to say, it didn't last long. (Laughter). It was shot to pieces.

And, see, that was one of Walt's favorite, one of his favorite places. It was called Celebrity because Burl Ives and Joan Crawford and Art Linkletter and Jack Benny all had a part of it, and Walt finally bought them all out. But it was a nice getaway for him, and it was a few hours by our company plane from Burbank over to Denver.

My boss, Jack Olsen, was the Art Director on it, and I would go up there with him, and we'd pick out new carpeting, if we needed, in the game room. And I learned such things as when you have a game room, in the carpeting pattern you put black. And that's so when they drop the cigarette butts on the floor and they burn a hole, it's not noticeable. So, he didn't like the idea of having to spend all of that time alone with Walt on the plane, and Walt could ask him all these questions about 'how's business,' 'what's going on.' And so he said, "Look, from now on I'm taking over administration." He says, "Nobody listens to an artist in this place anyway. You take art direction and you got Denver, too."

So, in the restaurant we had a lounge. And one night I was talking with Walt, and I said "Hey, Walt, do you remember a little kid from Buffalo, New York that used to write to you?" Now, I had a long Polish last name, it was Kwiatkowski. And it was hard to pronounce, hard to spell, nobody ever got it right so I changed it, legally, to Kent on my way out of the Army on my discharge, so they changed all my government papers and stuff like that. And so Walt looked at me and said, "Little kid from Buffalo... there was a little Polish kid with this long last name." I said, "Yeah! That's me!" And he raised his eyebrow like he always does and I went "oh, I'm in trouble." And he said "Why didn't you tell me this before!" And I said, "Well, I was in awe of you, and I still am now!" And I always was.

You know, we had a great relationship. It was like a father and son when, actually, he could have been my grandfather. But, anyhow, he always called me "kid." And we just laughed the rest of the evening and told stories and stuff like that.

Lou: Ralph, you also designed one of the first Mickey mouse watches. Tell us a little bit about that.

Ralph: Yeah, we used to go to... right across from Disney was a place called the Jolly Roger, and it had a lounge in it. Jack would go up to Burbank either to WED Imagineering or to the Studio and get all of his business then. And he'd come back and fill us in at night. And one time he came in and he said "Remember the old Mickey Mouse Watches for kids and the arms used to go <sound effect of moving arms>." And I said "Yeah," and he said "If I made one, would you wear one?" I said, "Yeah, but you're talking to the wrong guy: this is a Disney Nut. I'm a Mickey fan!" He said, "Well, look, what I want you to do is go back tomorrow and design one for adults, and we're going to show it to Walt, we're going to take it to him... see how he likes it."

So, we did, and Jack came back and he said "Walt likes it so well, he wants 25 electrics made. And what he's going to do is give them out to his top executives." So, we did, and Hamilton made the watches for us. And, as always, I forgot to put the copyright on it. So before we could go any further, we had an engraver come in and on the back of the metal case he engraved: Copyright, Walt Disney Productions. And so Walt passed them out, and I got the 25th one because I designed it. And it was the first time an adult watch was made.

And then we went to Helbros, and they made the $19.95 watch that we sold at Disneyland. Now, we went to Ingersoll first — Timex — and they had the right of first refusal, but they did not want to gear up for such a short run for a theme park, and make the hands and all of that stuff. So then Helbros did it for us. And, then as our execs — we always flew (separately), not only in a company plane, but commercially, too; so if anything happened, any of the planes went down we wouldn't leave the company stranded without any upper management. And so then we always flew first class, Walt said "I've got a First Class organization, I don't want any of my guys sitting in the back of the plane and somebody ask them 'Who do they work for' and they say 'Walt Disney.'" He said, "I want you up front." And so the stewardesses were first to see the watches and word of mouth spread, and then it took off. And that was 1966.

Then in 1969, Timex came out with a Mod Mickey Watch, and they took credit for the new adult watch that was on the market. The non-believers. We now do over 100 different designs a year.

Lou: How did you eventually come to Florida and to work for the Walt Disney World Parks?

Ralph: Well, one day I was talking to Walt, and he said "How would you like to work in Florida? How would you like to relocate?" And, at that time, we didn't know about Disney World. We were working on it, and when I was working on it we called it Project X. There was no location, and nobody was quite sure. Everybody was doing different little parts. So I said, "Look, I'll work any where you want me to. Do you want me to go to China?" And now we're IN China! And I said "Sure, I'll go." And he said "Well, I want you to double your art department right now. And then we're going to fly all of you guys out there with your families, and half of you can stay back here and half can move out there." And now, by that time we knew it was Walt Disney World. In '65 we announced it here in Florida, and Walt was here with the press and all that.

So, that's what I did. I went out and hired more people. Five of us decided to come to Florida, and the other five stayed back at Disneyland.

And from there we formed WED down here, the WED Imagineering Office. That was in '79; we had combined over 350 people. And that was artists, and craftsmen, and sculptors, and, then, all of our clerical staff—which was a big part of our operation; we couldn't have existed without their help and their being on the phones all day and helping us administratively. So from those five people we branched out. We ended up doing the Village, the Shopping Village, and designing that; designing the Empress Lilly, which we named after Lillian; and the Tree houses in the Village and all of that; that was all part of our group and it was done here in Florida under the direction of Imagineering in California. They were always the final say on everything that we did as far as the buildings and architecture and things like that.

Lou: You were the head of Imagineering East by this time?

Ralph: Right. The title was a Director at that time. And when we were doing Epcot, we would have meetings here and then go out to California for a week or two. We'd go out to resorts, get out of California, like Palm Springs and places like that. And then we'd have our timelines with construction, and everybody would go through their discipline. Of course, I'd go through what was going on with the creative staff. And, mainly, Imagineering here—80% of our job was support, supporting the California operation. But the reason I was even involved in that was because, by that time, I had been around so long I knew everybody and I had the contacts. So, if we knew something had to be done over here, I could make the phone calls and get that going underway.

Lou: Speaking of Epcot Center, considering that you knew Walt and worked with him so closely, and unfortunately his untimely passing in the late 60's: Having worked on Epcot Center — what it eventually became — how did you feel, knowing that it was so different from what Walt's original concept was?

Ralph: Well I knew that there was only one Walt, and it would never be what Walt realized. Only Walt could convince a government to have a city that would be totally under his control. It would not be a democracy. He did remarkable things, like coming down here he got Osceola County and Orange County to allow him to do Reedy Creek Improvement, which wrote all the building codes, and he convinced both governments that we would make them more stringent than any codes they had now in existence. So, he could do that. People believed in Walt.

I was sorry to see the city go because Walt never knew, really, what a great humanitarian he was. When we went to the World's Fair, he looked all the different countries, and he felt sorry for the little guys who only had little pavilions because that's all they could afford. And, what he wanted was what became World Showcase, and that still hasn't reached its potential. But he wanted facades that were all the same and then the interiors behind the façade could be as big as the country wanted. But what he wanted them to do was showcase their latest technology. And not only from a technological standpoint, but from a medical standpoint. He wanted to get all of the top doctors in the world in one place to solve all the cures for these diseases that plagued us.

And, then that city, when Herbie Ryman painted the dome that went over the city, he did that over a weekend for him, but that was just to show a controlled environment. It wasn't really going to have a glass dome that big with skyscrapers under it. And nobody understood the concept until now today when you go into shopping malls that have amusement parks in them, and they're all enclosed in their own environment: that's what Walt was getting at.

And he wanted the monorail to go around that city to take you from one big distance to another. And if you were just going from one block to another, then you used the Peoplemover, and that was linear induction. No air pollution by either one. And then when you were on the ground for a pedestrian, then you could have the moving sidewalks or you could just walk on your own. Three layers down you'd have the deliveries; you'd have the cars parked on one level, all the trucks down on the lowest level, and you'd service everything from underneath the ground like we did in the Magic Kingdom.

The reason we did that is, when Walt would walk through Disneyland, he had the burm around it to keep the outside world out so when you're in Frontierland or Tomorrowland it was like walking into a three dimensional experience based on one of his movies. At 4:00, though, the stock boys would run through the parks and restock, because at Disneyland it's a false perspective—the floor on the bottom is only 7/8^{ths} inch scale and then it goes smaller and smaller. So, the windows on the second floor were on the floor and there wasn't any room for stockrooms up there or anything. And he said "You know, that breaks the illusion, I really don't like that. In Disney World we're going to change it." And so that's when he came up with the elevator systems to service it. And he came in to me one day and he said "I want you to go to Engineering and get the schematics and the elevations of Main Street and I want you to go from the Railroad Station to the Castle, and when you get to the Castle I want that two stories high off the ground. And so I did that for him, and then he had the Engineers look at it. They said, "You know, people are going to be walking up an incline, and it's a slight incline, but it's an incline. Older people, especially, are going to start to get worn out and they won't know why." So what he did was, here in Florida, when you get off the monorail you go down and then you come back up. And then actually, the ground floor of Disney World is the second story of the park, actually. And so what they refer to the basement underneath all of that is not a basement, it's the first floor because in Florida you can't go down because of the high water table. A couple of feet and you're in water. So, he had that way of solving all these problems. His mind just kept going all the time.

Lou: It's amazing to hear you and some of the other people who knew Walt speak about him the way you did. I've seen much of the concept art for the early designs of Epcot the City and for what he wanted the World Showcase to be, with the circles that would have the same frontage.

Ralph: Right, right.

Lou: Having worked with him like that—you mentioned before about being in awe of Walt and, by the same token, having a father-son relationship. Did people have more of a reverence for him and an admiration for him, or was it more of a camaraderie kind of experience?

Ralph: Well, let's see… they had the greatest respect for him. And a lot of people were afraid of him because he was a hard taskmaster. If he knew you could come up with something more than you did, that your potential was greater than you were performing, he was very disappointed. And the last thing you wanted to do was disappoint Walt, just because of the person he was. There was a great camaraderie; we were smaller then. And when you were talking about my association with him, actually I only knew him for a couple years, and, those times, I didn't not see him or work with him on an everyday basis. I took opportunities when they arose to gleam as much as I could and pick his brain and stuff. (Laughs) But there are a lot of other people in the company that had much more experience with Walt per se than myself: I'm just a little Johnny-come-lately in the company. Actually, I was in the middle. The guys had started in the 30's, and then we came along in the 50's and 60's, and — what we didn't know was we were pioneering a whole new industry called Theme Parks. And, with all my friends out there, in 2005 they all became Legends, all the people I worked with at Disneyland. And I always wondered why I got a trophy, because all these Greats are in there. I had mine the year before, but I was in with the WED people that worked on the World's Fair, too. But when I saw all the Disneylanders, I said "Now I know what they're doing. They're giving awards to people who started out in the industry and started a new one." So, it started to make sense.

Lou: You actually led me to where I was going next. You can't downplay your career at Disney, everything that you did, including at the end of your career you were with the Disney Design Group as a corporate trainer, you did so much. You were with the company for 41 years and then, eventually, you received what I know we all consider the highest possible honor, which is to have a window on Main Street. And, actually, your window in my estimation even has a more prominent place because so few windows face the Castle. At one time, only Walt's did, and yours does as well.

Ralph: And it faces Walt and Mickey.

Lou: That's right; they face the Partners Statue, that's right!

Ralph: And, if you use your imagination, he's almost pointing to it!

Lou: Many people have speculated over the years as to what exactly Walt was pointing to. (Ralph laughs.) So, he's pointing to Ralph Kent's window, we finally have the answer! (Laughter)

Ralph: I doubt it! He's pointing to the Future, I know that.

Lou: I agree. The window actually reads... "The Ralph Kent Collection. Fine Art and Collectibles. Anaheim, Lake Buena Vista, and Tokyo." Obviously, all the theme parks that you had some sort of hand in.

Ralph: Right.

Lou: That's extremely impressive, and now, sitting in your home, I see the miniature version of it hanging in your bookcase. That is quite an honor, you should be very proud.

Ralph: And that's not too miniature! (Laughter.)

Lou: Yeah, I'm hoping you're going to turn your back for a few minutes so I can shuttle that into the car...

Ralph: It's heavy!

Lou: As your career with Disney wound down, from what I understand and looking around, I see that your fascination with Pinocchio still seems to continue.

Ralph: Yeah

Lou: You have a number of Pinocchio items in your case, and your woodworking here, your handiwork is very impressive as well.

Ralph: Yeah, Pinoc... that little naïve wonderment that he had as a little boy of the whole world and the way he'd just go "Wow" and "Oh." I identified with that so much.

Lou: I think a lot of us do. I think the people that really love Disney the way we all do, we kind of get that and we have that same kind of 'Wow' about so many of the things that, maybe you even as an Imagineer almost took for granted, the things that we see every day, the things that you people worked on—and you specifically—I know impress us all.

Ralph: Yeah, you really don't realize that you're doing anything special. You really don't. You enjoy what you're doing, and this is what you've always wanted to do. And then when you realize... like if you're on an airplane and you see somebody carrying something that you designed or wearing your shirt, a Goofy shirt or something like that... Somehow it's surrealistic. You can't believe that you're a part of it, but you are. You don't let that get in the way, you just... We had things to do. And you just go ahead and do them, and all of the sudden it's 40 years. And you go, Wow, where did it go to?

Lou: Before we came here, I had a million questions, and the more I have spoken to you, the more questions have come up. Really, it's an honor for me to be invited to your home. The work that you have done is appreciated, by not only me, but by millions of people. You have become Geppetto, in more ways than you think that you have.

Ralph: I'm honored to have you here. It's really a pleasure.

Lou: Well, again, Ralph Kent, Disney Legend. Thank you very, very much for your time and for inviting me into your home.

Ralph: Thank you.

George McGinnis sketch

George McGinnis

In 2007, I began a new series on my WDW Radio podcast, which I call, "Legends of Walt Disney Imagineering." In it, I interview and highlight the personal and professional careers of those individuals whose contributions to the Disney Parks, Resorts, Company, Film, and Television, warrant special recognition from those of us who continue to enjoy and appreciate their work.

My very first guest in that recurring series certainly qualified to bear that title and introduction as a legend (although at the time of this writing, he has not been recognized as a Disney Legend by The Walt Disney Company. The Disney Legends Awards is a program established in 1987, which recognizes individuals who have made extraordinary and integral contributions to The Walt Disney Company.

While attending the Art Center College of Design in Los Angeles, McGinnis' senior project was for a high-speed train that caught the eye of Disney. George was invited to work at WED Enterprises when he graduated in 1966, and began work on miniature transportation models for the Progress City display that was being created for the Carousel of Progress attraction.

George McGinnis was the last Imagineer personally hired by Walt Disney, and played a large part in the creation of the Mark VI monorail, Space Mountain in Disneyland and Walt Disney World, Horizons, 20,000 Leagues Under the Sea and countless other attractions and vehicles in Walt Disney World. In my exclusive, one-on-one interview, Mr. McGinnis shares stories of being personally hired by Walt Disney, the triumphs and challenges in creating such attractions as the WEDWay PeopleMover, Space Mountain, Communicore, the "Mighty Microscope" inside Disneyland's "Adventure Through Inner Space," and countless others. He reminisces about working with not only Walt Disney, but a who's who of Disney legends, including Dick Nunis, Marty Sklar, John Hench, Bob Gurr, Roger Broggie, Claude Coates, and so many others. It is truly something special that I think you're going to enjoy and was a personal privilege for me to do. And listen very carefully, as he also shares a secret about a change that is likely coming soon to one of his Walt Disney World attractions

Tom Fitzgerald, Creative Executive at Walt Disney Imagineering who served as a writer on the Horizons Pavilion, said, "He loved designing for Disney, and put his heart and soul into every project. From Space Mountain to Horizons, monorails to countless other ride vehicles, his imprint on Disney Parks was unique and timeless."

Disney Legend and former vice chairman and principal creative executive of Walt Disney Imagineering (WDI), Marty Sklar said of McGinnis; "George was a disciplined pro... a designer who truly paid attention to every detail." Sklar said in a statement: "I was just writing something about the Horizons pavilion in Epcot at Walt Disney World, and found this quote from George: 'We're convinced that even though environments will change, people won't. Teenagers in our show will still monopolize the phone; kids and dogs still exasperate mom and dad. We believe one of the main differences high technology will make is that it will give us more choices."

George wrote a book about his experiences at Walt Disney Imagineering that was published in 2016, "From Horizons to Space Mountain: The Life of a Disney Imagineer."

George McGinnis passed away in 2017 at the age of 87.

This interview is taken from my conversation with George on WDW Radio Show # 27, in August, 2007. You can listen to the full interview at WDWRadio.com/27

Lou Mongello: Today is one of those rare, very special opportunities where I'm fortunate enough to meet and speak with somebody whose work I've enjoyed and admired for so many years at Walt Disney World. His work is legendary and includes helping to create attractions in Walt Disney World such as Space Mountain, 20,000 Leagues Under the Sea, the Big Thunder Mountain Railroad, the WEDway People Mover, Spaceship Earth, World of Motion, Kilimanjaro Safaris, the Mark V and VI Monorails, and countless, countless others. And he's primarily responsible for Imagineering my personal favorite: Horizons. His work has extended beyond the theme parks into Disney feature films, and it continues to be enjoyed by millions of people worldwide.

So it's my distinct honor and pleasure and privilege to introduce a man who really needs no introduction, he is former Walt Disney Imagineer Mr. George McGinnis.

Mr. McGinnis, welcome to the WDW Radio Show.

George McGinnis: Thank you.

Lou: I have to not only thank you for taking the time to speak with me today, but I have to admit really what an absolute thrill this is for me personally to be able to talk to somebody who's so inherently instrumental in creating something that's such an important part of my life, and I really do appreciate it.

George: Thank you, Lou.

Lou: Mr. McGinnis, you really have one of the longest and most storied and, certainly, most successful careers at Walt Disney Imagineering. How did you begin with the company?

George: I was a student at the Art Center College of Design in Los Angeles. In 1966 I was finishing up my senior year and I did a transportation project that caught the eye — or the ear — of Walt Disney. The school Acting President was having lunch with Walt, and told Walt about my project. It was a high-speed train underground between Boston and New York and on to Washington, and it handled the way stations on the northeast corner with a shuttle that would zoom down; a linear motor powered shuttle integrated with the train, which had a station car in the middle and two 4-semi-circular compartments would rotate taking people on and off, with their luggage, in 8 seconds. And then the shuttle would return to, maybe, New London. And all the transfer took place in 2 and half minutes.

So, Walt came over to the school with Dick Irvine, the President of WDI (which was WED Enterprises at the time), Roger Broggie, Bob Gurr, who was responsible for the Monorails up until the Mark IV, and then John Hench was along. And, after Walt ran the train — it was a model that rotated the semi-circular compartment, and Walt invited me over to see the PeopleMover that Bob Gurr was designing, and they had a test track at that time. This PeopleMover was for Disneyland.

So, I started in June 1966, and I worked with… Walt had me do some special projects, and he died, unfortunately, in December that year. So, I had 6 months and about 6 meetings with Walt. And it was really a privilege, because he was so excited about everything he was planning. He had a love of design and entertainment.

Lou: Notwithstanding the list of people that he brought with, being as incredibly impressive as that is, what's it like for you when you're a student and somebody says to you, "Walt Disney wants to come over and see what you're working on?" I mean, what does that feel like?

George: I couldn't believe it. I had entered my train in the Alcoa project at the school, and my train came in second. I was a little disappointed. An aluminum garden cart came in first place. So, I told the Acting President, "I'm going to write to Time Magazine and tell them about my train." And a couple of days later, he told me that Walt wanted to see the train. He told Walt, "McGinnis will carry it over on his back," (Lou laughs). And Walt said, "No, I will come over." So that was very nice of Walt to show that interest.

Lou: Well, fortunately, one of your areas of interest and expertise was in the field of transportation and, specifically, trains, which we all know Walt had an interest and affinity in as well. And as you were talking about your initial project, you mentioned something that I think, for a lot of people, instantly raised a red flag which was "linear induction" type of technology. So some of your earlier work actually revolved around using that, and, again, on one of my favorite attractions: the WEDway PeopleMover.

George: Well, Bob Gurr did all the transportation for Disneyland. He was there from the beginning. I came 10 years later, '66, so Walt said "We could use another industrial designer at WED." And Bob Gurr told me that Walt said that in the car returning to the studio. So I joined. ... Actually, I started at the school as an automotive designer, and I switched to product design when I came back to the school in '64, and more diversity in product design. But, I did do a transportation project for the final project.

Lou: And your work on the PeopleMover wasn't just for the theme parks, correct? Because this was meant to be a real working transportation mode in Epcot — the city, not Epcot the Theme Park.

George: Yes, Walt had asked me to do a larger PeopleMover than the one planned for the Magic Kingdom, so I did that and — it was not my final design — but it's now running at the George Bush Intercontinental Airport in Houston. So, WDI did that with the Linear Induction Motor.

So Bob Gurr's PeopleMover at Disneyland, the quaint one with the tilting roof? (Lou acknowledges.) It was powered by rubber drive floats in the track against a Platon on the bottom of the train, a four or five car train. That worked well for Disneyland, it would get up and down hills and preview the shows along the way. Walt had a great idea there.

In Walt Disney World, because the linear induction motor had a very close gap that it had to maintain, didn't make grade changes. It was level all the way around. You may have noticed that.

Lou: How different was what ended up being in Walt Disney World from what possibly would have gone into Epcot the City, had it been built?

George: Well, the larger PeopleMover I designed would carry much more people. I did an illustration of the PeopleMover for Walt's so-called last film. It was the film he did to show to the Governor of Florida for promoting Epcot. I believe he showed that to the Governor in October, and I did illustrations for that film showing the

Monorail and the PeopleMover moving through the International Area, which became World Showcase, eventually. So that illustration is prominent in the film. In fact, they do computer graphics in the film of the area changing and being built in the computer. It's interesting. I think that's on the DVD just simply titled "Walt."

Lou: Right. I've seen the film before, and it's amazing the foresight and the engineering that was going to go into that, had it actually been built.

George: Yes, Walt was very interested in Victor Gruen, the architect from Vienna that is responsible for the "malling" of America. But Victor Gruen had these garden city ideas, and they were circular plans. So Walt's original plan owed much to Victor Gruen's concepts.

Lou: We're going to talk a little bit later on about some of the things that you did as far as attractions and, specifically, attraction vehicles. But your work wasn't just limited to that: you also did a lot of work on other transportation systems such as trams. But more importantly, I think, the design concepts on the current Walt Disney World Mark VI Monorails. You also had some work with the Mark IVs with Bob Gurr, correct?

George: Bob Gurr did four Monorails: Mark I, Mark II, Mark III, and Mark IV. And the Mark IV was done for Walt Disney World. The Mark III ran at Disneyland. Well, Bob left the Company and started his own business, and I kind of took over the transportation. But I spent about half my time on shows and half my time on ride vehicles. So the Monorail, Mark V, I designed it, made 12 trips to Germany following it through production, and then right on to the Mark VI for replacing the Mark IV at Walt Disney World. And I made similar trips to Bombardier in Canada on that production follow-through. So I did Mark V, Mark VI, and I started Mark VII, but then Bombardier reneged on doing such a small order. And I think the Mark VII for Disneyland is in design or maybe in production stage as we speak. But I didn't do the design; they're going back to a retro design similar to Bob Gurr's original Monorails.

Lou: Wow, interesting.

You also were very, very instrumental in the plans for Epcot Center, and, when it was announced, you actually became the Manager of Industrial Design for the entire park. What did that job entail for you?

George: Well, I wouldn't say I was instrumental in Epcot Center's planning. I was doing a lot of designs for the Magic Kingdom, but when Epcot started they knew they needed a lot more designers like myself. So they had me interview a bunch of students, recent graduates, from the same school I went to: the Art Center College of Design. And I recommended seven of them, and they hired them all. (laughter) So I told my boss, Marty Sklar, I was less interested in managing and more interested in design. So the managing of all the paperwork, I didn't have to handle it. It was handled by George Windram in Show Set Design. That relieved me of the time sheets and all of that.

So, I was designing on Horizons at that time. So, these young fellows came along, and one lady. They came along at the right time for handling a lot of details for the Communicore; I worked on many of the shows in Communicore, and these recent graduates were great at detailing the designs. In fact, we got into a little problem there, because these students were trained like I was: to do models, work between models and also, perhaps, drawings, and to come up with a design. So they produced detailed drawings. Well, the Model Shop had just changed to dimensional design; they were now designers rather than model builders. So when they received drawings from the Industrial Design Department, they complained that they were too detailed. They were used to sketches, and then they would build the models from sketches. So I got a little complaint from them that we were giving them too much design. They wanted to go back to the rough sketches, which they would interpret in model form.

Lou: You had mentioned, when we were talking about Epcot, exactly what I want to touch on next. We recently did something as part of an Epcot retrospective series on this show about one of my favorite attractions which is, unfortunately, now extinct and, I think, missed by many generations of fans, and that's Horizons. You developed some of the earliest concepts for the pavilion, including the multiple-screen Omnimax Theater and the ride vehicles, as well as one of the most memorable parts of the show: the ability to choose your own ending. Tell us about some of the things you designed for the pavilion.

George: Well, I started on the pavilion in '79 with Collin Campbell, and we researched a lot for the Edison Lab concept. Well, when we presented that to Reginald Jones, the Chairman of General Electric, he rejected it. He didn't want history; he wanted the future. So we went back to the drawing board, and, working with the General Electric Team and our own show writers, such as Tom Fitzgerald, we came up with a concept of Past, Present, and Future, with the Omnisphere handling the present.

Marty Sklar asked me to see if I could fit an IMAX into the pavilion. And I know Claude Coats was working on an IMAX concept, while I chose the Omnimax. And I had three screens circling around, and the vehicles would travel two times through the experience. Then, later on, when I had to reduce the size of the pavilion — Marty asked me to take $10 Million out of it; usually the engineers have to take $10 Million out. But, it shows how important the

Show Designer is to the cost. So, I took 600 feet of track out of the pavilion and didn't lose any story. The way I did it, my first design for the Omnisphere had three screens, as I said. I reduced it to two screens. And it went in at the bottom and it came out at the top to the level of the next scene after the Omnisphere. So, that was the biggest reduction in track. And then I combined two scenes, scrunched them into one scene in one bay, thus shortening the pavilion. And that, when you went through one side and you went through the back side, you were seeing the next scene.

And then I shortened the front of the building, making the pre-show and post-show very small. Now, we lost the post-show; I had done the post-show concept with Marc Nowadnick, but the incoming Chairman-to-be, Jack Welch, shot that down. So we only had a Bob McCall painting in the post-show, and I put three mirror illusions in the pre-show. So, all in all, the building became shorter in front in back, and two scenes combined, and a lot of track taken out of the Omnisphere. And I never heard whether we reduced it by $10 Million. That was not important to the Show Inventor. Just accomplish it, but never hear the details that resulted.

Lou: Not only did you cut it back in size while keeping the integrity of the story, but you were still able to get to the scheduled opening date of October First of '83, which is even more impressive.

George: Well, one of these things that I had done: the Omnisphere for the ending, the final ending, but the story team put it in the middle. So Marty asked me to come up with a "weenie," as Walt referred to them, for the ending. So I took something from the post-show that I showed to Jack Welch—traveling screens. I knew that there was an ability for projections to travel from one screen to the next. So I suggested that for the ending. I didn't come up with the idea of Choose Your Future; I came up with the technical concept. I offered an idea, which turned into the Choose Your Future.

Lou: One of the things for me was that Horizon really embodied so much of what Epcot as a whole represented on so many levels. It was representative of the themes of Epcot, and Future World specifically, and I think it was, really, the singular attraction that encompassed all of the themes of Future World. But I think, more importantly, it carried over the central themes of everything that Disney does, from its films to its theme parks and every form of entertainment — and that's the concept of family, and the importance of family.

George: Yeah. Some people said that the Horizons show should have been in Spaceship Earth, because it explained the reason for Epcot so well. So, that was someone's concept.

Lou: Yeah, and we talk about the connections to the Carousel of Progress, and, again, the whole idea of family transitioning to the next generation. Speaking of family, your own kids can be found on the attraction, right?

George: My kids were about 5 years old; my daughter was 7, my boys were 5. And Tom Fitzgerald suggested they could be in the scenes. So, Reed is the boy floating in the Space Shuttle that's docking, and Scott is the little boy with the seal licking his face in the undersea classroom, and Shauna is tapping her foot, with the long blonde hair. So, they did a good job on the kids, they did a good likeness. We always enjoyed that part of the show.

Lou: I couldn't imagine becoming a permanent fixture in Epcot and having an AudioAnimatronic.

Let's just stay at Epcot for a minute, because you created some special effects in Communicore, which you mentioned earlier, over at the Astuter Computer Review. Tell us what you created there.

George: Well, I laid out the show and the narrations and all that, and Tom Fitzgerald wrote the story. Tom and I worked on several shows, he being the story person and I being the show designer. But, the Astuter Computer Review, as it was called, had its beginnings in Alice in Computerland, a show that RCA was to produce, and John Hench did the concept. So, old concepts never die. So when RCA went out of the computer business, and they were to sponsor Space Mountain—which I was working on—Disney offered Space Mountain for them to sponsor. So Alice in Computerland died for a while, but it was reincarnated into the Astuter Computer Review for the Communicore.

Lou: And you did some of the effects for that, did you help design some of the special effects, specifically?

George: Yes, the major special effect was similar to the Haunted Mansion scene where you see the organist and the ghosts. We used the same effect, and it was very effective for the little dancing person on the computers. But Tom Fitzgerald secured the people for the parts and all; I laid out the... underneath the guests... where the monitors and all, the special effects were moving around, unseen by the guests.

Lou: Again, we're talking about some of the extinct attractions that you worked on. You worked on Dreamflight and Take Flight in the Magic Kingdom...

George: I did the storyboards for Dreamflight, and that's all I did. Larry Gertz followed that through.

Lou: You also worked on one of my favorite extinct attractions, and that's 20,000 Leagues Under the Sea, where you designed the actual ride vehicles, correct?

George: Yes, that was one I did very early on in my career. I'm very disappointed that they removed that ride and filled in the lagoon. Because it had as much, and maybe more, potential for a new show than the subs at Disneyland, where they put the Nemo ride in there.

Lou: You are not alone in your sentiments, I can assure you.

George: They never did a proper show for the 20,000 Leagues in Florida. They brought the show from Disneyland with minor changes, and it didn't relate to 20,000 Leagues Under the Sea, the movie. Can you imagine what they could do with that movie if they had wanted to? They brought, basically, the same show from Disneyland, just like they did the Pirates of the Caribbean. They had an all-new audience in Florida, so they didn't have to do a new show. But I think Michael Eisner missed the boat in taking out the 20,000 League's subs. Now, albeit they don't have a lot of capacity, and right now at Disneyland you wait in line for a long time. But it's a good show, and 20,000 Leagues could have had a wonderful show, based on the movie. That's my feeling.

Lou: I agree, being a fan of the attraction and a fan of the film. And it's unfortunate because it sounds—and, again, I haven't ridden Disneyland's Nemo Voyages yet—but it sounds like it's suffering the same issues that the Walt Disney World version was, which was accessibility, load times, the ability to get guests in and out of the attraction very quickly.

George: The sub rides?

Lou: Yeah.

George: Yeah. It wasn't a high capacity ride. But Walt didn't mind that. He wanted you to be entertained in the queue, and we always tried to make the queues interesting. As long as people are walking along, they are happy.

Lou: That's a good segue to talking about one of your greatest triumphs, I think, and one of the things you are most noted for, which is your work on a true classic attraction, and that's Space Mountain. And that must have been such an incredible project to work on for so many different reasons, from the engineering and the technical challenges to the concepts themselves.

George: Well, Walt Disney came up with the name. He is reputed to have said, "We have a Matterhorn Mountain, why can't we have a Space Mountain." And he assigned John Hench to do that. But it didn't come about for many years after Walt's death. I started on it in '71 for Disneyland, believe it or not. We had a 200 foot circle of space between substructures at Disneyland. So, I started on it and Bill Watkins, the engineer I worked with on many rides, he was responsible for the track design. Of course, I did a small wire model, and I showed it to Dick Irvine. It was a two track model that eventually went into Walt Disney World. And Dick Irvine looked at it. "Can it be more pyramidal?" Dick said. And so, shortly after that, they decided to put the Space Mountain in Florida after RCA became the sponsor.

So the track that was designed for Disneyland, although it wouldn't have fit in very well, was now going to be in Walt Disney World. So, in '71 Roger Broggie told me to go over to John Hench's office, and I did, and John put me on Space Mountain, told me have a pre-show and a post-show along a belt going in and a moving belt going out and have the load area at the back end. So, I laid that out, and Bill Watkins did the track around my show concept.

I went right on to Space Mountain for Disneyland after that, in '75. There had been some work done on it, showing the load area outside the mountain. Well, I gave a big challenge to the engineer. I took the load area to the bottom floor of that 200 foot circle, and I entered 30 feet above that. So the queue walking along, they saw into the ride, and the luminescent vehicles zooming around were the pre-show. And then they got into the load area 30 feet below the entrance. What I did was produce a headache for the track engineer; it got so tight at the bottom that, in order to get the vehicles back to the load area, they had to dig out some of the embankment and surcharge the foundation for Bill's track to make it back to the unload. I'm sure that boosted the cost of the Mountain considerably. They were hoping for a $1 Million structure. I didn't hear how much it cost, but I'm sure it went over because of that.

Lou: See, that's why they made you cut back on Horizons, because of all the money you spent on Space Mountain. (Both laugh).

George: Well, it's always the time to reduce costs.

Now, at that time, we didn't have project management, all the people that are concerned with that. Project management came with Epcot. Bill and I, the engineer and the show designer, worked together and we designed the ride. Later on, we had more people to make happy, with the project managers and bean counters.

Lou: One of the elements of Space Mountain that I believe you helped work on was the Star Tunnel. For a lot of people, including myself, it really is one of the most exciting parts of the ride; it's really very exhilarating in what you created there just as the attraction begins.

George: Yeah, I wonder if you mean the revolving tunnel that was to be on both Space Mountains, but ended up being at the end for the fiery re-entry. And the illusion of turning over didn't work in the 4 seconds it takes. You pass through that so fast there was no illusion of turning over. But that brings us to the Space Mountain that was re-designed for Disneyland that opened in 2005. I did the redesign on the vehicle, bringing the speakers into the seats and making the seats much more comfortable. That was the last real project I did as a consultant for Disneyland.

Now the Space Mountain at Disneyland has the revolving tunnel I designed for Walt Disney World, and then I designed it for Disneyland, and they put versions of it at the ending, but the effect didn't work. But it works very well at Disneyland now: you feel like you're turning over.

Lou: I have yet to experience it, but from what I hear the effect itself is incredible.

Back at Walt Disney World, as the park continued to grow and as the property continued to grow, you continued making some of that magic: a lot of the new ride vehicles over at the Studios as well as over at Animal Kingdom, you worked on the Studio Tram, the Honey I Shrunk the Kids play area, Kilimanjaro Safari, the Wilderness Express, the steam train, the Dinosaur—actually, the Countdown to Extinction—ride vehicle, as well as the Kali River Rafts. Tell us about some of the things you worked on.

George: Some of those things I worked on as a consultant after I retired in '95. I worked about 8 years as a consultant after retiring.

But, the Star Tunnel—back to that—the Strobe Tunnel that I put in to Walt Disney World's Space Mountain. When Space Mountain was for Disneyland, I wanted to make, after Dick Irvine asked me if it could be more cone shaped or pyramidal, I took Bill Watkins' track, and tried to make a cone out of it, letting the track go outside the cone. They were in the design called Satelloids by John Hench. He was disappointed that they finally went away when the design went to Walt Disney World, and we had a 300 foot cone that contained the whole track. But I did the Strobe Tunnel to get the vehicles to the front of the mountain before they went up the lift. And I called it the Strobe Tunnel... blinking lights.

Well, Tom Fitzgerald was a cast member of Walt Disney World at the time, over at Haunted Mansion. And he put in a suggestion that we add sound in the tunnel. I didn't think of that. So the tunnel has an ascending sound... ascending in that it always is going up. That was a wonderful addition. Now, Tom was interested in bringing the Strobe Tunnel to the new Space Mountain re-do at Disneyland. It's at the top of the first lift, you go in to the Strobe Tunnel and then you go into the Revolving Tunnel up the main lift. So, I hope your listeners come to Disneyland so they can experience that.

Lou: Yeah, again, from what I hear the enhancements are just breathtaking. And I know there've been rumors for some time that Walt Disney World may be getting some of those same enhancements as well.

George: Yeah... the man that did the special effects for Disneyland, Mayrand is his name, he told me he was working on Walt Disney World's Space Mountain, so I hope they get the same effects.

Lou: Wow. I do as well, again, from what I hear.

Back in the 80s, if I understand correctly, you were appointed by Marty Sklar as head of the Industrial Design Department. What was it like — and you alluded to this before — what was it like going from the hands-on approach to Imagineering and creating to more of the role of a Director?

George: Well, I don't know that there's much change. I was directing, as I said, seven designers. I kept on my job, and gave them jobs that came in. So we were all sort of on this same level, as far as I was concerned.

Lou: I have to admit that one of the accomplishments on your very, very extensive resume — and, again, we talked about your other work over at the Studios and the Animal Kingdom as Walt Disney World began to grow was actually the creation of one of my favorite characters from my childhood, and that was Vincent the Robot from the Black Hole movie. How were you recruited from working on Theme Parks to designing a robot for a feature film?

George: I did so many things, from the Rocket Jets, which was one of my first designs for Disneyland... even did the mailbox for Tomorrowland. Yeah, Peter Ellenshaw was our director on that film, the late Peter Ellenshaw, and he was doing a wonderful job but he was having problems with the robots. So, our Vice President of R&D was the astronaut Gordon Cooper, he was Vice President of R&D at WDI and he came over one day and, our offices were just around the corner from each other. And he said "George, I have Ron Miller in my office; we want to talk about robots for the Black Hole." Well, I went over with him and Ron explained he wanted a small, cute robot. Bob McCall was working on the film, and it was called Space Probe 1 or something like that, but Ron wanted to call it the Black Hole and have a cute robot. And I kind of argued with Ron, I said, "Do you want to compete with R2D2?" (Laughter)

I didn't want to, but he said "Yes, we're going to do a small robot." So I did the robots, all the robots, and my only screen credit. And it was quite a privilege. And the movie... Roger Broggie said that the robots were the best thing in it.

Lou: I have to agree.

George: I like that compliment.

I was Director-level at the end; I didn't know that, I wouldn't have known it because they never told me. A support person told me, "George, you can fly first class because you are Director-level. Do you mind not flying with the rest of the team?" I said "I have no problem with that." And so I was able to use my—we were getting triple points there with American Express and so I took my family on one of the trips to Munich, and we have wonderful memories of that.

Lou: The incredibly talented people that you were able to meet and work with at Disney is just mind boggling. The list is just a veritable Who's Who of Disney history, like you said, Dick Nunis, and Marty Sklar, and John Hench, and Bob Gurr, Michael Eisner, X Atencio, and, of course, Walt Disney. What was it like working with, and learning from, and, eventually, teaching people whose names are synonymous with making Disney Magic.

George: Well, you learn a lot of things from the people you work with. John Hench was always reminding us we were getting an education at Disney that we could get nowhere else. And I think that was true. The understanding of how important story is to an attraction. Having the success and momentum behind us with the successful attractions already built. And especially learning from the animators that Walt brought over to Glendale to design Disneyland: Herb Ryman, of course John Hench, X Atencio, and... I could name a lot, if I had the list in front of me. I had that list of Mahogany Row when I first started there. I wondered if I made a mistake—I left a job with the City of Los Angeles where I had a beautiful electric drafting table, all modern equipment... and they threw a 4×8 piece of plywood on two sawhorses and I had my drafting table. But I didn't realize how blessed I was: there was Marc Davis right beside me? And Chuck Myall, and Vic Greene, and Herb Ryman, and others who were right in a row. And they were just in a cubicle without a door. Dick Irvine had the only door on his cubicle where I interviewed with him.

I was in a perfect place to learn, and I remember Walt Disney coming in to see Marc the last time he visited WED. He went in to talk to Marc right beside my door, which was out in the middle of the floor. WED's only computer was to the right of me. And Ken Klug and Jim Cashen were working on the Monorail track on the computer. So I was right there, and the Architectural Department was one area adjacent to it and one of the persons who was very welcoming to me was Sam McKim.

Lou: Wow.

George: He was wonderful to bring me up to date on what it was like to work at WDI. He first informed me I didn't need to wear a necktie. Working for the City as a draftsman, I had more formal clothing. I came in after finishing at the Art Center, I had taken a leave of absence from the City. And, as I said, when they dropped down that sawhorse and the 4×8 piece of plywood I wondered "Did I make the right decision?" (Laughter) But it worked out wonderfully, I worked there for 5 months, for 6 months, and Dick Irvine sent me over to Engineering to work beside Bob Gurr, my office was next to his, and I learned <u>a lot</u> from Bob.

Now, 20,000 Leagues submarine: there's a story there. I like detail, and submarines had detail on the outside, and I was in the process of adding the detail to the inside, like the Grand Salon, as much as I could. Well, I passed Dick Irvine in the hall one day, and he said, "George, are you glossing the goose over there?" And I thought "Oh, oh, something's going to change..." And, sure enough, Roger took me off the project, put me on another, and Bob Gurr finished the submarines in the field. He went to Tampa Shipyards to follow through the construction.

Lou: Mr. McGinnis, just to wrap up, what do you think with all the accomplishments that you've done with Disney and elsewhere, what do you think your greatest accomplishment is while when you worked for the company, or what are you most proud of?

George: The Horizons Pavilion.

Lou: I was hoping you were going to say that!

George: Because we had a great team. Horizons opened late, and the best people were retained after Epcot opened, and they worked on the Horizons project. So, we had a great team with General Electric, their persons were fun to work with, and I think I, in coming up with the Omnimax, I gave basic form to the pavilion, and George Rester, the architect, gave it its design. I worked from '79 from the Edison Lab concept to when it opened. And we had a wonderful opening day experience in Florida. So that encompassed not only all the stories of Epcot, there were so many different areas of design in the pavilion and its special effects. I really enjoyed laying out the pavilion and saving $10 Million and all that went into it. It was the best and largest project of my Disney career.

Lou: Mr. McGinnis, there's so much more that you've done in your career at Disney that I know so many of us recognize and appreciate. And your creativity, and your talent, and your inspirational work embody the true definition of an Imagineer, as your imagination and your engineering created what was the essence of Disney Magic. I think that you faithfully carry on Walt Disney's values and his optimistic views, and you integrated them so well into everything you did throughout all the theme parks worldwide. Walt was quoted as saying that all he asked of his designers was that his guests leave with a smile on their face. And I can testify as being a guest that you have accomplished and exceeded that goal many times over, and I really want to give you my sincere thanks for taking the time today to share your stories with me and my listeners, and I hope to one day have the opportunity to meet you in person sometime in the future.

George: OK, Lou. Thanks much, and, if you get to California, I want to take you on the trolleys I've been designing.

Lou: I would absolutely love that, and I appreciate that offer. I will promise to definitely take you up on that.

George: Thank you, Lou.

Lou: Thanks, Mr. McGinnis.

George McGinniss sketch

Alice Davis

In 2010, I had the honor of spending the day with a fascinating woman and true Disney Legend, Alice Davis. Born in Escalon, California, in 1929, Alice received a scholarship to attend the celebrated Chouinard Art Institute from the Long Beach Art Association in 1947. The Institute was quickly becoming the renowned training ground for Disney artists, and it was there that she met her future husband, Marc, who was an instructor at Chouinard for more than 17 years.

In what I can only describe as a one of my fondest and most treasured personal Disney experiences, I was invited to her home, and we spent hours together not only touring her home and Marc's studios, but Alice also shared so many personal stories about each of the incredible pieces of memorabilia she and her husband had collected and displayed over the years.

In our interview, Alice discussed her fairy tale story of how she came to work for and with Walt Disney through her marriage to Marc Davis, one of Disney's Nine Old Men. In addition to discussing her relationships with both, we also closely examine her work on classic films such as Sleeping Beauty, and attractions such as it's a small world and Pirates of the Caribbean. Alice shares her very personal stories and humorous anecdotes about her work and life, from her early beginnings to the World's Fair, to her ongoing connection to Disney enthusiasts today. Alice was honored with a window on Main Street, U.S.A. at Disneyland, appropriately next to her husband Marc's, on May 10, 2012. Her window reads, "Small World Costuming Co.," "Alice Davis," and "Seamstress to the Stars," and includes an "it's a small world" doll dress from the famed Disneyland attraction.

This interview is taken from my conversation with Alice on WDW Radio Show #193, in October, 2010. You can listen to the full interview at WDWRadio.com/193

Lou Mongello: The name Davis is one that is synonymous with Disney magic and Disney legends. Marc Davis was extraordinary. Well, his wife Alice's accomplishments are equally as impressive. Her story is a true Disney fairytale from the fortuitous meeting of her husband and fellow Disney legend through her work on classic films such as Sleeping Beauty, and attraction such as it's a small world, and Pirates of the Caribbean. I am truly honored and privileged to welcome Disney Legend Alice Davis to the show.

Alice: Hello there. Glad to be requested to speak in front of your audience.

Lou: Well, before we get started, I can't tell you truly what a thrill this is for me on a personal level because of the admiration and the appreciation I have for your work and your husband's work. So when this opportunity came up I was excited personally as well as just for being able to share your important stories with my audience.

Alice: Thank you very much.

Lou: So I wanted to — before we start talking about the work with Disney talk about your early career. Because I think it's a fascinating journey going from really designing ladies' undergarments to becoming you know, a Disney legend and really now kind of a Disney household name. Tell us a little bit about that, those early days which are your education and your early work.

Alice: Well, I think that the interesting part of my walk shall we say through the youth of my life was I won a scholarship to Chouinard Art Institute out of high school. And when I went up to sign up for this school, I said that I wanted to become an animator. And Mrs. Chouinard, fortunately, was the one helping the registrar, and I happened to get her to register me. And she said, well, we don't train girls for animation because the animators are all men and the girls are the ink and paint artists. And I said, well, that's like, I don't want to be an ink and paint artist because that's like coloring a coloring book when you're a child putting color in between lines and not going over the line. And she looked at me with knowledge of knowing what I was talking about and so she said, but I can't put you in school for two years.

We have a two-year waiting list because it was right after the second world war and all of the young men who blew their first chance of getting into school had on the GI bill to go. So they were all signing up for art school because they wanted to go into advertising and things of that type and also into the motion picture business. So she said, just a minute, I started to cry because I knew that if I didn't get going in school with the scholarship, I would never get to go. And so she left and she came back and she was standing in the doorway with a woman with a white smock on, with a tape measure hanging around her neck, and then they walked away. Mrs. Chouinard came back a few minutes later and said, you're starting school Monday morning and you're going to be a costume designer.

You're going to be in the costume design department because that's the only opening I have in the school. And so I said, fine. But I didn't know Dior from a shoe. When I had the first test I had in the class, I got zero because I never heard of the people before. So I knew I had to keep a B plus average to keep my scholarship. So boy, I had to really dig in, and study. But, Mrs. Chouinard said at the same time, and this is the interesting part is that she said, I know you have your heart set on being an animator, but she said, we have Mr. Marc Davis who is starting on Monday, teaching animation drawing on Tuesday nights. And she said, if you'll call the role for me in the evening classes I'll let you take his class for free.

So I studied with Marc for two years, and called the role and then continued — oh, and I had to take two pieces of perfect white chalk to Mr. Davis for his lectures when he talked with the class. And so, I did that the whole time I was a student at the school. I will take the chalk to him and everybody tried to make big things out of hanky-panky going on and so on. And I've heard all kinds of marvelous stories, but they never happened. I mean, he was Mr. Davis. And I remember when he started the class, you know, everybody was calling him Mr. Davis. And he said don't call me Mr. Davis; just call me Marc. Nobody would because it was a matter of respect in those days to call people by their last name. So he never got called Marc. It was always Mr. Davis. In fact, even when we started going together and I was still calling him Mr. Davis, and he finally said, the name is Marc, but that's the way it was.

And so the day I graduated from Chouinard, I got a job right out of school designing braziers and girdles and lingerie. And I learned a lot about elastics and that was very helpful to me. Plus Marc's class and learning how the body works and functions and the structure and the gravity and everything else was the best thing I had in regards to designing clothes because I knew how far you could pull an arm, how far you reach with the arm. Also in girdles, in that, you learn where you can hold things tighter with elastic and not have them roll or move around. And I always felt it was a good profession to be in because you never saw the wrong person wearing one of your garments with the fat rolling over the top and the bottom. So I'd always think to myself, that's not one of mine.

So one day I got a call from Marc and he said, you're the one that I think can help me more than anyone. He was working on Briar Rose Dancing in the Forest. And he said, we're going to take and shoot part—do some live-action shooting of her dancing to get the footwork in that. And he said I want this skirt to work a certain way. And he said I know that you know what I'm talking about in regards to the movement of the figure and how the skirt should work with it. And so he said, would you make the costume for me? And so I said, yes, of course. And I made the costume and it worked out just great. And the dancing that you see in a sleeping beauty of Aurora in the forest with the Prince was the garment that I made and the way the skirt worked in that, so I was very proud of that.

Lou: And you finally got to work in automation, sort of roundabout, and that love of animation that you must have had at a very early age. Do you remember when that got started and was it sort of the Disney films that impacted you as you when you were younger?

Alice: Oh boy did it. We lived right near the Disney studio and there was a big sign on the top of the building of Mickey Mouse and you know, we'd go by and oh boy that's where Mickey Mouse lives, you know with big eyes. And then, my mother during the depression, it was very tough to get anything. In fact, the vet for my dogs was telling me that when he was a young boy in grammar school and Snow White opened, his father couldn't afford to buy tickets, but he was able to buy round trip ticket on the streetcar to go from the house to the Carthay circle where Snow White was showing and see the placards out in front.

And his father took photographs of him standing with snow white and the doors and that. And he was big-time at the school for over a month showing the pictures of how he got to go and see the theater where Snow White was showing. Well, my mother saved money for about six months and for my eighth birthday she took me to see Snow White and of all things that I fell in love with, I fell in love with Grumpy playing the organ and all the different animals and such bouncing up and down and such on the organ. And that was the day I was a Disney fan from there on.

Lou: So it really was a dream come true. And I can't imagine what you feel like when your mentor slash boyfriend teacher tells you, you finally have an opportunity to come and work for Disney. Tell us what that was like and then sort of how you were able to—did you stay on with the company right away?

Alice: No, no, this was a freelance from the side. I wasn't an employee. I just made the costume and there were a couple of others that I made, but nobody knew I was working for Disney. I was kind of like a jobber is what you call it. You would be paid by the day or by the hour, and you do what they asked of you. So we bought this house after we got married and I was stripping wallpaper and all the good things that you do when you buy a house and move into it. And I was very tired this one day, and I called Marc at the studio and said, you're taking me to dinner tonight because I'm too tired to cook. And so we were sitting, having a cocktail at the Tam O'Shanter which happened to be one of Walt's favorite restaurants.

And we're having, as I say, a cocktail and this hand came down on Marc's shoulder and this voice said, "Marc, is this your new bride?" And I looked up and it was Walt Disney. And he sat down and joined us, and he had a cocktail with us. And he started quizzing me on what I did before I got married, how I supported myself, and so on. And when I announced elastic, he said, "I don't know anything about elastic." He said elastic is always fascinated me. And they started asking me all the different kinds of elastic and whether it was synthetic or with cotton or with wool or whatever. And we had a conversation for at least a half an hour just talking about elastics. And he was fascinated with it, but he always was anything that he didn't know anything about he immediately started asking all kinds of questions and got very interested in anything, everything interested him.

So anyway, he finally said, well, I think I better let you get to your dinner and that, and he said goodbye. And he started walking away, and he turned around and he said, and he pointed his finger at me and he said, you're going to work for me someday. He didn't know I did the other things. A lot of people work for them all their life and never know him. So I was lucky from that standpoint, very lucky.

Lou: And that was your first ever meeting with Walt? I mean, what was that like when Walt Disney comes over and certainly your husband had worked there, but when he comes over and says to you, basically, unbeknownst to you, him saying, your dreams are going to come true and you're going to work for me someday,

Alice: I didn't believe in it at first. I thought to myself, oh, sure, sure. You know, and then as the months went by, I was positive I was never going to hear from him. And it went maybe two years, and one day the phone rang and it was his secretary. And she said Alice, Walt wants to know if you want to do the small world costumes. And I said, do I? And she said, well, be here tomorrow morning at nine o'clock, so I was, and I got the job. And we had one year to do the whole thing, to do the research, the costumes, the patterns, arrange all the things so that each costume could be made in a matter of hours if something happened, you know, like if there was a fire or a flood or something. And they had never had a system, and they never made the costumes out of the pattern. They would just make a costume and use it as long as it would last.

And then when that went, it would be a number of days, or even a week or so before you'd get another costume and things would have to shut down. So, I insisted that they have two costumes so that if something happened, you could make another costume in no time at all, and you would have a filler to take care of the situation until you got the next group of costumes made. So it was very fast, there wasn't time to do any color sketches or anything, but I didn't have to make any color sketches because I got to work with Mary Blair, which was a thrill of my life. And she set all the costume colors up, and I got to work with her with that, and she was an absolute joy to work with.

Lou: You mentioned the research process. Can you tell us about that? Because I always wondered, you know, how do you go about — ? How are you tasked to go about and accurately portray authentic dresses from around the world, and also, one that would have to be somewhat timeless because you knew that this attraction was going to last, and be seen by millions of people over literal generations?

Alice: Well, the best research that I was able to find was they had Disney studios in the library. They had some national geographics that were before the turn of the century. They were 1890 up to 1900, and that's when they had the best research for costumes of peasants and of different countries, and that was a great help. And they had a number of other fashion books, but it was mostly national geographic. And there was a magazine from England that was national illustrated or something like that that had a lot of wonderful festivals and such. You could get different costumes from, and then just look up lands and people that had a lot of wonderful costumes in them, but it was the older ones. The new ones, they were not that interested in costumes, shall we say, but it was — the research also was to find out what colors you shouldn't use or what shapes you shouldn't use.

And Mary wanted to put the bare skin hats on the guards of the Buckingham palace in bright red. And I said, I know I read somewhere that they had to be black and I can't remember why. And my oldest brother was a history nut, so I called him and asked him if he'd look it up for me, please. Because I was short on time and he found it and it was. They had to be black; if he made them any other color; you did not accept the fact that the British beat Napoleon at Waterloo. And so they went black and stayed black.

Lou: And in addition to — and I mentioned about the collaborative process with Mary Blair, which also worked with Harry Burns and Joyce Cross, I mean, it really was a team effort. Tell us about the process of all of you working together to put this together in such, like you said a very, very short amount of time.

Alice: I think one thing that Walt did that was I thought most unique. We never spoke to each other by the last name. Everybody spoke to each other by their first name, including Walt. If you called him Mr. Disney, an eyebrow would go up and you knew you goofed. His brother, same thing, everybody was first name, and we didn't have titles, so there was no competition to get somebody else's title or anything like that. It was a very happy place to work. In fact, I thought, boy, has it ever lucky to be able to be working here because you were enjoying it so much you were eager to get to work early just to do more of it. And I didn't mind working on weekends and all that because it was a joy to do

Lou: And I think a lot of that still sort of carries down to people who do that. I think that's why what distinguishes working and going to Disney as opposed to anywhere else because people love what they do. But Walt also gave you some relatively unprecedented free-range to a certain degree and maybe something that wouldn't happen today when it came to things like budget and what those costumes are going to cost. Tell us about the sort of freedom that he gave you when you were designing the costumes.

Alice: He gave us great freedom. He would say what he wanted and then he would ask you, when do you think you'll have it ready for me to see? And you'd say maybe Tuesday of next week. And he said, okay, I'll see you Tuesday at two o'clock. He never wrote anything down, but he was there Tuesday at two o'clock and you had better be there too, because that's one thing he did not appreciate, and that was anyone being late. You had to have an awful good reason why you were late. And if you had your work done, and whether he liked it or not there was never any anger. Sometimes he would be upset with you, but it was done in a very mannerly way. It wasn't screaming at you or anything. And he would say, let's see what we can do to change this and have it come around the way I think it would work better.

And he said, sometimes you can get something better out of something that you have to redo. So it was then, you know, sometimes if he had to have it before the date you gave him, he would have his secretary call on the phone and say that he was being pressed and pushed to have it ready ahead of time. And could you possibly do it and have it ready by such and such a time and you do your best to do it. As far as how much you would spend on costume and that, I asked him how much I would be allowed to have on the budget that I shouldn't go over for a costume. And he said, Alice, and he looked at me kind of like, oh, for heaven sake, you know. He'd say, Alice, I want you to do the best costume you can possibly design that any woman from the age of one up to a hundred would want to have herself, would enjoy looking at and having it.

And he said, we don't worry about what it costs. You always give the public more than they expect and they will come back. He said, if you cheat them, you're never going to see him again. So he said we'd do the best and give the audience the best, and we will have a good show for everybody, and they will enjoy it and we will enjoy seeing them enjoy it.

Lou: Yeah, and I get the sense that it was—you did the best work that you could, not just because you wanted to be proud of it, but you wanted Walt to be proud of it. And he knew how important it was for the guests.

Alice: You wanted to have Walt pleased with it. That was the most important thing is to please him because he was so wonderful to work with. And you've got all these different people, we all got together and would come out with the best we could possibly put together and that would please him. When you didn't please him, you felt like a monster. You went home with a long face and you tried to figure out what you could do to improve what you goofed at. And you always—the other thing, he wasn't very good at telling you what he thought of what you were doing. He would say something about, well that'll work or something like this. And then he always knew who your close friends were and on his way to wherever he was going, he would just happen to go by to see them and say, "Hey, you ought to go over and see what Alice is doing. She's really doing a good job. What she's doing now is really coming out nicely." And that was your compliment because he knew that they would immediately run it and tell you. But, it was very difficult for him to tell you how he felt about something.

Lou: And everybody seems to, that I've had a chance to speak with who worked with Walt and with is the operative word there hesitantly. There wasn't that fear of Walt being mad, it was that you didn't want to disappoint Walt. And I think the fact that you a couple of times said that working with Walt, it never seemed like it was working for Walt, that you were all working together. And he was almost more like someone that worked with you as opposed to your boss.

Alice: Right, very much so. He was the top man and you didn't have a whole bunch of meetings. You had a meeting with him when he comes through the shop and if it was something he wanted to see or make a comment on, he would come by and speak to you and set up another date to see you later. But, there were never all these meetings. I think on Small World, I was maybe in six meetings with a group, a large group. Otherwise, he would see—and we got a lot more work done that way too. Because when you had a group of a whole bunch of people, by the time everybody got finished putting in their 2 cents worth, half the day was shot. And this way, he got everything done the way he wanted and we put in a full day.

Lou: You think that Walt seemed to have a trust in the people that worked with him and a knowledge that although you may not have ever done this before, he knew that you could get the job done.

Alice: Yes, and he could put together people that didn't like each other very much and it was almost if it was competition to put out the best. He always knew, he would go around and it was like—what's his name? The one that did—the head of the sculpture department, he was an animator, and Walt was looking for a sculptor. And he decided that Blaine would be the one to do the sculpting because he was doing little sculpting things on the side that he sometimes had in his office. Walt put him to work doing the sculpting for the Small World and also them for the Pirates, and he did a magnificent job. And he did this sculpting of wild standing with Mickey Mouse. It's there in the center hub of Disneyland; it needed a wonderful one of Roy, Walt's brother sitting on a bench that's sitting in the hall of the Handprints of the Legends. But, he always got the right people together. And what you spoke about Harriet Burns, I called her the mother superior of the shop.

She never missed a thing, and she was always the perfect lady and always dressed beautifully with scarf and everything else and she'd be working in all this gook and stuff making skins and so on. And she'd never get anything on her clothes. She was always immaculate and it just astounded me, and I loved her dearly, and she's been a terrible loss; terrible loss.

Lou: Well, you know, we mentioned your name and Harriet Burns and Joyce Crossley and Mary Blair; you spoke about how women weren't allowed to animators, but here you were working on arguably one of the most important projects in a long time, which was going to be something for the World's Fair. Did you realize at that point that maybe you had broken a barrier or that what was giving you an opportunity?

Alice: Oh, Walt gave me a marvelous opportunity. He gave all of us, and Carlton, Joyce Carlton; she was somebody else. It was terrific; just marvelous. And she spent her whole life with Small World. She was in ink and paint, but she could match paint. You know, the paint was one color when it was wet and when it was dry, it was another color. She could mix it and make it so well that when it dried, it would match perfectly to the dried one. I've never seen anything like it. She had a wonderful eye for it. And Ward Kimball's wife Betty, she also was very good at mixing paint and matching it up, and that's not easy.

Lou: So, what was the opening of the World's Fair and the opening of Small World to an incredible response like for you personally?

Alice: Well, there were some funny things that happened and some things that were kind of wild. But, I think one of the funniest ones was the skin on the dolls. Where there were dolls that were dancing, like the CanCan girls doing the kicking. The skin on the knee would tear before 17 hours. They had to go 17 hours a day, seven days a week. And the first day after just a few hours, the skin would rep. So, I had designed the costumes just like they are in France with the little panties, ruffled panties on the skirts. So what were we going to do about the skin because we couldn't get it to work? So I put long pantaloons just below the knee with a little ribbon and lace, you know, and so on.

And it was about two days before the show was to open and we had everything up and working. And Walt came through with his Admiral and General; General Potter and Admiral Fowler. The Admiral was standing up in the back of the boat. The only thing missing was he didn't have his hand inside his vest. And Walt was sitting in the front of the boat with General Potter who was making all the—later on, made all the waterways and everything down in Florida. And well saw me—there was a bridge that went over the top where you come in with a boat to change to get out of the boat and get into the boat. And Walt called me; I was walking across on the bridge. I was about the center of the bridge, and he said, "Alice, how come you put long pantaloons on the CanCan girls?" Well, I knew he didn't want a big long story about what happened in that.

So I looked at him and I said, you told me you wanted a family show. And then, I took off around like crazy getting off the bridge so he couldn't ask me anymore questions. Working on the show's opening at the World's Fair, the Small World part was marvelous. But I was scared to death because they were having the UNICEF people coming in with their children and also having the United Nations come in with their children, and all of these people from all these different countries. And I was thinking, what are they going to tear apart, you know, oh God, and I was just a nervous wreck. I was shocked beyond belief. I didn't have a single complaint, not one. And I couldn't believe it; then I didn't know quite what to do whether I was walking or floating, but that was one of the great joys of doing the Small World and have it come out so well. And I owe a great deal to everybody that worked with me, you know, it was a group effort.

Lou: When the attraction opened, when the fair opened, you went up to New York and did you stay up in New York for awhile just to make sure everything was okay, and then eventually go back.

Alice: I went to New York ahead of time to dress all the figures and it was difficult to do because the unions in New York or something else and you're not allowed to touch the fabric. So if you're trying to tell them how to fix something and that you can't touch it, you have to try to explain to them. And of course, they wanted to get as much hours in as possible so they don't understand what you're talking about. So, I would wait until everybody left and then the things that I wanted to have done that I had to touch, I would take home and sit up all night at the hotel doing it all by hand and running back before anybody came to work in the morning and putting it up.

Lou: So I want to talk to you, obviously, a little bit about Pirates of the Caribbean. Obviously, your husband Marc, does the concept sketches, but then you have to go from working out every little girl's dream, to dress up dolls all day, to turning his two-dimensional sketches into three-dimensional costumes and really pieces of art. Tell us about that process.

Alice: Well, the first thing about it that I used to say about it was I went from sweet little children to dirty old men overnight. And also that Disney got a three and one when they got me to do the designing. Because when you graduated from — when you got a graduation certificate from Chouinard Art Institute in costume design, you had to be able to do children's clothes and the patterns and such. You had to do women's wear and the patterns and cut and you had to do men's tailoring. And I thought, I don't know why I have to take those, I just want a woman. And they said, if you want your certificate, you got to do all three. And I had to keep the grades up and the whole bit. So it turned out that whenever they tell you, you have to take something you don't want to graduate, take it because you never know.

It turned out to be the best thing that ever happened to me there too. Chouinard did a lot of good for me. That was really the beginning of everything for me is to be able to go to Chouinard. But, doing the pirates, there was a lot of things in the pirates. The sculptors were very difficult to work with at first, and I would try to tell Blaine certain things in Blaine would turn red and get very embarrassed and wouldn't be able to talk about it. But, they brought in some sculptors from New York that were very, very good at doing the classic figure, and they were very good for doing the bodies for the men and women and the pirates. And the problem was, is that they would do—when a woman got older, she would have sagging bosoms, they would sculpt the sagging bosoms and it would be cast in solid butyrate; you can't change the shape of it.

It's a show but this is very strong stuff. In fact, a lot of the figures are still the same ones from 67. So, anyway, I would go over and tell them that women wear corsets in that and so the bosoms are where they should be. And some are bulging over the top purposely by pushing them up, and they just didn't understand. So I went and bought a bunch of—I went to the department store and bought a bunch of braziers and brought them back and put them on the figures and said do you see? It's changed. And this time I finally got that through to them. But then the other problem came too with the way they were sculpting the gentlemen. And so, I would say to him, you're giving me a big problem because you're sculpting men just the way God made them. But they said when you put pants on them, they wear them—they dress themselves to the right or the left?

And so, they got very angry with me. "We sculpt the way God made them" and that was it, and they wouldn't change. So I told them it would be very difficult to dress them in the way they're doing this. So, I had to drop the crotch about eight inches to make room for it. And it looked like I didn't know what I was doing. And I was angry because it was making me look bad and I couldn't get them to understand, so they auctioneer, I was working on the auctioneer. Walt wanted to see the auctioneer first, and that's the only figure he ever saw. He passed away before he saw any of the other pirates. And he was so looking forward to the pirate show it was a shame.

But anyway, I did the costume for the auctioneer and he had a vest that came just above the knees and I knew it was going to happen. And he had the fancy lace cuffs and collar and all that, and the hat and the scarf around his head and the wig and so on, and he was perfectly dressed. He looked magnificent. And then, when we turned him on, his face worked and all of a sudden everybody was just in awe. We know he'd never seen anything like this before. And so, I knew that there was going to be a problem though because the way they cut the figure to make it works, they take and cut the backside of the knee out and have the calf of the leg and the thigh come together, but to be able to bend your knee in that you can't have the butyrate in the back.

So that would be cut out, and the inside of the arm would be cut out, so you could bend at the elbow. And you would cut the waist, a section of the waist out, so they could have the rib cage and the pelvis work separately. And you'd cut the thighs out of the pelvis so that the pelvis could work separately to the thighs, and so on. And when they turned on the—I had all of the sculptors, all of the machinists; everybody come to see this working. And so everybody that worked on it got a chance to see it the first time it went to work. And when the auctioneer was throwing his arms around and talking and so on, he was just terrific, perfect movement, very smooth. And when he leaned back and said, how much am I bid? His erection came up through the vest.

[Note from Lou... While this was an hysterical story, you could imagine my face when she said that to me. When it came time to post the interview on the show, I felt uncomfortable leaving that word in there, as my podcast is (and always will be) 100% family-friendly. I didn't want a child to be listening with a parent and have to ask what that word meant. So, I "bleeped" out that single word with a sound effect from Pirates of the Caribbean, and inserted an audio clip of the Auctioneer saying a line from the attraction, *"No need to expose your superstructure!"* In my more than 15 years of interviewing and podcasting, I find it so sweet and funny that adorable little Alice Davis was the one and only person I ever had to "censor."]

All the sculptors were like, "Oh my God, now we understand what you were talking about." And Walt was going to be there and a half an hour. And they said, what are we going to do? What are we going to do? And I'm the only female there. And I said, you get a Hacksaw and saw it off. And there was quite an emotional moment with all of them, and they finally did. And the sculptors came and apologized to me for not understanding what I was telling them. And it was a shame that Walt didn't get to see it, but we weren't sure whether he'd blow his stack or laugh, you know, it was a serious moment. He had an awful lot of money invested in that. So, unfortunately, he passed away a few weeks after that. So even if he got angry, I think he would have laughed when he got away from us and got his nickering, but it's probably not the best thing for the public to know what happened to that. But, it was an interesting moment in regards to the pirates.

But, there were lots of other things that there were, you know, that happened. And when I did a remake on the General Electric Show, there were a lot of funny things have happened in that too. But some of the things weren't so funny, so they kind of — but when you're doing something like this that had never been done before, it was, I don't know, you felt like a pioneer being. And I don't think I could make clothes for a human being again because I'd be looking for where the hydraulic tube came through with the red oil that stained everything when it burst and would ruin the costumes.

But, the idea of my making two costumes instead of one was one that nobody bought. And I said, but if you don't have a costume to fill in, in case something should happen, you're not going to be able to keep the ride open for a week or more until you get everything made. Because some of the hats take a whole week because you have periods you have to sit and wait for it to dry, and then do something else and wait for that to dry. So, I was told to go to the pencil pusher and tell him how many yards I needed for each shirt or each pair of pants. And I had a book this thick of all these orders and so he would okay them, and he didn't know what I was talking about. And so, I was ordering material for two costumes, not one.

And I had them all made and I had one set in back because the girl could cut them out at the same time. There was, you know, if you did a time emotion study, I saved lots of time for that. And then when they're putting them together, they can put two of them together much faster than one and then go back to do a second one sometime later and try to remember how it fits together. So oddly enough, I think it was about five weeks later after when the pirate ride opened, there was a fire and the sprinklers went on and it ruined a whole section of the fire area. Oddly enough, the fire was in the fire, but it wasn't because of the fire, it was because of some electrical, something in the building. And so Dick Irvine, who was the president of Imagineering, he came running out to me and saying, "Alice, how long is it going to take you to make the costumes to replace the ones that were damaged or ruined?

And I said, "Well, if you'd bring me the fishing pole that the hats are on for the pirate that's holding the chest, and then he's got some jewelry and such on it. And then he's got all these hats stacked on his head. Well, they're on a fish pole and it will move around, but the hats won't fall off. So I said, you can have everything in a half an hour. And he goes, "half an hour?" And his eyes got big and he didn't know whether to hit me or kiss me. He stomped his feet a couple of times and took off back up to his office. It was only closed for one day.

Lou: Yeah, and you alluded to — because I had to imagine being used to designing clothes for people and then designing clothes for the animatronic dolls whose range of motion obviously, certainly wasn't as much as an audio-animatronic figure, had to present a great deal of challenges for you. Because you are doing — you were doing something that nobody had done before, which also had that same challenge to a certain degree that you had at Small World, which was that level of authenticity and trying to create pirate costumes from the 17th, 18th century, trying to keep those accurate and authentic and then still trying to maybe tailor them for a Disney attraction.

Alice: Well, it was — Marc sketches more or less set up the, you know, the period and everything else for it. But also it was something there you had where you could put a lot of different things together because what the pirates were wearing were things that they pillaged. I can't say the word.

Lou: Pillage, plundered, rifle, and loot.

Alice: Yeah, they're plunder that they took — my tongue is not doing what I wanted to do today. Anyway, it was imagination. A lot of it was being this washed buckle bed of your childhood when they were doing all these films and such of the pirates. And so it was the imagination of yourself and things that you saw that were the pirates. And all the little kids were running around with sticks and so forth and having battles with it, so it was a — you didn't have people to imagine, you had to dress them to be what your imagination was and try to catch the imagination of others. But I think Marc did a marvelous job of putting it all together really. It was.

Lou: And again, you brought his drawings to life. If you can, what was the dynamic like working, especially on a project like this, probably so relatively closely with your husband? How did you sort of collaborate at work and then, were you able to sort of leave work at work, or was this always sort of the subject of dinner table conversation and you were talking and sketching?

Alice: No, no, Marc always closed the door when he came home. Once in a while I would be asking questions and so on, and he would take it for so long and then no more, but there was never any argument. We never had any arguments. And Mary was a great one to work with too in regards to what she wanted color-wise and that she was always very good at setting up the color patterns. But, Marc also was very good with color and good to set it up and they worked very well together.

Lou: When Pirates was updated back in 2006 were you consulted on, were you brought on at all for any sort of discussion about the changes? And then what did you think of some of the changes and the additions that came to pirates?

Alice: Oh, you're walking on difficult territory. I was not questioned on any of it. And also they changed so much of it in the staging and the staging and the lighting was what I complained about more than anything. I didn't complain actually to them. I asked them why they did certain things, and then I was surprised that some of them told me that Marc had left notes behind the sets saying how it should be staged and why. And Marc was a master at staging things, and I couldn't believe that they changed so much of it and it was not staged well. And I didn't spare any horses of stating that I didn't like the staging. And so, I wasn't invited to the opening. They finally invited me the day before it was to open with the red carpet and all this and I said, I'm very sorry, but there's no way I can possibly do that because I have to get somebody to stay with the house and the dogs, and I just said I can't go. And I said, if he would let me know ahead of time, and they said, well, we're so sorry, we forgot. And so it's imagination they're forgetting too, so I didn't go. I couldn't go.

Lou: You also mentioned working on, again, another classic iconic attraction like Carousel of Progress. I think maybe a lot of people aren't familiar with what you did there; tell us a little bit about your work on that project.

Alice: Well, I was doing a remake on it because General Electric wanted it to be brought up to date all the time because the last part of it was all the new things that they had to show that you could spend money on. So they wanted to have the costumes changed to go with the time, and that's what I was doing was changing the costumes. But, General Electric wanted to have as much publicity as possible from the show. And so, they eventually moved it from Los Angeles to Florida. Because here in Anaheim the majority of people that go to Disneyland are about 70% locals, and they would get a small amount of travelers. Where in Florida they get travelers from all over the world because it's cheaper to go to the United States and go to Disneyland than it is to go to Disneyland in France.

Lou: When you look back, and I know it's the unfair question, but one you have to ask anyway... was Small World sort of the thing that you look back on most fondly or most proud of?

Alice: I look back on it from being proud of it and for having things run smoothly and everything going together. But, I also look at it from the standpoint of the pleasure and the ability of being able to dress figures like that that you don't know where the controls are going to be coming out of or going into which you have to hide and have it looked normal and natural. There were so many different things that you had to use your imagination for. Sometimes I'd lie in bed at night wide awake, looking at the ceiling, trying to figure out how in the world I was going to get around some control that they had to have. And I don't know exactly what you would say was the hardest, but the part that I enjoyed the most of it was that I was a depression child. My father would say 1929 was bad enough to get through, but you had to come too; another mouth to feed, you know, which he meant as a fun and a joke, but no dolls, no fancy clothes or anything. So, they always say if you wait long enough, you'll get what you wish for. So, I waited until I was in my twenties and was pushing 30, I think at the time. And to be able to play with dolls, I had the best dolls in the world to play with, so that took away the part of not having the dolls when I was little, but I had the best there too.

Lou: Do you ever get a chance to go back and ride the attraction again as a guest and sort of look back at your work now?

Alice: Yes, but you know, Disneyland has never been the same. Because when you work on it, when you go through the ride and that you always look for something that's not working and you're very concerned about it, and you wanted to tell something, you know, to somebody. When I was doing it, I had a group of girls that would go through every morning before the show opened and would check all the costumes that they had, the wigs, everything else to makes sure everything was in proper order, and working before it opened up. And that doesn't happen anymore. But, it costs a lot of money to do that too, and the money keeps getting shorter and the problems bigger. Because most of the figures are the same ones, but now the ones for Small World have been changed; they're different sizes now.

Lou: I always, you know, in preparing to get a chance to speak with you, I pictured in my mind you writing Small World and getting off and saying, excuse me, miss, but the doll in France, there's something wrong. And them saying, "Lady, please just move along. You don't know what you're talking about."

Alice: No, no, I didn't do that, but I sometimes would see somebody I knew that was in the department and say so, and they say, what do you think of the ride? And I'd say, find accepting so and so isn't standing right or that the dress isn't fitting correctly or something like that. But I must say, I've gone to the sewing room a number of times and the girls that are working there are so proud of what they're doing. And they have my sketch and they hold the sketch up and say, see how close we are to doing the costume and that they're following. And the other thing was I may insist that there be a loose-leaf notebook of every figure with the fabric, the patterns, and I had it hooked with the patterns to scale, to make the garment from perfect patterns for everyone. And then, listed in the book are the fabric and so forth, and the colors, and so on. And they had never done this before and they had never made perfect patterns for the costumes before. And the last time I was there, there was a room bigger than this whole house and it's filled with all kinds of notebooks and such on every single figure and all the information and such.

They were so proud that they had kept all this and they wanted me to be sure and see it. And they have things in the department now where instead of having to go over and search everywhere for fabric to match, they have a machine now that you put the background fabric in and it will take—they make what they call a cartoon or a card that has the design or just the fabric itself with the design, and it will go through this computer and it will print the pattern onto the fabric. We were making block prints, or stencils to get certain little pieces of material for one little thing. But, it did my heart good to see that something that I, I started has gone through and now they have everything to where they can just go and pull out a book and there it is; everything that they need for each figure.

Lou: Can I ask you what you thought of the relatively recent changes to Disneyland where they added some of the classic animated film characters into Small World?

Alice: I'll tell you this, I am very proud of Kim Irvine and the job she did with changing that. Now, you have the superiors that make the decision that this has to go in the show and you have no control over it, but you have control of doing it in good taste. And she did it in the best taste possible, and everybody was on her back complaining, oh, it shouldn't be touched and it shouldn't this and shouldn't that. And then I said, how can you say what she's going to do? You haven't seen it yet. You know, you have to wait. And everybody was torn up over it.

I think I was more torn up over what they did to the pirates than to the Small World. But you know, it's like if you're going to make a film and say the film was built on the success of the pirate ride, why did they change it? I didn't understand that, but I'm one against many. The thing with Kim, I said when it finally came out; they were very kind and had a luncheon for me at the studio for my 80th birthday. The show had just opened, and they wanted to do a question and answer after the lunch. And so they were asking, I knew the first question they were going to ask was asking what I thought about the Small World ride and the change. And

I said, you know, I think we all should take a bow and take our hats off to Kim for the job that she did. I think she did a marvelous job under terrible pressure.

And I said that she was born with a Disney spoon in her mouth. Both her mother and father worked for Disney. She was second generation, and she did a very good job and placed the figures with good taste. And she had to do what was asked of her. And I said, you have to realize too, she has to pay the rent and buy food to eat just like the rest of us, and she has to do the orders that were given to her, else she'd lose her job. I said, I don't think any of us could do it any better, in fact as well. And so, she let me know she was very pleased at what I said and made her life a little easier.

Lou: Again, certainly incredibly high praise, especially coming from you.

Alice: Well, she earned it. She worked hard at it. She earned every bit of it. And she had known Mary and worked with Mary and she knew what Mary wanted too, so nobody had to ask. She knew what she was doing and she did a very good job of it; they were lucky to have her.

Lou: And again, keeping that integrity of the story and the characters carrying forward. If I can, I want to ask you about Walt and your relationship with Walt because I know people talk about Walt as a mentor, a father figure, a demanding boss, whatever it might be. But, can you tell us about what your relationship was like with him and sort of your memories of Walt?

Alice: Well, my relationship with him was a little different than most. And sometimes it would be difficult and sometimes not so difficult. But the difficult part of it was, is that he asked me to do the job and I didn't have to compete as hard as others to get the job. Also, I was Marc's wife, which was different too. Because when I worked there the first week or two, they didn't know who I was.

And then when they found out things changed a bit, but we still got along very well at work and did our job without any problems. Well, it was different at different times, like with everybody. And also, the other thing was, is very dear friends of ours were friends of — personal friends of Roy and Edna Disney.

So I had a different friendship there, which would show only and at the shop. And that was because when he would come into the shop, he would always come over and throw his arms around me and give me a big kiss. And that was — I always said it was the kiss of death because everybody thought I was freeloading and I wasn't. I was working my tail off and I was working weekends and all this and they didn't know that they were all making far more money than I was because I was hired as a job or I was never hired as an employee, and I never got paid for holidays. And if I worked weekends, I never got paid for that either. I just got paid for by the day. And if there was a day I missed that was no money. And they all thought I didn't need to be — how would you say an employee because my husband was and he was getting all the perks so I didn't have to worry about that.

Well, there were some things that weren't so good about it, but those are the things you'd take for getting to do what you wish to do. I decided to give all that up for being able to work there and I have never thought back about it or been upset about it at all. I was just overjoyed that I got to work at Disney Studios and get to know all the different people there who many are very dear friends and still are. And Walt was a good con man too. I think the biggest con he pulled on me was — Mrs. Chouinard was another idol of mine. And to be able to know her very well was another pleasure of my life.

She was losing the school because of some bookmakers that were — well her bookkeepers I called them. They were bookmakers because they were cleaning her blind. And Walt was very close with Mrs. Chouinard because when he wanted to do snow white, he knew his animators were — the draftsman that he needed to do live figures, and make people believe that they were real people and not just a drawing on the wall. So, he went to all the different art schools and this was during the height of the depression, and asking them if they could train his animators to be better draftsman and carry him on the books until the film opened and then he'd pay them because he had no money to pay for him at the time. He was lucky to be able to get the — in fact they were even washing the cells and reusing them.

They were so hard up for money, and he would say that, you know, would you keep, you know, I'll pay you when the film comes out and they say there's the door. So he went to Chouinard Art Institute; Mrs. Chouinard and he asked her and she said, "Mr. Disney, I admire what you're doing." She said, "The change from Steamboat Willie to the present time is amazing that you did it so rapidly and I admire what you're doing." And she said, "You are creating an art for America." She said, "The Europeans have the old masters. The Orientals have their Oriental work from years and centuries ago. The Eastern Europe, the same thing, but we don't have a true art for America." And she said, "You are building the true art of America." And he thanked her for that and she really believed it. And she said, "You send down your boys and we'll train them and whenever you can, we'll worry about that later."

And so she trained them for two and a half years. They went one night a week to this art school and studied with Don Graham. And he eventually, Walt hired him to come two days a week or so to the studio and continued training new animators coming along and the nine old men went to Chouinard at night. And my husband said that Disney Studios was the finest school he ever went to because Walt was constantly bringing in all kinds of foreign films and speakers and art majors — not art majors, but artists that were the major artists of the time to give classes and such at night to the animators and different people working at the studio. And it was better than any college or university would have. And what he was doing — and I really do think he has made the animation the art of the United States.

Lou: And I think the genius of Walt Disney was that from the very beginning, he always surrounded himself with the most brilliant minds and the finest artists. What was his passing like for you, because of your special relationship with him and really for the company at that time?

Alice: Oh, it was devastating, absolutely devastating. It was like your father died and in some ways worse. Just the genius of the man; he was always thinking 20, 30 years ahead of time, and he loved new and different things. Anything that was new, he had to know everything about it. And anybody who he admired their genius, he would always somehow get to know them or have them come to the studio and give lectures for the employees. He was always — even when he was under tremendous pressure, very seldom did he ever become irritated or angry about things. He always had a way of controlling himself. But sometimes if he did lose control, I wouldn't blame him the least. Because they — well, it was like with Abraham Lincoln; Abraham Lincoln was fantastic and nobody had ever seen anything like this before. When it first opened in the World's Fair, people were talking about how he stood up and walked forward. Well, he never walked forward, but they never saw anything like this, you know, and Harry would stand up out of this chair and start delivering a speech. In fact, one of the little kids in the neighborhood went to see Lincoln and she said, "Boy, he was really scary." And I said, "Scary." I said, "What was scary about it?" She said, "Well, he kept tapping the chair with one of his fingers," and she said, "We all knew he was dead, but he was moving."

And then when he stood up, she said, that was really scary, so it was interesting the different attitudes. But when they were trying to operate the figure beyond what anything had been created yet. It didn't have computers and so on, and they were trying to get this thing to work. And every once in a while he would stand up and he'd start this speech and then all of a sudden he'd sit down, something would — one of the controls would break down or something and he'd sit down and he'd just splintered the chair. The chair was a beautiful old chair that would just be splintered. He was a couple of weeks late opening in the World's Fair, and it was because you had to run him all the way through and make a perfect pattern.

And if there was the worst little glitch or something, he'd all of a sudden jerk up or sit down and mash the chair or something else. And then to add to it, when they finally got him working, if something needed just a little bit of touch up or something, or the machine needed to be tightened up a little, or whatever they do to solve that problem, they'd have to go out on the stage. Well, next door to the, the Illinois, the pavilion that he was in was a Japanese Pavilion and they were giving away free ball bearings. They had a new ball bearing that they were advertising and they'd give you a big handful of ball-bearings to leave with. And they didn't think Lincoln was an audio electronic figure, they thought it was a real person pretending to be Abraham Lincoln.

So they'd go over with a pocket full of these ball bearings and throw it at Lincoln and it would make the noises on that, but the figure would keep working and going on. But the poor guys that had to go out and make a change or something, and had to go out and they'd be sliding all over at these ball-bearings on this stage. And some of them had terrible falls and got badly injured. And so we finally had to go over and ask him not to give away the ball bearings anymore because of that. Everybody was getting half killed by them, but there were lots of things like that that happened. People throwing things at them because they didn't think they were mechanical. They thought they were real, so we were very proud and thought that it was keen that they thought they were real people, but we weren't pleased with their destroying with ball bearings and rocks and things that they'd throw.

I think all of us were extremely proud to be in the beginning of a new type of three-dimensional animation. And I think that we made Walt proud with it, and also, it was giving him something else to work with. In fact, he got so excited over that he wasn't too excited over the animation anymore, but his brother insisted that the animation continue because that's what made the studio, and that they owed it to the animators to continue with the animation.

Lou: Well, speaking of animation and sort of thinking about that legacy of Walt, about surrounding yourself with the most brilliant minds. When I started thinking about people like John Lasser, I started thinking the same way. And to segue in to that, you were actually called on by Pixar to consult on Up. And it's a Testament to the fact that still to this day; they want to surround themselves with the best minds and the most brilliant people. Tell us what John Lasser and the boys over at Pixar called upon you for to help out with Up?

Alice: My style of life, the way Marc and I lived in what we did. We were traveling to New Guinea and collecting things. It was kind of our lifestyle, I think more than anything. And we had what we called the Anther Biz fund and the Anther BizFund was—I had a very serious horse accident when I was young. I can't remember, I think I was 20 and I hit a tree trunk. The horse got frightened and it turned and went down this steep hill between trees and the horse leaned out and misses the trees, but I didn't. And I caught it with my left side and mashed the whole side of my face in, and broke all of my ribs, and cut this eyelid loose, and down the cheek.

And I didn't have any money I was living like a lion from zebra to zebra and never knowing when the next zebra was coming along.

And I had to borrow money from my brother to get out of the hospital. I didn't even have money to pay for the hospital bill. And when I got home, I opened up a letter that was in the postbox from John and Jane Anther whom I had met only twice in my life. And there was a good size check in the letter, and the letter stated that this was their fund. And when they were very young and first married, a very wealthy person drove into them and demolished their car and so on, but had the money to beat them in the lawsuit and such, and they were destitute. They had no money to pay for the doctor bills and they've had the loss, their car was destroyed and so on.

And so these people gave them money for paying off their hospital bill and paying for the car and the whole bit, and so they got a new start in life. And so, they were passing on the money the way the people gave them the money was if and when they knew somebody that had an accident happened to them to pass the money on to them with no strings accepting if and when they could to pass it on to somebody else. So, Marc and I put so much money away each year and we would give the Anther Biz fund to people. And we helped a lot of people, but nobody ever knows who they are because we don't tell anything. And it helps you, you know, like when the car's tire would burst or something, well that was an Anther Biz fund to where they could get another tire and so on.

I think it was just that they knew both Marc and I over the years and knew what we did, and that was—we love to go to foreign countries and studying and go through the art schools and see what they were teaching and so on. And they thought that was kind of Keen and they liked the way that Joe Grant and his wife lived pretty much. They were both artists and worked together and had great joy in meeting and seeing other people and seeing how they live and do what you can to help your friend. I always call our house, our church. If you live a good life and you help people in need, and you enjoy friendship; it's a good way to live.

Lou: Thank you for sharing that story and I wanted you to tell it because when I mentioned the film Up, I think a lot of people's minds probably thought they went to costumes or colors or whatever it might be. But, it really was about the special relationship that you and Marc had, and that's what the Frederickson's were. And that's what they came to tap into you to sort of share those stories with. And I think hopefully the next time people watch it, they'll have a better understanding that that's Marc and Alice Davis.

Alice: Well, I can't think of anything more flattering. In fact, I felt like I should take my head to keep it from swelling after I saw the film because the film was—then there was a complete surprise to me, you know? I think about three years before the film opened, I knew nothing about it. It's just that Pete Doctor called me, whom I admire. He's fantastic. He and his wife bot; they're lovely people. He called and asked me if he could bring his animators down to see our house; go through the house in Marc's studio? And I said, "Sure". And he said, "Well, would next week or something, be good to see it?" And I said, "Fine". He brought all of them and they brought all—I was surprised because they came with all kinds of cameras and everything else known to man. And they spent at least three hours or more going around photographing everything inside of the house, the outside of the house, and Marc's studio and so on. And the day that it opened, before I went in to see the film, one of the young animators came up and said, "Do you remember me, I went through your house?"

And I said, "yes, I remember you." And he said, "Well, I think you'll be surprised with what you see in the film." And I said, "Oh, what's that?" And he said, "Well, just see what we saw." And I don't know if you know when it's coming down the stairs in the chair, it's not the paintings that are on my wall, but there were paintings on the wall and the rail and such was part of the house and there were a number of things that picked up on it. The first half-hour of that film made you laugh and cry at the same time. It was absolutely—I love that film. And when I saw my — everybody said, you have to stay with it to the very end of the credits. And when I saw my name there, I almost lost my teeth.

Wow, this is my moment of fame. And then at the Academy Awards, I was the loudest one screaming and yelling that he got the Academy award. And then, I was at the governor's ball having dinner afterward and I was sitting at this table, and all of a sudden there was this great, WHAM! I was sitting talking to the person next to me, and the whole table shook and I looked and there was the Oscar. And sending it back at me was Pete Doctor and he said, "Look, our Oscar!", and he crammed it on the table. And I jumped out of my skin, but I leaped up and gave he and his wife both big hugs and kisses. It was a marvelous, marvelous moment. I was so sorry Marc couldn't be there.

Lou: I'm sure he would be proud. But do you—have to openly talk about your moment of fame. But, I think something has happened over the past number of years or so, and even in the past couple of days, things like Disney's D23 and the events have brought you and personalized to Alice David's for us, the Disney enthusiasts. And you have—liked it or not, Alice, you've become a Disney celebrity and you've become very, very well recognized over the past few years. I mean, did you ever imagine when you first started working on some of these attractions that this is what it would be? And look, I sat in on a number of panels and discussions that you've been at over the last couple of years, including one just a couple of days ago at Destination D in Disneyland. And I watched the crowd as much as

I watched the panel because more so than any of the other events and presentations over those two days, I think that is where people would be fascinated. And Marty Sklar kept you going longer than the hour and a half or so, but we would have sat there for hours. I mean, how does it feel to you now to be sort of, you know, people are asking for your autograph and for your picture and to be sort of thrust into the Disney celebrity status?

Alice: I still feel like I should go home and take my head to keep it from swelling, but also, it's like old family meeting, you know, because they keep coming back. They keep coming back, just like Walt said they would. And they become friends and I ask how their son is doing or their children and this and it's like a family reunion I think I would say more than anything. It's a family reunion and they're all there and its hugs and kisses, and I thank them for coming because I said if it weren't for you and your eagerness, I would not have food in my mouth or a house to live in. You know, it takes two to tango.

Lou: Well, your work is certainly very well, very much appreciated and respected. Certainly, you were named the Disney legends 2004. You followed in the footsteps of your husband who was given that honor in 1989. What did that recognition from the company mean for you?

Alice: It meant a great deal, a great deal. And again, I wish Marc could have been there and been able to enjoy it with me because I think I owe a great deal of it to Marc and to Mary and to all the people that I worked with. I didn't do it by myself. It was a group effort by all of us. And that's the way it always has been. And it's why it's still a joy to see each other and catch up with time.

Lou: And we see that sort of love and admiration and mutual respect and that sense of family that all of you and people like Marty and X. Atencio and Bob Gurr and some of the other people that you work with decades ago; you still carry that forward today. You're certainly so well-deserved of that and that award and all the recognition that you get, your work continues to bring laughter and smiles, and incredible memories to generations of Disney enthusiasts like myself.

Lou and Alice Davis

Alice: It is a good job to have. It's the best job. You know, this is the other part, it was so wonderful not only to work there, but to have people enjoyed seeing, and coming back to see what we worked at and accomplished. And I think that's the best part of all this is to sit and watch the people enjoy what they're seeing.

Lou: Well, you should be very pleased and proud to know that the work of you and your husband will continue. Your legacy will go on to thrill generations of Disney fans from around the world. So for that on behalf of myself and my family and I'm sure the other people who appreciate your work, I want to thank you for welcoming me into your home today and for sharing your stories with us and for all the work that you and your husband have done.

Alice: That's my pleasure. But, I have to make one remark of a story that I told the other night, and that was the first time I went to Disney Land and took this little girl who was crying because she couldn't get in and I tried to pay to get in and I couldn't. And because they said they closed up the park one hour before it was to be closed, in other words, not letting other people in because they were going to try to get them out. And when the time came and this little girl started crying and she was going home to New York the next morning and she'd never get to see Disneyland. So that's why — and I don't know why it came into my head to do it that way, but I had to get her in there somehow. And so I'm waiting — I should finish by saying that — I said we'll just stand over there by the exit where they're coming out and talk and just walk backward, be facing the same way but walk backward through the crowd.

And we got in and they were very kind, and she got to go on the rides. Fortunately, Marc had given me some books that had the key on it that employees had so I could get her on the rides with the key book. And they even kept one open for one more go around so she could see it, so she could see everything she wanted to see. And I'm waiting for now since it's gotten out. I know my mother never even knew it. The only one I told was Marc and it was almost the end of a good friendship because we weren't married then. So anyway, I thought any day now I'll get a bill from them for going into the park. But that's the only time I've ever done anything like that, and I felt guilty for a long time, but at the same time, I was proud of the fact that I got her in to see the show.

Lou: Well this is good. This is very cathartic...

Alice: I'm getting it off my chest.

Lou: You know what, though? You bent the rules to make magic and I think that was the important part.

Alice: Well, I hope they keep it; everybody keeping the magic going because it is magic and it's a place—I've had a number of people say, "Oh, Disneyland, I'm not going there." And I finally talked him into going and they become rabid fans now and they say it is a place where you can drop all your troubles and worries and go down and have a wonderful time. And it's true, and we hope that magic keeps going for many years in the future.

Lou: I'm sure it will. Again, the legacy of Walt, and you, and Marc, and so many of the people that built the foundation for what is to come in the years that followed is definitely being followed through. So, Alice Davis, Disney legend, and so much more, thank you again so, so much for your time.

Alice: Well, thank you very much for thinking of me and giving you the choice of being able to spread more of the magic around.

Dave Smith

In September of 2010, on WDW Radio show #188, I was pleased to welcome to the show a true Disney Legend, and someone whose name is synonymous with Disney history. From founding the Walt Disney Archives in 1970, to authoring numerous books, Dave Smith's 40 year career with the company afforded him the opportunity to preserve the magic that began with Walt himself. Dave joined me on the show to discuss his career, including not just his role in the creation and legacy of the Walt Disney Archives, but its challenges, personal highlights, changes and his future, as he prepares to retire from this "temporary" job that lasted four decades. It's a fascinating conversation not just about the Archives, but the person who made it a reality.

Walt Disney Archives founder and former chief archivist David R. Smith officially joined The Walt Disney Company on June 22, 1970, but his interest in compiling an extensive bibliography on Walt Disney started back in 1967.

When the Disney Company decided to preserve Walt Disney's memorabilia and legacy, they reached out to Dave, who was then selected as archivist. Dave went on to not only curate the Archives, but wrote extensively on Disney history for The Disney Channel Magazine, Disney Magazine, Disney Newsreel, and countless articles in other major publications. Dave is also the author of the official Disney encyclopedia Disney A to Z, co-authored four volumes of The Ultimate Disney Trivia Book; and with Steven Clark co-wrote Disney: The First 100 Years.

Dave Smith was named a Disney Legend in 2007, and passed away in Burbank, California, on February 15, 2019 at the age of 78.

This interview is taken from my conversation with Dave on WDW Radio Show # 188, in September, 2010. You can listen to the interview at WDWRadio.com/188

Lou Mongello: A name very well recognized and synonymous with Disney history has had a long tenure with the Disney company as not only the head of the legendary Disney archives, but also as an author with numerous titles and publications to his credit. And what was supposed to be a temporary role in which he was given an empty office and told, "Just start," he went on to establish what is regarded as the model for corporate archives worldwide and personally acts as the final authority on all matters of Disney history. He has a Master's degree in Library Science from the University of California at Berkeley, and he interned with the Library of Congress in Washington D.C. In his forty year career with the company, Dave has witnessed transitions, growth, and the spreading of Disney magic to countless smiling faces worldwide. So it is my distinct honor to welcome somebody to the show who I've had the pleasure of meeting and speaking with in the past, chief Disney archivist, Dave Smith. Dave, welcome to the show.

Dave Smith: Hi. Thank you.

Lou: It's great to be able to talk to you, and we're gonna talk about how you're coming to the end of your tenure with the Disney company. But before we talk about that, let's go back a little bit to the beginning and tell people how you went from being a librarian over at UCLA to working for and with the Disney Company.

Dave: Well, I sort of was in the right place at the right time. Disney was starting to wonder about what we are going to do about preserving our history and this was, of course… you know, it came to a head with the death of Walt Disney in 1966. So I was working as a librarian at UCLA, and I had done some work on a Disney bibliography. So I got to know some people at Disney. And so I was around when they started wondering how they could preserve the history of the company, and I thought I could help so I volunteered my services, and they didn't know anybody else that could do anything like that for them, and so they hired me.

Lou: So the Disney bibliography that you were working on, was this a personal project or something you were doing for the company?

Dave: Well, it started out as a personal project. I had done several other bibliographies, including a couple that had been published by UCLA. So I started it out this way, but as I got farther into it, the people at the Disney studio felt this would be something very useful to them. And so when I finished it, they bought it from me.

Lou: Hmm. So were you surprised when you were first talking to them, at that point in the company's history that there were no archives already in existence?

Dave: Oh, I don't know that I was surprised. I knew very little about archives. I never had a class in archives, but I studied library science, and I had worked in a number of different departments at the Library of Congress with rare books and manuscripts and prints and photographs and maps and all that sort of thing. So I was familiar with how to deal with different types of archival materials, but I don't think it ever crossed my mind that there were a lot of business archives in the country. And it was only after I started talking to Disney about an archive that I actually did a bit of research and found out there weren't very many business archives in the United States at that time.

Lou: So, did you basically get to live the dream and say, "Okay, here's my proposal for what I think I can do to set up this archive," and they say, "Yeah this sounds like a good idea. Go ahead. Go do it."

Dave: Yes, essentially! It just happened. I did about a two month consulting job for them in the fall of 1969, wrote my proposal around the beginning of January 1970, and took them six months to decide to go ahead. But they finally did, and we started the archives in June of 1970.

Lou: So, tell us what that, you know, I put in quotations, "That first day is like." They say, "Okay, Dave, walk into work on Monday morning." How do you start? How do you start putting together the Disney archives?

Dave: Well, you know, it actually started... There was a semblance of a start really when I was doing my consulting job for two months because I just went back to the same office I used during those two months. And during that few month period, I had contacted other companies to see what they'd done with their archives, but I also was going around the studio and various areas of the company itself to find out sort of the quantity and the quality of the materials that had been saved. So I was getting to know people in the company, and they were getting to know me. And so when I came in June of 1970, it was really just a continuation of what I'd started in the fall of '69.

Lou: Now you obviously must have been, I have to assume, a Disney enthusiast early on to have been working on this bibliography. I know I had read that you had met Walt Disney briefly as a child in Disneyland, certainly not in your capacity as an archivist, but you also, you worked with Roy. Tell us about his role in helping to set up the archives.

Dave: Well, the people that were thinking about preserving the history were in two camps. You have the Disney family camp, and you have the Disney Company administration. So I was working with both sides, and Roy was, of course, the one to make the decisions for the family side, and Card Walker was making the decisions for the company side. So I was working, as I say, with both of them and various assistants that worked with them. So I think Roy was very anxious to do something to preserve the history of his brother, and it just sort of grew from that.

Lou: And tell us the story early on about Walt Disney's office, how basically it was pretty much locked up after he passed away, and you were one of the first people to gain access to that and start archiving what was in there?

Dave: That's right. Walt's secretaries had actually stayed on the job for about a year after he died cleaning up the files and answering correspondence and things like that, and then they pretty much shut up the office. And then, so this would have been toward the end of 1967. I came along to do my consulting job two years later. So for two years it had been pretty much closed up, and the only one that went in there was the janitor who went in there and cleaned every week or two, and nobody else really had access to the office. So when I started, one of the first jobs they asked me to do was to make an inventory of the offices because they knew that this valuable space at the studio just couldn't be sitting there forever. They really needed that space and other executives needed offices and so forth. So they wanted to make sure that we documented exactly the way it was when Walt was there, and that included not only making an inventory but photographing the office from all angles and drawing up essentially blueprints of how it was laid out.

Lou: And I have to assume that that task fell on you because you were the Disney archivist at that point.

Dave: That's correct. It was just me (laughs). They gave me a secretary from the publicity department to help me for a few months. So she and I would go into the office, and she had her little steno pad, and I would read to her the things that I was coming upon, and she would put down the list.

Lou: I have to assume, and I've sort of put myself in your shoes… Forget the fact that it's overwhelming, just in scope, but a daunting task because you, they open that door and you sit down at Walt Disney, I mean it's Walt Disney's desk. And I think that there's, you know, there's something about the fact that it was his desk that had to have had some sort of special meaning for you.

Dave: (Laughs) Sure, there was that aura around the offices. And being the only person having access to the offices really seemed very sort of eerie to me as a brand new member of the staff of the company, and so I had a heavy mantle on my shoulders. (laughs) I was hoping that I would be worthy of the task.

Lou: I could just imagine sitting down and, you know, taking a deep breath and saying, okay, I have to forget about the fact that I'm sitting in Walt Disney's chair and looking at all the things that he was the last to touch before he passed away and sort of kind of go through the process of documenting everything. I mean I have to assume you had to go down to the most minute detail because it was so important to document exactly the way it was.

Dave: Sure. I mean, I counted the paper clips in the desk drawer (laughs). But I mean the exciting thing would be opening a drawer or a cupboard and finding something that was really iconic in Disney history that one wouldn't really not have expected to be there in his office. And that happened several times.

Lou: Yeah and were there things that, I mean you know, we hear about how much time Walt spent in his office, it was almost probably more of a home to him. Were there a lot of personal things there that really weren't appropriate for the archives and you had to sort of distinguish what should go to the archives and what should go to his family?

Dave: There was not a lot of personal memorabilia or items primarily because the family took them home. As I said, the office was open a year after Walt died, and the secretaries were in there so I know that Mrs. Disney came in on occasion and took some of the personal things home. So there wasn't a lot of that when I came.

Lou: And then tell me about sort of the growth of the archives. Certainly after you finished the job over at Walt Disney's office, it must have snowballed, I guess, pretty quickly because you know, there was film, there was television, there was animation, there was so much going on. Was there any sort of rhyme or reason or direction, or did you sort of guide and just started going out and collecting what you could?

Dave: Well, two things. I tried to first find all the oldest stuff I could find because that was the stuff that was in the most danger of being lost, the things that were not in people's offices and had been stashed away and people had essentially forgotten about them. So that type of material I tried to get into the archives right away, but at the same time, when you start an archive you have to start collecting current materials too because that's going to be the history of tomorrow. So I had to make contact with all the different areas of the company, get onto the distribution lists when I could, and just sort of keep in touch on a regular basis to make sure we were getting the things that we felt were important to tell this history of the company.

Lou: And so for people that maybe don't, have never visited or aren't really sure, what were the kind of things and what are the kind of things over the years that you collected and are found in the archives? I think many of us have this impression of sort of the last scene of Raiders of the Lost Ark, this giant warehouse with crates that are locked up but it may not be very far...

Dave: Exactly! That's us (laughs). First off, let me say what we don't have in the archives, and that's a lot of artwork. There are other departments in the company like the animation research library and Walt Disney Imagineering that maintain the artwork for the animated films and for the theme parks. Practically everything else, we have here. Well, one other thing we don't have, the films. We have a separate film library in the company, but everything else is represented in our collection. It's everything from correspondence files of Walt's and Roy Disney and other Disney executives to books and magazines and comic books and photographs and awards and just a little bit of everything.

Lou: Now in addition to some of the art and things like that, I think a lot of people would also probably be surprised to find out that, and may be disappointed, that the archives doesn't necessarily keep things like attraction props. You don't have a 20,000 League sub, you don't have Mr. Toad's car, you don't have a Skyway bucket necessarily in the archives, but you do have files for every theme park attraction, correct?

Dave: Well, you know, actually this has changed a bit in the last few years. As Bob Iger has said in some public statements, there is the thought that the company might want to do a museum someday so three or four years ago, we were asked if we would collect some more props and costumes and set pieces from the movies as well as iconic things from the parks. So we got more warehouses, and we got more staff, and we started doing that. So we do have a lot more of those large pieces now than we used to have. In the olden days I think people, while they thought maybe we were like a museum, we really weren't because people were coming to us for information, not to see things particularly. And that lasted through our first 35 years or so. Today, as I say, we're getting more of the things, and we'll have more of a museum collection eventually.

Lou: I want to talk to you about what that change that Bob Iger brought about, but before that, before Bob Iger, when you know, you start out as a young man at the company, was it difficult to acquire some of the things that you wanted? I mean, how does the new kid with the empty office go about, and go into the different divisions, saying "I need this. I need to take this and bring it to the archives." Did you meet with any sort of, you know…

Dave: (Laughing) Well, you had to be very diplomatic. You had to convince the different departments that you were going to be around for a long time, you would take better care of their files than they were and they would still have access to them. Those were the main things that the departments were worried about. Now, there were some departments that were a bit reticent in turning over their file sets of their materials because these were things they needed to get into to on a fairly regular basis and they wanted to make that they were still going to be accessible to them. On the other hand, there were other departments that welcomed the archives with open arms because they needed the space. "Here, take all this stuff. Get it out of here." (laughs) So we had both sides of the coin and pretty soon we had pretty much convinced all of the departments that we were going to be around a while and their materials would be safe with us.

Lou: And as you alluded to, Bob Iger obviously seemed to be very much aware of the importance and the value of what you're doing. And tell me if this is true, that he basically sort of gave a mandate to all divisions that said, look if Dave Smith and the archives want it, you get it. And you know, is that sort of like you having your search warrant to go in and sort of pick and choose want you needed?

Dave: Well you know, he certainly reinforced that but that started back in 1970 with Card Walker sending a memo out to all the divisions saying "We started an archive. Dave Smith is running it. Please give him all the help that he requires" essentially. So Walker did essentially the same thing that Iger is doing today, but Bob certainly reinforced it and had it apply to more things like the museum objects and so forth which we hadn't been collecting in the past.

Lou: Yeah, in 1970 did you have to walk around with a copy of that in your pocket just in case?

(Laughter)

Dave: No, I don't think I ever had to pull it out and show it to anybody!

Lou: Let me ask you this. You know you talked about the growth of the company and the expansion of the company, and even early on, there was so much going on with live action, and animation, and TV, and the theme parks, and now it's growing so much more. Obviously, way back when, it was just you, and your staff grew just a little bit. How do you and your staff, I mean, how do you kind of be in every place at once with so much going on to make sure that you are able to gather all that you need to? Or do you find that the different divisions are voluntarily sending this stuff to you?

Dave: Well, the archive staff has grown as the company has grown. So as there are more demands on our time and more people need information from the archives, we've been able to add staff members. So there were maybe 10,000 employees in the company in 1970 and now there are 150,000 employees so it's a much different company, But we had one person in the archives then, and we have about 8 people in the archives today. So we have grown as the company has grown.

Lou: Have you found it more or less of a challenge as time has gone on? I mean, obviously part of preserving the history includes things that you spoke about before, such as documents and memos from Walt Disney and executives. As time has gone on, obviously, computer, e-mail, mobile technology, is that more challenging now for you to sort of gather and archive the electronic media?

Dave: Well, of course, there's more of a challenge today primarily because there's more stuff to collect. And there's always the problem of the electronic media. E-mails for example, the company saves some of the e-mails of the top executives but a lot of other stuff from various departments is done with e-mail and on their computers, and there are no hard copies made so nothing is available to be archived. It is a problem that all archives in the world are facing.

Lou: And what about, in time the acquisition of other companies. So I'm thinking about things like Pixar and Marvel. Is that something that, as these companies are acquired, they start to be added to the archives at all, or is it from that acquisition point forward?

Dave: We are... we collect basic materials on the acquisitions and of course keep track of newspaper and magazine articles that are written about our acquisition and about the companies once we have them. But if you talk about Pixar, and you talk about Marvel, they both have their own archives already. And so those are existing, and so we don't have to go back and archive things from before the time that we acquired the companies.

Lou: One thing that was always disappointing to me as an enthusiast, as a researcher, is that while the purpose of the archives is to collect and preserve all of this history and make it available to people, it really has always been for the internal company's use, for cast members, for executives, for whoever might need it. It's never really been open to the public for research purposes, correct?

Dave: Well, no, don't say never. It was originally and probably for the first 30 years or so we were open to students and writers outside the company, but the company just grew so large and the demands on our staff grew so great that we just didn't have the time to work with students and others that wanted to come in and use our materials and so we had to stop it at that time. And so today, yes, we are only open to employees and cast members of the company.

Lou: I missed the boat by just a few years! But, let me ask you this, though, How, What about the relatively recent opening of the archives to Disney enthusiasts, certainly not for research but through things like the D23 Archives tours and the D23 Expos, how has that changed things for you?

Dave: Well, I like it! It hasn't really changed anything for me. It's just that I've been able to acquaint more people with what we have done here. And I love doing the D23 Archives tours because these people are so entranced with the type of materials that we have in our collection, and they just love to see some of the special things that I bring out to show them, as well as, of course, having a chance to look at a few of our display cases and things that we regularly have on display here. So this is just another type of outreach that has been very gratifying.

Lou: Listen, you went from the empty room to a Disney celebrity, Dave. I mean, you're the face of the archives and really the face of the company for a lot of people whether they see you at events or meet you at some of the special events or they...

Dave: Well, I don't always realize that, and then when D23 decided to throw me a retirement banquet down at Walt Disney World on the 15th of October as part of their Sip and Stroll event that they're doing tied into the Food and Wine Festival, I thought who's going to want to come and have dinner with me. But they sold out in a day and a half so I guess there's more people that want to have dinner with me than I thought!

Lou: You're really a Disney rock star, Dave. You have to come to terms with it. (laughter) Well ,I mean, you mentioned the Archives tour, and I had a chance to do that myself. I was part of the group that had the very first tour that D23 gave, and I have to tell ya, it was the highlight and still is of anything I have ever experienced as far as my passion for Disney is concerned. To be able to, not just see you of course, but to see some of the things and to be in a place where so much important information and props and materials was being held. What's been the reaction of other fans? I have to assume it's got to be just the same way.

Dave: Yes, I feel it is the same way. I get a lot of feedback from people that have been on those tours, and the archives is their highlight of their visit to the studio, and they're just very thrilled to have a chance to at least see what the archives is. Sometimes they're a little disappointed because they expect a Raiders of the Ark, Lost Ark warehouse, but, and maybe our display area isn't as big as they might have envisioned in their mind, but I think they come away with an appreciation of what we've done and how we've done it here.

Lou: I know for myself and for a lot of people when we were on the tour, I was almost watching their reactions as much as I was sort of in awe of where I was and there were so many gasps and "Oh my God, I can't believe this. I can't believe that" as they were walking from case to case, and I had even videotaped it and some of those reactions were caught on there. And you could hear people's just joy and what they were seeing. What do you think that the one things is that people have come into the archives that seems to maybe amaze them the most or that they comment on or are surprised by most? Cause I have one in particular for myself.

(Laughter)

Dave: Well, maybe you're thinking of ticket number 1 for Disneyland. I usually pull that one out for the groups, and that's always a highlight thinking that, yes indeed, this is the very first ticket that was ever sold in Disneyland.

Lou: And as impressed as I was with that, you know, and I was happy to see that ticket number 1 was preserved, for me, Dave, it was the bird. And I tell this story to anybody that will listen, and even some people that won't, about going on the tour, and I've, we've always heard the story about Walt Disney finding this animatronic bird, and I have this vision of this larger bird that Walt gave to the Imagineers and they disassembled, they reverse engineered it and so goes the birth of audio animatronics. And you start talking about the bird and you reach over casually on the stand to the side, and you bring over this little birdcage with this little tiny, I don't know, 4 or 5 inch bird . And you talk about how this was the bird, and there you are you're just picking it up and handling it and winding it. And I'm looking at it like it's the holy grail. I'm like, "My God, man... Put on some gloves! It's the bird!" (Laughs)

Dave: I guess we get used to some of these things that we see everyday.

Lou: Yeah, I mean, and it was such a thrill for me to see that, you know, and I look back and I laugh. And again it's just sort of part of your normal day to have the bird there. And what that represents for us was just like, you imagine that it should be in some sort of like, hermetically sealed case. But let me ask you this. For you, especially because you were a Disney enthusiast, was there anything that you found during your 40 plus years that was your, and I have to assume there was many, that wow moment like, ahh, I can't believe I'm holding Walt's paperclip. Whatever it might be.

Dave: (Laughs) I think a lot of the things that most excite me are the things related to Walt himself. And I'm still terribly thankful for Roy E. Disney who brought us a tin box that he found in his garage that had belonged to his grandfather, Elias Disney, which had all of his important documents and papers in it. And one of the things I found in that box was a postcard written by Walt when he was 15 to his mother with a drawing on the back, a beautiful drawing showing that this guy really had art talent even at that age.

Lou: Yeah, and it's so wonderful to know that those things from his personal childhood before he was Walt Disney the icon are preserved there as well.

Dave: Right.

Lou: I think when we were talking, especially about the theme parks before, I think people may not realize that in addition to the archives and what you've been able to do by kind of sort of opening the vault and sharing with fans, you as the archives also had a role in the creation of something that I hope all Walt Disney World fans have had a chance to visit and go through and appreciate, which is Walt Disney: One Man's Dream over in Hollywood Studios. That opened back in October for Walt Disney's 100 Years of Magic celebration and really is a tribute to Walt Disney, the man behind the mouse, but there's a lot of authentic artifacts on display. Can you tell us about the creation of that attraction and your hand in it?

Dave: Sure, it was Walt Disney Imagineering, of course, that designed the attraction, but they came to us in the archives, and we discussed various things from our collection that would be nice to have on display down there. And through the years we've switched out some materials, and we are doing that right now. The attraction is currently closed, I believe, until November, and we have some of the old toys that were on display have come back to us. And we've gathered some different ones to put on display down there so all the Disney fans that think they've seen One Man's Dream are gonna have to go back again after November because there will be some different things on display.

Lou: I am excited. Listen, that is actually one of my favorite attractions because I think it is so much about Walt and the history of the company and you know, we talk about Walt Disney...

Dave: It's very important, I think, especially for the young people of today that don't really know of Walt Disney the man, and they know Walt Disney as a company or a place or a thing; they don't think of it as an actual person. And this is at least one place that we can testify to the fact that yes indeed there was a man who started this all

Lou: I agree. The fact that it personalizes him so well is why I love that attraction so much and why I think it is so very important and I hope it never goes away and continues to change. You know, part of the reason why I wanted to talk to you now, Dave, and have you on the show is, like I said at the beginning, I'm happy for you but I'm sad to see you go. You know, like many people in the company, you started out as, you know, what was to be sort of a temporary position, you were writing your little book and now 40 years later you're retiring ,and I'm going to ask you the difficult questions that I have to ask, things like you know, looking back, what might be sort of the most rewarding or the most gratifying part of what you've done with your career as an archivist for the company?

Dave: Well, the thing that I think I'm the most gratified about is something that most people probably wouldn't think of, but through the years I have been contacted by hundreds and hundreds of young people that are passionate about Disney. They have questions so they contact the archives. In a lot of these people, I have seen the spark. I have seen the desire to work for the company and to uphold Walt Disney's traditions and so forth. And I have encouraged these people. I have mentored these people, and it's so gratifying today for me to see dozens and dozens of people throughout the company that I met when they were children essentially. And now they are members of the company and serving the company very well. One good example is Clay Shoemaker, who is the current ambassador, one of the current ambassadors at Walt Disney World. I met Clay when he was 13 years old.

Lou: That's great. And, that's great, I mean the fact that you are able to help inspire people like that in so many different ways, I think is wonderful and certainly a testament to who you are as well. Looking back, did you find that there was anything sort of may have been your biggest challenge along the way that you were, either were or were not able to overcome but in your tenure with the company, or collecting things for the archives I should say?

Dave: Well the challenges of course, it's a growing company and realizing you can't save everything and trying to figure out, well, what of this stuff should I keep and what do I not need to keep? What are the employees of the company going to need to see in 10 years and what maybe isn't as important? So you have to make ruthless decisions sometimes because you just cannot save everything. And that's always a challenge, and it's always gratifying when you've made the right decision, but it's also a bit daunting when you realize you got rid of something you shouldn't have.

Lou: Is there anything you look back and say, "Ahhh, I can't believe I didn't keep this?"

Dave: Right. (Laughs) I want a time machine so I can go back.

Lou: Right! (Laughs) You know, I, it's still very much apparent that you are still very passionate about what you do. I mean, I have to assume, I know you had talked about retiring 5 years ago so, but it still must have been a tough decision to decide to hang it up.

Dave: Well, see, 5 years ago I was reaching 65 and I thought, You know everybody retires at 65. I should retire at 65, but I was still having fun. I wasn't ready to retire at 65 so, now this year I'm turning 70, and I thought, well, maybe this is the time.

Lou: And you're certainly leaving the archives in very able hands of Becky and the rest of the staff. Are you gonna stay on and help out or consult at all with the archives?

Dave: I'm very sure that I will be. I don't know just in what capacity. It'll probably be as a consultant of some sort. And they certainly will have me involved with the D23 events. They're already talking about several for next year, and I'll be retired but they want me to come back and do presentations at the Expo and things like that so I'm sure I'm going to be around. I just live a mile from the studios so it's very convenient for me to drop by if they have need of me for any reason, and so I assume that I will continue to work for the company as long as I can in some basis but not as a regular employee.

Lou: Well, we'll see. If you leave on a Friday afternoon, we'll see how long it takes on Monday morning before your cell phone starts to ring. "Dave, we can't find this."

Dave: Well, my retirement date is October 15, and I'm gonna be in Florida still on a business trip for 3 more days while I'm not longer an employee!

(Laughter)

Lou: So you and I spoke about 5 years ago, and I asked you the question that if on your last day of work you could walk out of the archives with one item as a gift from the company for all of your years of service and dedication, what would it be and I'm gonna ask you that same question now, you know, today, because you are about to leave, and they probably won't give you…

Dave: What answer did I give you last time?

Lou: (Laughs) Well, you can't cheat. I'll tell ya, you said that you couldn't come up with…

Dave: I don't remember…

Lou: You said that you couldn't come up with one because the collection was so very personal to you and so much of a part of you, I have to assume that's even more so for you now.

Dave: Sure, that's definitely true. And I just have felt that this is all my baby here so it's not going away. I can come back and visit it anytime I want. And so I don't really see that I need any of these things at my house because they're nearby.

Lou: (Laughs) Take the bird. I'm telling you, take the bird!

(Laughter)

Lou: You know, as long as we're sort of talking about your entire career, I'd be very remiss if I didn't point out to people that in addition to the archives, you know, in your spare time, you also author a number of books, including Disney, The First 100 Years, which you co-authored with Steven Clark, who's from D23, and Disney A to Z, which is the literal encyclopedia of all things Disney. Quite accomplishments on their own, not even including the archives. Are you going to continue to write or update any of those books?

Dave: I will, I am planning to continue to update Disney A to Z. I feel that's something that's important to the company as well as to fans and as most people know, I've been doing a monthly update of that on the Disney web site ever since the most recent edition, the third edition, was published in 2006. So I would assume that that's going to keep up. And as long as I have access to the information to keep it up. It's not going to be as easy getting the information when I'm not reading everything that's crossing my desk but hopefully the archive staff will set aside the things that I need to keep that book updated.

Lou: Well I was very happy to hear that you are going to continue to attend some of the D23 events. I know Destination D is coming up, you've got the Sip & Stroll, hopefully we'll be at the Expo back in Anaheim next year. Are you going to also continue the Ask Dave column? I know a lot of people like the fact that they can sort of reach, although they can't visit the archives, they can reach out to you via the web site and the newsletter.

Dave: I really enjoy doing the Ask Dave column and so I have offered my services to the D23 people that I would be willing to continue Ask Dave, and I think they're glad to have me do that.

Lou: That's wonderful because again it's a chance for us to sort of get to interact with you and pose questions that guests have that only you can answer, and I'll put a link on the web site in the show notes where you can go and you can post your questions to the Ask Dave column. Dave, I have to make a quick personal aside. I've told you this in the past but when I visited the archives and was able to go in there yes I was impressed with the bird and some of the Mary... and some of the things, but when you had told me years ago that you had put copies of my books in the archives, it was, that was my holy grail, that was my, you know, most incredible honor when you said that you had them in the office, I again cannot tell you what that means to me on a personal level. So, Dave, what I'm gonna do is first I'm going to post a couple of videos that I'm going to share with listeners from my Disney archives tour as well as something you did last year at the D23 Expo. You gave me a private tour of the archives exhibit, and I've been holding on to that, and I want to share it now with people as sort of part of your retirement, and again, on behalf of myself and everybody that's listening and all the Disney fans who you have impacted by the important work that you're doing, I want to offer you my sincerest thanks as well as my congratulations to your retirement and best of luck with everything going forward.

Dave: I thank you very much.

Lou: I look forward to seeing you in a couple of weeks at D23.

Dave: Okay.

Lou: Dave, again thanks so much for your time. I really do appreciate it.

Dave: Sure.

Lou: Take care.

Dave: Bye.

Lou: Bye.

Lou and Dave Smith

JULIE ANDREWS

Julie Andrews

Julie Andrews needs no introduction. In all the years I have been writing about Disney and hosting the show (going back to 2003), I have been fortunate enough to interview so many "Disney heroes" of mine. Names that meant something to me, but maybe not everyone else.

From Imagineers to writers, artists, and more, they were names I am quite familiar with, but I realized that for those people I know who were not as heavily vested in the "Disney world" as I was, they might not be as meaningful. But when I had the incredibly rare opportunity to sit down with Dame Julie Andrews for a one-on-one interview... this was one I knew I could go to my mom and excitedly say, "Guess who I just interviewed for my show?!??!?!" and she would know right away who I was talking about. How could she not?

"Practically perfect in every way," Julie Andrews is best known for her 1964 Best Actress Oscar® for her titular role of Mary Poppins.

Born on October 1, 1935, in Walton-on-Thames, England, Julie took singing lessons to keep busy when schools were closed during World War II, and it was at that time her incredible, rare, five-octave vocal range was revealed.

By age 12, Julie was performing at the London Hippodrome, which led to appearing in a variety of shows including Cinderella at the London Palladium and The Boy Friend on Broadway, which led to her stage role as Eliza Doolittle in My Fair Lady.

It was in the early 1960s when Walt Disney first spotted Julie while she was starring on Broadway as Queen Guinevere in Camelot... a story she shares during our interview. And the rest, as they say, is history.

In the early 2000's Julie continued her relationship with Disney by starring in a pair of royal roles in 2001's The Princess Diaries, and 2004's The Princess Diaries 2: Royal Engagement.

In 2005, Julie served as the Official Ambassador of Disneyland to celebrate its 50th anniversary during the park's 18-month "Happiest Homecoming on Earth." The following year, Julie narrated the Disney live-action film, Enchanted.

Julie Andrews was named a Disney Legend in 1991.

This interview is taken from my conversation with Julie on WDW Radio Show # 127, in July, 2009. You can listen to the interview at WDWRadio.com/127

Lou Mongello: How does one introduce an individual who truly needs no introduction? For millions of families spanning multiple generations, my next guest has brought joy to their lives on stage and screen by sharing her remarkable gift of song. Her storied career has rewarded her with a Tony, Emmy, Golden Globe, and, of course, Academy Award for her iconic role as the nanny who was truly Practically Perfect in Every Way. Mary Poppins is more than a timeless classic as, for many, its significance goes much deeper, thanks in large part to the title character brought to life by my next guest.

It is my true honor to have the opportunity to speak today with Dame Julie Andrews. Ms. Andrews, welcome to the WDW Radio Show.

Julie Andrews: Thank you. Very nice to speak to you, Lou.

Lou: With you, as well. Before we get started, there's so much I want to talk to you about; it's so hard to find a place to begin, but I have to say at the outset that, I mean it so sincerely, what a privilege it is to speak to you because of what the characters you brought to life mean to me and because of the happiness that you brought me and my family by sharing your gift.

Julie: That's very kind of you, thank you so much. They have also given me a great deal of pleasure, as you can imagine.

Lou: I'm sure. Your career began at such an early age; your first stage performance is at age two, and over time you have delighted audiences with legendary performances… I mean, stage and television and, of course, in film. And certainly, one of your most important roles was your very first movie role, and that was with Mary Poppins.

Julie: Courtesy of Mr. Disney, who I owe a great deal to.

Lou: I'm sure. As we celebrate the forty-fifth anniversary this year, can you tell us how it came to be that you were cast in that part?

Julie: Well, as far as I understand it, I was playing in a show on Broadway called Camelot, and it was recommended to Mr. Disney that he come and see me in the show because he was looking for a Mary Poppins. The first I heard of it was that Mr. Disney was in the audience and requested to come back stage to visit. I assumed he was just coming back stage as a courtesy, and I was very flattered. In fact, when he came back stage, he had loved the show — obviously, seemingly, had made up his mind about me — and asked if I would be interested in coming to Hollywood to listen to the songs, and see the drawings, and, really, the general feel of Mary Poppins: would I be interested? And, I remember saying to him, "Oh, Mr. Disney, how very, very kind, but I'm expecting a baby in about six months. And he very kindly said, "That's okay, we'll wait!" And he did!

Eventually, of course, I went out to Hollywood, and the rest you know.

Lou: Right, and clearly a testament to how much Walt knew that you were right for the part. And everybody really did, because the Sherman Brothers had watched you, and Don DaGradi, and they all sort of agreed before even meeting you that you were the person to be Mary Poppins.

Julie: Well, it was a wonderful, tremendous break in my life, as you can imagine. It was a major stepping stone. And, of course, I had never made a film before. I came out to Hollywood very green, but in the very good hands of Disney who looked after me and guided me and spoiled me, and I couldn't have been luckier.

Lou: And in addition to coming out to California and meeting the Sherman Brothers and everyone else, you also had the chance to travel to London and meet the author of the Mary Poppins books, Pamela Travers.

Julie: Yes, P.L. Travers! Yes, she was quite a character. She sort of was Mary Poppins, but perhaps even a little bit more strict, a little bit more quirky and unusual. She was quite individual, but very dear. I had tea with her. While we were making the movie in California, occasionally we would correspond, and I would tell her how things were going. She was, understandably, quite nervous about it, you know.

Lou: Certainly. She was very, very involved from the beginning — from the twenty years...

Julie: Wanted to be! Wanted to be! Until, I think, Walt said, "Listen. You have to trust us." I think she thought that she had to be (involved), but, in fact, Walt very nicely put her in her place, I think.

Lou: Well, after twenty years of trying to get the rights and convincing her, as I'm sure he was able to do, it's clear that she had that trust in him.

Julie: Eventually she certainly did. She said to me once, "You're far too pretty, but you've got the nose for that character." (Julie and Lou laugh.)

Lou: Let's talk about Mary Poppins, the character herself. She is somewhat different from the character in the books: still very strong, but what do you think makes her so special and so timeless. And how much, if any, influence did you have on her portrayal in the film?

Julie: Oh, gosh... I think that the influence and longevity of Mary Poppins is probably to do with the feeling of safety that she brings to children. Her world, and things she does in the world, are all fun. Even though she is very strict, there are boundaries. Children can feel safe while enjoying all the adventures and so on. She's just got such a spark of mischief and fun.

I was helped to find her character by my first husband, Tony Walton. He was the designer on the film — again, thanks to Mr. Disney's discerning, good eye. Tony did all of the costumes and most of the sets for the movie. When he was designing the costumes, he showed and indicated that although Mary Poppins had very formal clothes, if you saw a slash of petticoat or something like that it was quite often a beautiful bright orange or pink. He said "I think she's got a kind of hidden secret in her life. I think she's much more of a 'kick up your heels' gal than anybody would know. But that's only for her to know and no one else to find out.

So I sort of thought, well, that's a very nice thing to know while portraying the character; that she's actually got a kind of extra spark that not too many people know about.

Lou: Very interesting. And, certainly, much of the success is based...

Julie: I'm sure...I mean, I don't know if it was in the book or not, but it certainly seemed to help for the movie.

Lou: And the chemistry — it's so clear on screen with the other characters, and, certainly, with Dick Van Dyke — was so spot-on.

Julie: Oh, so adorable and such a lovely man. We really... we stayed great, great friends, and it was such a joy to work with him.

Lou: I can imagine. Again, we get so much from Mary Poppins, some of the characteristics that you talk about. But the film, I think, is so relevant and important because there are so many lessons to be learned from it, from a character that has all the right answers, all the time.

Julie: (Laughs) Yes, she does! We did a great deal of hard work, and (it was) a phenomenal lesson for me on the art of making a movie because there were so many special effects and so much waiting around. Movie making is holding yourself ready for that one moment when everything connects and makes sense on camera. But, in the case of the special effects, there was a great deal of patience required because they were the things that had to be made to work; especially when we merged with the animated sequences. There was a lot of choreography, too.

Lou: I'm sure that there are countless times during the production that just incredible memories were made. But is there any one moment during the filming that really stays with you or something that was profound or funny or very memorable for you?

Julie: Lots of memories. I mean, lots of them. We rehearsed on the back lot at Disney under big tarpaulins, but it was, like, September, I think. Baking hot, and I mean baking hot. And the idea was to toughen up all the bouncers in the heat and get us outside so we didn't swelter. Having just had a baby, for me it was like getting back into shape in rapid time, you know? That was one memory, it was mostly at the heat, which I had never experienced as I am an English gal and it mostly rains in England.

Other memories were loving and funny working with the children. On the last day of the shoot, I was...they saved all the special, difficult sets until the last week of the movie for me, in case of an accident, in which case most of the film was in the can. And so I was hanging up in the ceiling of this huge soundstage. I'd been waiting around for the cameras to roll and I was in an excruciating flying harness and I remember—I think it was my very last day—and I suddenly felt the wires that were supporting me give by about a foot. And I thought, "Oh, I must be imagining this." But I suddenly became very frightened that maybe my good fortune was running out and maybe something was going to happen. So I called down and asked that they be very, very careful letting me down when I did come down. And so, eventually, the word was passed about along the studio that when she comes down be sure to let her down easy. And, of course, at that point I dropped straight to the soundstage. I had counter-balancing equipment, which saved my knees but I did land extremely hard. There was this awful silence from everybody for a while. But, luckily, nothing happened.

Lou: And while the film itself is certainly remarkable for its story, the Richard and Robert Sherman music is nothing short of a masterpiece.

Julie: I know. They got it right, absolutely. And it had a kind of vaudeville quality which resonated with me because vaudeville was my early training and background. And so when they first played the music for me, it was so easy to say "I really relate to this." I really get that lovely kind of rum-tee-tum sound that they make: songs like "Jolly Holiday" or "Supercalifragilistic." They were all such fun. And were a joy to do.

Lou: I actually had the pleasure of interviewing Richard Sherman, and we spoke about how "Feed the Birds" was Walt's favorite song.

Julie: Yes, I heard that, too.

Lou: Did you ever get to perform it for him, other than while filming?

Julie: No. Not at all. I don't know why, but I guess he just loved to run the piece of the movie or listen to the recording.

Lou: Walt was so obviously a hands-on person; did he come to Soundstage 2 often?

Julie: Oh, yes, but not that often. Having said that, I know that he knew every single detail of what was going on, because that was Walt. He was meticulous that way. But he did trust his director, and he didn't intimidate in any way. And if he did come down, it was an event. Of course, he was involved in some of the publicity: pre-publicity and post-publicity for the film.

So it was a nice day when tea was set up for us both as a photo shoot. He and I sat and really had tea and chatted, and the photographer shot away, and it was very nice.

Lou: Did you — or maybe anyone else on the set — did you realize that you were working on something that was going to be so special?

Julie: No! I certainly didn't. I mean, I was such a rank amateur in terms of making movies; I was learning on my feet as fast as I could. Films are made in such tiny increments, you know, tiny pieces of a jigsaw that get put together later. And so much of the film was completed after I had finished my part because of all the animation that had to be done. So it was quite a long while before I saw it put all together.

But throughout it all, I have to say, the Disney Studios could not have been more kind, more loving, more nurturing to me. I really owe them a great deal of thanks for how they showed me how to make a movie, how to have a wonderful time while doing it, and meeting all these glorious people.

Lou: Do you remember how you felt when you first watched the completed film?

Julie: You know, that's a good question. I must have watched it in a room where, you know, they were just sort of previewing it or something. I think the thing that I looked for... yes, I felt a great joy, now that I remember it. But the thing that I looked for was did the very first take I ever took on the film — which was in the "Jolly

Holiday" sequence — did it look like I knew what I was doing. And, to my surprise, it did! So I was alright after that!

Lou: Well, certainly, for Mary Poppins you win an incredibly well deserved Oscar, and I'm sure you remember what that moment must have been like.

Julie: I do. I didn't expect it; it was a complete surprise. There was another wonderful film that Anne Bancroft and Peter Finch were in that year that was nominated called "The Pumpkin Eater" and I was convinced that she was going to get the Oscar for that. And so when they mentioned my name it was really a complete surprise.

Lou: Now, Mary Poppins is released just a couple of years before Walt's untimely passing.

Julie: I know, he died very shortly, much too shortly afterwards.

Lou: How did his death affect you personally?

Julie: Well, just the enormous loss, the weight of his personality was suddenly gone. He's still a benevolent and wonderful presence in the Studios, but just not to see him in the commissary, just not to see him coming down the Animation Building steps, to not have him in our lives... it felt very strange and very sad.

Lou: You know, Mary Poppins is still regarded as one of the very few, true masterpieces of film making. What is it about it that makes it so? And why does the film continue to stand the test of time for so many generations of families?

Julie: I think it's the perfect movie for families, in general. For parents and children, they're both going to get something good out of it. It's not just a movie for children or just a movie for adults. You could really — the grandparents can go, parents can go, children can go — everyone can have a great time. And it was the pioneer, it was the one that said 'you can combine live action and animation and make a musical out of it.' It was an amazing vision that Walt had for it, and such a clever idea and, at the time, it was so totally original. Yeah, and I think it's just a wonderfully joyous film; it's about all the good things, and gives one great pleasure to watch it, of course.

Lou: Absolutely, and I can't believe it's been 45 years. Disney released a commemorative edition with really wonderful bonus features. And to see you and Dick Van Dyke and Richard Sherman around the piano singing is priceless.

Julie: I can't believe it's been this long, either. I mean, it seems like yesterday.

Lou: I can imagine. But there's so much more ahead for Julie Andrews, too. And I want to start off by talking about an opportunity that people are going to have to meet you in person at an in-park signing at Disneyland.

Julie: Right! I will be coming out to Disneyland, which I really look forward to, on August the 29th. And copies of my latest book will be pre-sold at the event, and I'll be signing special commemorative illustrated — one illustrated image from Mary Poppins. And I will be hosting that afternoon, too.

Lou: I will certainly put more information about it on the website. You've got many more things coming forward: in 2010, you've got the "Tooth Fairy," you have "Shrek Comes Forth," you've got "Despicable Me,"

Julie: That's right.

Lou: So, so much more to delight new generations of Julie Andrews fans. Again, please indulge me as I sort-of step out of the role of interviewer and into that of admirer. I have to thank you for your body of work, including and especially your role as Mary

Poppins. It had a profound impact on me as a child, and, again, as a parent. And I'm grateful to be able to share something that has meant so much to me with my kids. It is such an honor and such a privilege to be able to say 'thank you' to you personally.

Julie: Well, you are very kind. Thank you so much, Lou. It's been a great pleasure talking to you.

Lou: You, too, as well. Thank you so, so very much.

Julie: You're welcome.

Richard M. Sherman

Have I mentioned that I consider myself to be the luckiest, most fortunate, and blessed man I know? Why? First and foremost, because of you. You afford me the opportunity to do what I love and share my passion with you. And as a result of that gift, I have had incredible opportunities to meet, interview, and share my conversations with people whose work I have enjoyed and admired for years. There are some cases, where I am not only privileged to have occasion to interview them for the show, but there is a friendship that forms with them that goes beyond the confines of a podcast episode.

That is how I feel about Richard M. Sherman.

I remember, going back to early 2008, wanting to interview someone whose work I had enjoyed since childhood. Mind you, this was a time long before what we currently have with social media, etc. Additionally, it was pre-D23 (the community for Disney fans which, through a variety of content and events, showcases and highlights the work of so many extraordinary individuals. Learn more at D23.com), which means that we, as fans, did not have access to, or even knowledge of, many of the people whose work we reaped the benefit of.

So after a long period of investigation and research, I was able to track down a telephone number for Mr. Sherman. Nervously, I called the number and, in my state of nervous anticipation, almost hung up when a woman answered the phone. Thankfully, I didn't. The woman was Richard's wife, and after I explained who I was and what I wanted to do, she and I spent the next 45 minutes just casually chatting as though we had known each other for years.

Fast forward a week or so. I was sitting by the phone, nervous as a highschooler waiting for a call to be asked to the prom, when the phone rang. On the other end was Richard Sherman, who instantly made me feel at ease. I was, and still am to this day, incredibly shocked when, just a few minutes into our conversation, he genuinely asked me if I was sure I wanted to interview him. Again, this is long before Disney Legends such as he were brought to the forefront through Disney-created content and events. I wanted to ask him "Don't you know who you are?!?" but instead reassured him that because of my love of his work since childhood, this was literally an interview I had (unknowingly) waited my entire life to do.

We spoke at great length, even after the recording had stopped. Little did I know at that time that a true friendship was forming. We would keep in touch over the years, and in 2011, I called to ask him a special favor.

Each year, I host a WDW Radio group cruise on Disney Cruise Line. In my ongoing efforts to "plus" these everts even further, I thought about asking Richard if he would be our very special guest.

I distinctly remember calling and asking him, and him immediately saying yes, but with one caveat... his only, simple request, was if he could take his beautiful wife with him.

In November, 2012, we set sail on the Disney Dream out of Port Canaveral, Florida with 500 members of our WDW Radio community and what would be one of the most special and memorable weeks of my life.

Richard not only performed a private concert just for our WDW Radio family in the Walt Disney Theater onboard (I STILL smile and get a little choked up when I think about that), but he and his wife were the warmest, kindest people you could ever want to meet. There was no sense of "celebrity" about him at all. He was so incredibly generous with his time and talents to anyone and everyone who wanted to meet and chat with them.

And for me personally, there are two moments which I know I will never forget.

This cruise was just days before my daughter Marion's ninth birthday (She was born on November 18, which coincidentally, is Mickey Mouse's birthday. Yes, of course we planned that). . As a special treat, we had a pre-birthday cake for her... with a surprise.

We brought her into the Sherman's stateroom, where Richard, his wife, and some close friends were waiting. I'll never forget the look on her face when she walked in. It was only eclipsed by her expression as Richard put her on his lap, and sang "Happy Birthday" to her.

There wasn't a dry eye in the room, myself included. I remember my daughter running over and hugging me after she blew out the candles. It was at that point that I jokingly whispered in her little ear, "You better remember this moment for the rest of your life!" (And yes, I reminder her of that quite often).

The second mental image is one that will forever remain in my mind's eye. One night at dinner on the cruise, Richard, sitting at my right, leaned over to me and asked if he and his wife could take my children to the evening show, which was starting soon in the Walt Disney Theater. I said that wasn't necessary, and as I started to take my napkin off my lap and stand up, Richard placed his arm around me and said, "Would it be OK if my wife and I take them?" Not knowing how to respond, I looked over to see my children already standing up, flanking his wife's chair. I, of course, said that it was fine, and I would be happy to go with them. He told me not to worry, stood up, and took both of my childrens' hands.

I will never (ever) forget seeing Richard M. Sherman, a man who, at that moment, was more grandfather than Disney Legend, taking our children by their hands, walking and laughing on the way to the theater to see a Disney show.

I sat there. Silent. Mouth agape at what was happening. And shed a silent tear.

Thankfully, my children remember and cherish that moment as much as I do.

I may even be a little choked up now as I reminisce and write this.

But back to Richard...

I will let him share his personal story and journey with you in the interview, but suffice it to say that Richard and his late brother Robert Sherman are the quintessential musical voices of Disney.

From Mary Poppins to The Parent Trap, The Jungle Book, Bedknobs and Broomsticks, Winnie the Pooh, and Walt Disney's Wonderful World of Color, the Sherman brothers' 13-year career at Disney (1960–1973), brought them four Academy Award® nominations and a Grammy® award. Richard and Robert wrote more than 200 songs for 27 films and dozens of television productions.

Enter any Disney theme park around the world and their timeless classics still play in attractions and shows, including Disneyland's Enchanted Tiki Room, Epcot's Journey Into Imagination, and Tokyo Disneyland's "Meet the World." Arguably the duo's most well-known song, iconic "it's a small world" continues to delight park goers, through a song that Richard considers "a prayer for peace."

Their 1998 autobiography, <u>Walt's Time: From Before to Beyond</u>, is available on Amazon.com, and the brothers' life stories were told in the documentary film The Boys: The Sherman Brothers' Story.

Richard M. Sherman was named a Disney Legend in 1990.

This interview is taken from my conversation with Richard on WDW Radio Show # 80, in August, 2008. You can listen to the interview at WDWRadio.com/80. You can also watch video highlights of Richard on our Cruise on the Disney Dream, a portion of his private concert, and listen to a follow-up interview with Richard from 2009 at WDWRadio.com/RichardMSherman.

Lou Mongello: As I've always said, everything we see and experience in Walt Disney World is about a story. And it's a story that's being told to us, a story that we're an interactive part of. And story has always been of primary importance, not just in the parks, but, of course, in the movies. And the concept of good storytelling first came from Walt Disney himself.

And an integral part of that storytelling in both the films and the parks is unquestionably the music. It sets a mood, immerses and inspires us, and, in many cases, defines a film, a show, or an attraction. And it's what connects us. And, for so many people, it's one of the reasons they love Disney the way they do, and maybe even makes us believe in that Disney Magic that we talk about as if it's a tangible thing.

And the name that for decades has been synonymous with Disney music and classic films and theme park attractions is none other than the Sherman Brothers. And their credits read like a "Best Of" of Disney films, television shows, and attractions, having written more musical scores for motion pictures than any other songwriting team in history. Including timeless classics like the music from Mary Poppins, the Jungle Book, the Aristocats, the Tigger Movie. Theme park attractions like It's a Small World, There's a Great Big Beautiful Tomorrow, so many songs from Epcot's Imagination Pavilion, the Tiki Room, and countless others. In 1965, they won two Academy Awards for Mary Poppins. They have received 9 additional Academy Award nominations, two Grammy Awards, four additional nominations, Tony nominations, they have had Number One pop songs, and an astounding 23 gold and platinum albums.

So today it is my absolute honor to be able to chat with a true Disney Legend, and one of the brothers from that creative team that has changed the world with their music, Richard M. Sherman.

And, Mr. Sherman, I want to thank and welcome you to the WDW Radio Show.

Richard M. Sherman: Oh, thank you. It's great to be here talking to you. I'm looking forward to whatever questions you're going to ask me, so shoot!

Lou: That's the thing — there's so much that I want to talk to you about, it's almost difficult to find a place to begin. Maybe let's start with the simplest question, which would be how did you and your brother start to work together and become a songwriting team?

Richard: Well, actually, it was almost inevitable. Father was a wonderful songwriter, his name was Al Sherman. And Al Sherman in the 20s, 30s, and into the 40s was writing hit songs, very big songs that today many of them are forgotten, but some of them still linger like the famous football song, "You've Gotta Be a Football Hero," that's one of his. It's a wonderful, wonderful song. And for the great Eddie Cantor he wrote "Now is the Time to Fall In Love — potatoes are cheaper, tomatoes are cheaper…" The older generation would know those songs; they were big, big popular hits.

I got the bug, I guess, to be a songwriter when I was in college. I started writing songs for college shows, things like that. My brother was going to write the great American novel; he wanted to be a writer. I wanted to write music for plays and shows. What happened was after college we both were living in a little, tiny apartment, and my brother was writing the great American novel and digging a hole in the ground, and I was writing the great American musical and digging a hole in the ground. And our dad came up, he was this pop tune writer, and he said "I'll bet you guys couldn't write a popular song that some kid would give up his lunch money for to buy a record." And it was like a challenge. Well, he sensed that if we pulled our wits and actually worked together as a team we'd come up with strong ideas for pop songs.

And so that's where it all started. And it truly is this: a song — a good song — has a story in it. And you always have to dig for that story, that angle, before you start drawing. I think that's the thing that attracted Walt Disney to our songwriting is we always had a kind of a hook, and angle. It wasn't a straight ahead statement, it was a song that had either a question in it that made you think or a statement in it that made you think, a hook.

And, basically, that's what Bob and I did, we started writing pop songs. Through sheer luck a little girl named Annette Funicello recorded a song of ours called "Tall Paul" back in 1958, only 50 years ago (Richard and Lou laugh). And, that song in 1959 became a top ten song, a big hit. And Annette, who was a Mouseketeer for the Disney Organization, needed new songs and so the publishers at Disney Company asked us "do we have any more songs for Annette," and, of course, we wrote song after song for her, and made many records with her. And, little did we know this, she was one of the pets of Walt's organization, and he had discovered her, and was listening to all of the songs that she had recorded. And, basically, what happened is that he said he was going to put her into a film, and he said "those two young fellas that are writing these cute songs, I'd like to meet them, maybe they'll put a song into this picture I'm going to put Annette in, because she's now so popular with songs."

That's how we met the great man. And that sort of brings you up to a very crucial part of our lives, and that's when we met Walt Disney.

Lou: And what was that first meeting like? You're told now that you're going to be brought before Walt Disney who, obviously at the time, was so successful with what he was doing. Tell me, what was the first meeting like for you?

Richard: Well, I can remember very vividly what it was like, because it was amazing! We walked into this office — we didn't realize we were going to play the song for Walt Disney himself, we played it for this music executive and he said "Yeah, that sounds like a great song for the picture. You've got to play it for the boss."

And I said "Who's the boss?"

And he said, "Walt Disney, of course."

So I said, "You mean we're going to play for this icon?" We never realized that we'd ever meet the man.

And so we were in this office, and he brought us into the actual offices of Walt Disney. And he was sitting behind a desk very occupied, writing, signing some autographs or something like that.

His opening line to us: "Are you fellas really brothers, or are you just using that name? Because when I was in vaudeville we used to have brother acts and we never were brothers!" I can't believe he threw it, he was so funny and sort of friendly.

And I said, no, no we have the same parents, Mr. Disney."

And he said "No, call me Walt, call me Walt." He didn't like to be called Mr. Disney. So then he said, "Let me tell you about this picture," and he launched into describing a picture that had nothing to do with the film that we had written the song for. He was describing what became The Parent Trap, the Haley Mills picture.

We had written a song for a picture called The Horse Masters for Annette Funicello. So he was into this long description of this picture, and my brother, Bob, who is very brave, said, "Mr. Disney… uh, Walt, we have come with a song for Annette Funicello, we don't know about this other picture."

So he says, "Oh, well why did you let me go on like this?" (Lou and Richard laugh.) How do you tell this man, this world famous man, that you're talking about the wrong picture? You stop him. So he said, "Okay, let's go into the other room, and let's hear this song."

So I played this song, the Strummin' Song for him, this song we had written for Annette. And he said, which is typical of Disney, "That'll work. Now, I wasted a lot of time on this other thing…." so, he actually had given us a huge compliment, because Walt never said anything more than 'that'll work' to people that were working for him, because he didn't want to spoil them. He'd never say "Wonderful, Great, Perfect." He would just say "That'll work." But, at the time, we thought that was kind of a put down for this song that we slaved, we really worked hard to get the right song for that picture.

So, basically, he started on this other picture, and he handed us a script, and the script was called "We Belong Together," and that was the picture that became The Parent Trap, which is our very first Disney major picture that we had done.

Lou: Yeah, I tried to imagine what that must be like, and then hearing the story about how you don't want to interrupt the man as he's on a roll, but… we'll talk specifically about some of the films you worked on and some of the attractions, but you worked for Disney during, really, what was a Golden Age for the Studios.

What was it like working with and for Walt Disney? What are some of your fondest memories during that time?

Richard: The thing about working at the Disney Studio under Walt was this: he was a member of the team, he was a great sparkplug. A listener, a remarkable listener; he could discern what would work and what wouldn't work. He inspired everybody that worked for him, and everybody was trying so hard to please the boss, I mean that was the whole thing. And if he told you a story, it was the most important story that ever was told by humankind. He had this ability to hypnotize you, to get you so excited about some episode of Zorro or something, that you just would kill yourself to write the perfect number for it. Or write the perfect dialogue, if you were a scriptwriter. Or design the perfect setting, if you were a setting designer. I mean, the whole thing was he was hypnotic about the way he inspired people. And it was great, it was wonderful working for him. He never talked about how much it's gonna cost, and this is the bottom line, and this is the blue, this is this..., he never talked about that. It's just the quality of the product. And that's all he cared about.

That abruptly changed when Walt passed away; it totally changed. But when he was alive, nobody ever thought about anything but doing a great job on the product.

Lou: And, obviously, like you said, we keep talking about story, and story was really of paramount importance to Walt and, I assume, for you and your brother, as well, as you were writing the songs.

Richard: Well I think, basically, the key to our getting jobs as staff writers for Walt Disney was our sense of story. Because all good songs, as I said earlier, have good story in them, good hook lines. And, when we were handed, eventually, a book called The Stories of Mary Poppins, by Pamela Travers, Walt Disney knew full well that there was no story line in the Mary Poppins books, they were just episodes. They were just wonderful, wonderful episodes with an incredibly delightful character, Mary Poppins. And they each had self-contained story lines, each chapter was another adventure. But there was no through-line, nothing really happened to the family. It's just that Mary Poppins would come into the Banks' household, have wonderful adventures with the children, and fly away again.

So, Bob and I, when we were handed this book, 'cause one day he handed us the book after we had done about six or seven assignments that he had given us, and he liked them all, he said, "Read this and tell me what you think." He didn't say "I need a song for this sequence" or "I need a title song for this movie." He just said "Read this and tell me what you think."

And Bob and I read the book, and we were thrilled by the fact that he gave us a book to read. And, secondly, we were kind of disappointed because there was no storyline. So we said let's take six juicy chapters, that we thought were really outstanding, put them together, and make a story out of it. Let's say there was a problem in the family, let's just say the father's not paying attention to the kids and the mother's off busy doing her things, and so Mary Poppins is needed. So she comes into the family, and she changes things. She gives little life lessons to the kids and to the family itself, and unites that family so that when she flies away, she's done a job. This was our concept. And we came in with a story concept, not just some song ideas or "yeah, that's good, Walt, it could be something." We came in with a real idea. And, also, we came in with a period. We changed the story from the 30s, which was depression England, back to the turn of the century when it was still colorful and charming and English Music Hall style songs could be used. We came in with all these ideas. And so we weren't just songwriters for him, we were story men.

When we sat down and talked about this project and what it could possibly be, that's the day he said "You fellas really like to work." I said, "We sure do, Walt." And he said, "How'd you like to work here?" Of course, we flipped, we flipped, we said "Oh, my God, yes, sir, we'd love to." And that was August, I think it was, of 1960. And so from that point on we were the staff writers, and we worked on everything.

But it was always story, story, story. I mean, that was what it was all about. And that was our key to our being successful at Disney.

Lou: And I think that was the fascinating part: you weren't just songwriters, you really were involved in the creative process of the films themselves, and I think that's why the songs work so well.

Richard: Well, thank you. That's very nice for you to say that. But, actually, we were very fortunate. We weren't just like augmenting or adding something to a film, we were actually helping to paint the picture in our way. And sometimes it was merely a title song for a film, sometimes it was a whole musical with storytelling throughout and character development throughout. It all depended on the project; each project was different.

In all, we did about thirty-six films at the Disney Studio in those days, and then we subsequently came back and did others. But ten years there was very, very, let's say, prolific. We worked every day, and we loved it.

Lou: Going back to stories and writing for the films, is it fair to say, maybe, that you wrote songs for the characters in the films as opposed to the actors themselves, even though you have the benefit of working and writing for people like Julie Andrews and Dick Van Dyke and Louis Prima?

Richard: You're absolutely right, you've said it all; I'll just repeat what you said and say this: we wrote for the character. We never wrote for the actor. On rare occasions when we were told 'we're gonna have Maurice Chevalier in a film, we need a number for him,' we could hear his voice when we were doing it. But all the songs for Mary Poppins and in Jungle Book when Louis Prima sings "I'm Wan'na Be Like You," I mean, we had no idea Louis Prima was going to do it. All we knew was that we were writing about this ape, and we had to write a funny song about a scary ape and make him to be fun instead of scary. And so we made him the king of the swingers, and that gave us a jazz number.

I mean, these are things where we just wrote the song. And when we were finished with the song, then we would talk with Walt and we would talk with the other producers and directors about casting. And when we found the person that we wanted, we'd come and test him and make sure he was right. So, all these things are ingredients in the creation of the film. But, in the case of the Sherman Brothers writing for Disney, 95% of all the songs we wrote, we wrote for the character and not for the actor.

Lou: Around the same time as Mary Poppins—early to mid-60s—the 1964–65 World's Fair is approaching, and you are asked to write for two attractions, the Carousel of Progress and It's a Small World. I'm going to ask you about each of these individually, but first tell us about the challenge of being presented with writing for an attraction versus writing for a motion picture.

Richard: Well, each and every assignment that we had was an individual unto itself, because if you you're going to have to write for a stuffed teddy bear or a tiger who is called TIgger and jumps around, it's just as much of a challenge as to write for a concept that's a Carousel of Progress that's going to be putting people into this auditorium that swings around so that there are six different stories that are being told. Each one of these was an individual challenge, and it was fun, it was great. Because we never knew what we were going to do from one day to the next.

I recall, the first challenge was the Carousel of Progress. They were constructing this for the World's Fair, it was going to be sponsored by General Electric, and it was going to tell the story of how electricity has changed man's life. And how we came from an ice cube sitting in a bathtub for cooling the house to electronic devices. You know, it was just remarkable how this was done and depicted. It would take me two hours to even describe it. Let me just say we were given an assignment, by Walt, to write a song that would tell the story with broad strokes of how life has changed through man's ingenuity, of man reaching further, challenging the envelope and going further. We had to have a king of a song that would change in period from the turn of the century, which would be ragtime, to the jazz age, which would be jazz music, to the swing period, which would be 30's and 40's Big Band Era, and into the 60's which would be the current day at that time, and that would be the sweet music, sort of Mantovani strings and things. So, basically, one song could be played in different guises, different arrangements. All of these were little buttons that were pressed to us, and then he said 'I need it yesterday,' because he always needed it right away.

I remember vividly the inspiration for "There's a Great Big Beautiful Tomorrow," which is the theme song for the GE Pavilion, which was the Carousel of Progress. We started talking about it, and said 'Well, another one of Walt's big dreams and we have to sit there and create something for him.' So, we said 'well, Walt has a dream, and that's the start.' So we started with that, and he said 'we cant say like that in a song.' If you listen closely to the lyrics, there's a line that says "MAN has a dream, and that's the start. He follows his dream with mind and heart. And when it becomes a reality, it's a dream come true for you and me." That's all part of the lyric of "There's a Great Big Beautiful Tomorrow."

And so, basically, Walt Disney was the inspiration for the wellspring that gave us the key to writing that song. And he loved it, he liked the play on the "Bs," with the great Big Beautiful Tomorrow. Shining at the end of every day, very optimistic. Walt was definitely an optimistic man, he liked to look at the bright side of things. And it was Walt's song, and he loved the song very much. Of course, he never said anything but 'that'll work' to us. But to everybody else he'd say 'they wrote the perfect number for this,' and that was it. That was Walt's way.

That was the one song for the World's Fair, which became a permanent attraction at the parks, and the other song that we wrote was "It's a Small World After All." Here we were like troubleshooters. Because they had this incredibly beautiful concept of a boat ride through the water, the audio-animatronic dolls all beautifully gowned and costumed, singing. And they were singing national anthems of the various countries, that was the concept on paper. And they started recording these voices to do that. And, as you can imagine, it was an absolute disaster. Because, if you walked through this—it was not boats at the time, it was a mockup—and you'd walk through the serpentine trail listening to these voices, the first three or four groups were kind of charming and delightful, and all the sudden you heard nothing, it was all swishing together and it was cacophony. And so Bob and I were called in to come up with a simple song that could be translated into any language. It had to have sort of simple repetitions in it. And so we were told 'like the simplest possible song, but saying the most you possibly can.'

It was a salute to the children of the world, and it was call Unicef's Salute to the Children of the World, that was the working title of it. And we said, 'Walt, can we come up with something better than that,' and he said 'well, yeah, if you can, but remember it's about the small children of the world, the hope of the future.' He gave us that to start with, and so we came up with the concept "it's a small world, after all. Let's not blow each other up. Let's learn to respect each other and love each other." And that's what we were saying without saying those words, we just said "It's a small world, after all. It's a world of laughter, and a world of tears; a world of hopes, and a world of fears. There's so much that we share that it's time we're aware it's a small world after all." That's what we said in the song. And if you want to hear it as a jingle, you want to shoot us. But if you hear it slowly and hear the words you say 'hey, it IS a prayer for peace, isn't it."

And that's what we wrote. And it became, I'm told, the most performed song in the world, with all the parks that are playing all the time. And everybody knows it, which makes me feel very happy.

Lou: Yeah, and I'll have to admit, to hear the person that wrote the words say and sing the words, really, is a privilege. Those four words, even with all the amazing things you and your brother have done, sort of immortalized you. Correct me if I'm wrong: the original way that you had written the song, you originally thought about it to be performed in somewhat of a different style?

Richard: Oh, definitely. When we first wrote the song—you know, when you write anything you don't write it fast and in tempo, you write it slowly and carefully. And we were playing it and singing it, and Bob was coming up with wonderful words for it, and I was coming up with words on it, we were both working on the music because we always collaborated on everything, we actually were writing it like a prayer for peace. "There is just one moon. And one golden sun. And a smile means friendship to everyone.

Though the mountains divide, and the oceans are wide, it's a small world after all." That's what we're saying: Let's be loving and kind and reach out to people. But we didn't say 'reach out to people, loving, kind,' we'd just sort of imply it because Walt would never want us to lay it down with a trowel, just put it on with a feather. And so we just implied that.

He loved implied ideas. He was very quick to grasp an idea, like "a spoonful of sugar helps the medicine go down." And it has nothing to do with sugar and medicine, it has to do with an attitude. If you have a bright attitude about something, a sweet attitude, a tough job becomes easier. You look at the bright side of it. "See the birds, tuppence a bag." It has nothing to do with the price of bread crumbs, two pennies to buy bread crumbs. It says 'it doesn't take much to be kind and do a kind deed. To give love, it costs nothing. Tuppence is nothing, no money. It's just giving it, from your heart.' But we don't say those words, we just say "Feed the birds. Tuppence a bag." And the implication was there. He always dug the fact that we imply things. And it was the same with Small World, "It's a small world, after all." And the "after all" was the hook.

Lou: And you obviously followed your father's advice, which was to keep it simple, keep it singable, but, most of all, keep it sincere.

Richard: Oh, my goodness, you really are a researcher, that was great. Yeah, that's exactly what he said to us when we were young guys starting out, he made the challenge: he said keep it simple, keep it singable and sincere. And as he was walking out the door he said "and make it original." (laughter).

And so he'd always guide us in those early years until we finally got the right angle on things. I remember we had written many, many songs. Country music was very big back in the early 50's, and we finally wrote a song which we had a hook on, and he liked the hook.

And that was, we wrote a song, a blatant line: "Gold can buy anything." And then we had a cadis: "But love." Gold can buy anything but love. And he said, "Now you have a hit song, now you have a possibility of a hit song. Go out and try to sell that one." And that was our very first published song. It wasn't a hit, but it did get published.

Lou: In addition to "It's a Small World," really, two other small words that really define, to a certain degree, your work are obviously Mary Poppins.

Richard: Well, yeah, that was a major, major jump for Bob and myself. You know, we had never done a full musical score. We've had pictures with songs in them, and we've had popular song hits, a couple of big ones. But the thing is that this was a giant, giant step forward for us. Of course, it put us into the position of writing musical films, and that's where we started doing. From then on, most of our pictures were musicals.

But Mary Poppins was the perfect cast, the perfect creative team. I mean, my praise goes out to so many people involved in that film, from Bill Walsh and Don DaGradi, who did this incredible script, and Walt himself who was hands-on the entire time, pushing everybody and creating the final product. And Peter Ellenshaw, the incredible mat artist who did the mats—there in Burbank, California we were in Edwardian England because of his artistic creativity. There were so many people who contributed, and I haven't even mentioned the superlative cast, with Julie Andrews and Dick Van Dyke and Glynis Johns and David Tomlinson. All these wonderful people that were part of our cast. It was a labor of great love and great talent on many, many parts. And Bob and I were lucky enough to be the songwriters. We really loved working on it and helping with the story, because that's what we did.

Lou: I applaud you for crediting so many people, but I have to say that what you did and what your brother did on this work made this film the timeless classic that it remains. And, to your credit, in addition to receiving your Oscar, you also coined a word that's a staple of every Disney fan's vocabulary, you put it to song, and you have to allow me to just step through the songs that you wrote for the film so as not to minimize your impact on it: A Spoonful of Sugar. Jolly Holiday. I Love to Laugh. Chim Chim Cheree. Feed the Birds. Step In Time. Stay Awake. A Man Has Dreams. The Life I Lead. Let's Go Fly a Kite, one of my personal favorites. Fidelity Fiduciary Bank. The Perfect Nanny. And, of course, Supercalifragilisticexpialidocious.

I don't think that I'm exaggerating when I say that what you did qualifies as a true masterpiece.

Richard: Well, you are very, very kind to say that. I'm very proud of it, I know Bob is. And we feel it was a big, big leap forward for our career, and we were very lucky, I think, to have a boss like Walt Disney who helped select what was going to finally wind up in the film. Because, as you see, as we developed this film, we were developing many of the chapters that we were exploring to see which other chapters he might use. And so a lot of songs were written for the film that we never used. Some of them found their life in another film, and we'd change it a little bit and use it someplace else, but basically, the songs that were selected were really the very cream of all the things we were doing. They really were story, each song had a story. A part of the story was being told through the song. I think the key to a really good musical is if you don't have the songs, you don't have a picture. And I think that's what we had here, we had hunks of the story, I mean huge hunks of dialogue were just sung. And people didn't even realize they were hearing songs performed when they were doing it because it was so woven into the film.

One of my favorites of all the songs in the picture, there are two reprises that we used near the end of the film when the father and Bert had a conversation. And the father things his life is falling apart because he's been fired from the bank for causing a ruckus, you know there was a run on the bank because the little boy didn't want to invest his tuppence in the bank (laughs), and so everything falls apart and he's very sad and he says "A man has dreams of walking with giants, to carve his niche in the edifice of time." And he's feeling sorry for himself, and he says "it's Mary Poppins; she's the one that caused all this trouble."

And then Bert pipes in, "Oh, yeah, she's the one what sings 'A spoonful of sugar that's all it takes, it changes bread and water into tea and cakes. Tea and cakes, indeed." And they're having this conversation that is all sung! The whole thing is musical comedy, the way it's sung, and that's a really well integrated show. That's the way we were writing it.

Lou: And is it true that "Feed the Birds" really was a personal favorite of Walt's and one that he would often ask you to come into his office and play for him on the piano?

Richard: That's absolutely true. Walt fell in love with that song when he heard the first time, that first propitious meeting when we first told him our idea of how we could do Mary Poppins as a musical. He asked at the end of that meeting, 'play that Bird Lady thing again,' so I played — it was not completed, it was just about 16 bars — I sang it for him, and he listened to it intently. And he said, "That's the whole story, isn't it?"

And we said, "That IS the story, Walt. That's the story: the father doesn't give the tuppence to the kids." Meaning, he doesn't give them attention. He's so busy making money and supporting the family, he's not giving himself to the kids. And the mother is so busy with her life, she has to have a nanny take care of the kids because she's not doing it. So then, symbolically, at the end of the show, we have this song "Let's Go Fly a Kite," and the opening line is "With tuppence for paper and strings, you can have your own set of wings." And the father, mother, kids run out to the park and fly the kite.

That is all symbolic. It's Walt Disney's way of doing things. He doesn't say, 'hey, listen, families, get together, go to Disneyland and enjoy each other.' He doesn't say that, he says 'let's go fly a kite." That's why Disney dug us, because we understood what he wanted to say to people. And that's the secret of the whole thing

I don't know, I think I drifted away from answering your question.

Lou: No, not at all. It was beautiful. And because "Let's Go Fly a Kite" is a personal favorite of mine, I really can appreciate your explanation of it.

Richard: Actually, that's something that came from our father. Our father used to make kites for us when we were kids. He said, you know, it's one thing to go out and buy a kite and fly it, that's great fun: we used to do that, too. But, he says, if you make a kite, then it's really yours and it's a piece of you up in the air.

He used to make kites for us, and then we'd go out and fly them, as youngsters. And we were trying to think of a good ending for the show, and it just came to our minds: what about if the father mends the kite that was broken at the beginning of the movie, and he says 'to heck with all of this worrying about the bank, I'm going to take my kids out to fly a kite together.' And they all go out and fly the kite. People were crying at the end of the picture. Why? Because it's so pretty, it's a statement. Without insulting anybody by telling them what it is. You just felt it in your gut. And that's we tried to do.

And, in answer to your question about "Feed the Birds," yes, it was his favorite song. And many times on Friday afternoons, he'd call us up and say 'what are you working on,' and we'd come over and tell him. We knew that's not what he wanted to hear. He knew what we were working on. He said, "Okay, play it." And he'd look out the north window of his office, and I'd sing and play "Feed the Birds" for him. He'd say, "Well. Have a good weekend, boys." And he'd send us off.

He was very sentimental, he loved that song. I'll tell you a little story: about five, six years ago, the Disney people decided to have this statue, this wonderful bronze statue of Walt and Mickey Mouse called "The Partners," officially dedicated out in Disneyland. And so they had a big ceremony on the 100th anniversary of Walt Disney's birth. And I was asked to come and play some of the songs we had done for the parks and some of the things, which I did. And there were thousands of people, maybe 2500 people out on Main Street, in Disneyland. I remember I was playing this white piano, and there was a hush. I had finished playing one of the songs, Small World or something, and I said "I'm going to play this one song just for Walt. It was his favorite." So I looked at the statue and said, "This one's for you, Walt," and I sang and played "Feed the Birds." And you could hear a pin drop in this setting, it was just amazing. And toward the end of the song, just as I sang "Tuppence, tuppence, tuppence a bag," one bird out of a clear sky—there wasn't anything, not even a cloud, in the sky—came flying out of nowhere right down swooping under to where I was with the piano, right past where I was with the piano, and up into the sky again as I finished the song. And I heard an audible intake of breath from 2500 people on Main Street in Disneyland. And then, I couldn't even believe it. They applauded, of course. I said "What was that" to one of the officials there, and he said, "Well, Walt came down and said 'thank you.'" And I said, what do you mean? He said, "One bird came out of the sky." And I said I can't believe this. Well, there were newsreels that were shot of that, and there's that bird coming down as I'm finishing the song. So I know that Walt loved that song, let me just say that. I think it was him.

Lou: And I'm sure that everybody else that saw that felt the exact same. Without speaking a word, they all thought the same thing.

Richard: Oh yes. Definitely, definitely. Walt was a great believer in people, he loved people. He loved that song because that song said it doesn't take much to give love. Give it.

Lou: A testament to, maybe Walt's... the way he was: during this time in the late 60s, you're working for the company, and you're asked to work on a non-Disney project. You were asked to work on Chitty Chitty Bang Bang.with Albert Broccoli, your first project in some time outside the company. Yet, Walt gave you his approval to do this, didn't he?

Richard: Well, actually, Cubby Broccoli, who was the producer of all the James Bond films, had acquired the one Ian Fleming story about the magical flying car that Ian had written for his son. Because his son said 'you write about all these Maseratis and Porsches and all these fancy cars, why don't you write a story about a car I'd like to have?' So he created this magical flying car, Chitty Chitty Bang Bang — made that funny sound. And Cubby got the idea, because he loved Mary Poppins so much, he wanted to have Walt Disney co-produce with him. And he could, you know, get all the people. Most of the people, like Dick Van Dyke, were independent, they didn't have to get Walt Disney's approval, but Bob and I were under contract to Disney. So he wanted to do a co-production, and Walt's plate was very full. He didn't have the time or inclination to do a co-production. But he said, if you really like this project — and I liked Cubby, I think he's a nice guy, a good man and a good producer — I'll give you a leave if you want to take it. So we were given a leave of absence from our exclusive contract with Walt Disney Productions to work in England with Cubby.

And that's the kind of a man Walt Disney was, he just gave us this permission, he said 'it'll be good for your career to do an outside picture.' And so we did "Chitty Chitty Bang Bang," which was a huge hit for us. Yes, it was, again, a tribute to the genius and the kindness of Walt Disney.

Lou: And, for you, Walt was right once again because you received your third Academy Award nomination, so...

Richard: That's right! We were nominated for that. And also, years later it became a successful stage show, and it's going to be coming back to the States as a touring show very shortly, I think in the latter part of this year.

Lou: Excellent. I was a big fan of it as a child, so it's nice to know that it's coming to the States like so many of your other shows, like Mary Poppins.

Just back to Walt for a minute...

Richard: Sure.

Lou: ...how did his passing affect you personally and professionally, maybe with your work with the studio?

Richard: Well, let's put it this way. How do you feel if your father dies? It was devastating, absolutely devastating. We loved him very much, and we depended on him—we never realized, when he passed, that things would change so radically. But, unfortunately, that's what happens. The people that took over, meant well, they tried very hard, and they weren't Walt Disney. For many, many years the Studio did not produce any greatness for a long, long time. They were doing adequate sometimes, but not great.

It was later years—certainly the advent of the resurgence of fine musical scores in films like the Little Mermaid and Beauty and the Beast the greatness came back. But there was a long period of time with a tremendous lack of, let's call it, spark.

Lou: So many people talk about "spark" or lack of direction. People almost seemed lost because their mentor was gone and didn't know what to do.

Richard: Well, yes, you said it. They said, 'well, what would Walt do." I mean, that's not a way to think. You have to say 'what would we do,' and you want to carry on creativity and everything, but let's not just keep repeating just what we did in the past, or do the safe project. Walt was always taking chances and going further. And, so, I guess maybe the lack of further thinking... see, Walt was such an outstanding storyteller and a super genius and didn't have anybody that, really, was that capable. There really wasn't anyone around, I guess. I can't give you exact reasons, but how do you replace somebody as great as Walt Disney? You can't. You just can't. A long, long time has to pass, and then, eventually, things come together and the right people assemble, and then, yes, great things can happen. It took a long time. Great things are happening now. People at Pixar are geniuses, they're terrific. But they weren't around then. There was nobody around then, so it didn't happen then. Now it's happening again.

Lou: I agree. There's certainly no comparison, but... I think, like Walt Disney, Bob Iger is doing what Walt did which was surround himself with the very best people in the industry. And I think we're seeing, like you said, a resurgence of greatness and creativity and it's a very exciting time for the company and to be a fan.

Richard: Well you have to have a great leader who doesn't necessarily have to be creative himself, but at least respect and honor the creative mind. And help steer them and help guide them, let's say. Guide the ship. But basically you have to have people sensitive to creative thinking.

Iger's doing a great job, I think he's doing a wonderful job. He made a major step forward when he said, 'let's not start this bickering of who gets what, let's work together.' And so he and Pixar got together and made one organization out of it, which is fabulous. I mean, that's a great step forward. I think the entire industry is better off for that.

Lou: I agree. As fans, we also, too, are feeling the wonderful effects of it. And like what happened so many years ago, the company is making wonderful films again. It's also having a trickle-down effect on the theme parks, and you and your brother, of course, not only wrote amazing songs for films, but beyond the World's Fair attractions, you've also written a number of theme park attraction songs. How were you first approached, what was it like writing that first theme park song and what was it, if you remember.

Richard: Well I think the first theme park song we wrote was.... (laughs) there's a funny story with it ... we were invited to go down to a sound stage and look at something. I remember Bob and myself and about five other people came down and we sat on bridge chairs in a tropical room that was all dark and everything, and Walt said 'Okay, turn it on!' So on comes the lights, and we see we're sitting in a tropical room with flowers like orchids and everything just started singing songs. And then down from the roof came birds, and the birds started singing. And it was the first audio-animatronic experiment they were doing, and it was called The Enchanted Tiki Room. And we didn't know what the devil it was because you had never seen anything like it before. There were carved tiki poles that started chanting—"Uggabugga, uggabugga." And it was weird. And I remember one of the fellas in the room said "What the devil is this, Walt?" (Richard and Lou laugh) And Walt looked at Bob and myself and said "You guys are going to write a song that explains what this is all about." And we said, "We are?" And he says "Oh, yes, yes, you are. And it's going to be a song that explains the Enchanted Tiki Room." Well, all of the sudden Bob and I are looking at each other and we said, 'well, there's no parrots, no parrots. I think at least if you had a parrot you could understand dialogue and lyrics from him.' So we said, "If we had a parrot, maybe the parrot could sing it." So Walt immediately said "Four parrots. We'll have a French parrot, we'll have a Dutch parrot, a Spanish parrot, and..." he was plussing the idea. And he says "now, what kind of song are we going to do?" And I remember the first thing that popped into my head, I said "well, it's a tropical room, let's do a tropical song like a calypso." He says, "okay, it's calypso, going to be sung by parrots... I need this right away because we're going to have to start the whole thing with a song."

And I remember, Bob and I being songwriters, and he said "Tiki's a great word. If we played with the word Tiki, Tiki, Tiki, that sounds kind of cool." So we said, "What if we called it the Tiki, Tiki, Tiki Room..." He said, "That's it! Okay, you're going to write me that song and explain what it's all about." And with that we were ushered out of the door and we went off to write it in a hurry. And it's the longest running show song, I think, that's ever been performed. It's made all kinds of records now, 40-some years that it's been playing. (Sings) "In the tiki, tiki, tiki room." That song.

Lou: Yeah, to call it a classic would be an understatement.

Richard: And the birth of it was simply a need to explain what the Tiki Room was all about. But once you heard the birds singing 'welcome to the tropical hideaway,' and they say 'in the Tiki, Tiki, Tiki Room' everybody starts singing along with them. And that's, of course, just the fun of it all. Just an invitation to enjoy yourself, and the birds are your hosts, and they explain what the Tiki Room is all about in several silly verses that we wrote and funny jokes that Larry Clemons added. So we had a lot of fun doing that.

Lou: And it's funny to hear just how quickly the creative process took place. You opened your mouth, you say a couple of words, and Walt says 'good, that's it, go do it,' and you're off writing songs.

Richard: Show me the executive today that can do that, and I'll be amazed. Because Walt could grasp two words, an idea, and he would know exactly where you were heading. He could finish it for you. We were so close in our relationship with Walt that, sometimes, when we had an assignment, we'd see him in the hall and say 'Walt, I think we've got the idea' and then I'd sing him two bars of a song. And he'd say, "yeah, that's it Finish it." I mean, it was just like that because he knew what we were going to do if we could give him the approach. It was a marvelous symbiosis that we had between us of really understanding the need for a certain statement and how we could do it or how we could enlarge on it. We've never had it since. I must say that I've had some wonderful producers and creative people that I've worked with over the years, and they're all inspiring guys. But there's never been anybody like Walt Disney. He was only one of a kind. Maybe one in a century comes along like that.

Lou: And, obviously, this shows the trust that he had in you and your brother, that he could just hear those two bars and know that the rest of what you would create he didn't even need to hear.

Richard: Yeah, I think that's the kind of a mind he had. He knew us pretty well, he knew his artists. Many times an artist would show him a sketch and he'd say 'yeah, that's it, work on that.' or 'I think the chin's a little weak, do something there.' And he would sort of make suggestions, but he was so confident with his team of great animators, and he had some wonderful staff writers — like Bill Walsh, who is a brilliant writer. He'd say 'I need a scene where this thing happens...' and Walsh would go off and do it. That's what were talking about.

That's the kind of a boss he was, he'd sort of steer you. With our songwriting it was that kind of a thing. I remember walking down the hall one day, and we were writing a song for Maurice Chevalier to sing in a picture called "In Search of the Castaways," and Haley Mills was in it. They were stuck in an ombu tree after a big flash flood had come, and they were really stuck and they're hungry and they want something to eat. So this professor, who was played by Chevalier, said 'use the things we have around us. There are some bird eggs over here and we can fry 'em on this pan, and everything….' And he starts building an omelet with spices and everything he finds in the tree, and he sings this song. And Walt wanted him to be singing a song as he's doing this. So we said "we have an idea, and the idea is "Enjoy it." And we said "why cry about bad weather, enjoy it. Each moment is a treasure, enjoy it."

And I sang that little song to him, with the melody, that much. He said, "Yeah, that's it. Finish it." And that was it. That became a classic Walt Disney moment in that film, it was just wonderful when he did that with Haley, they sang a duet together. It was lovely. But it all started when he heard two lines of a song and he said "yeah, finish it."

Lou: And, you know, that song, like most else of what you have written — including the theme park music — is that same happy, uplifting thing. For example, for Carousel of Progress you wrote the "Great Big Beautiful Tomorrow," again, one of my personal favorites. And I have to say that video of you and your brother singing that at the piano with you and Walt with the GE Jackets on is one of my favorite videos anywhere.

Richard: (laughs) Well that, again, was where he wanted to get some more money to finish the pavilion, it was running over budget. We had just finished this song. This, he didn't discuss this with us. We were just the kids on the block, we were writing our song. And one day he called up about three days after we had played the song for him, and he said his classic 'that'll work,' and he said, "on Friday, put a tie on. I'm doing some lead-ins, I want you to come down to Sound Stage 2 after lunch."

And we said, "Okay, Walt." So we wore a jacket and a tie and as he was being made up he said "we're going to do something together." They pinned the GE Logos on the back of our jackets, and he was doing a big sales pitch on what they were doing for the Carousel of Progress, and he wanted us to sing the song. We didn't know he would sing it with us! And he said, "prop the lyric up so we can do it together." So, on the piano there we did one take, really, and sang the song, and he said "kick your heels up when you go off, when I tell you to." So, okay, we did that.

And then, for the one and only time on film, he actually said, "the Sherman Brothers write a lot of the wonderful songs at the Disney Studios." Well, he said 'wonderful songs' to us, but not directly to us, he said it to the GE people. Well, sure enough, he got his money and he finished his pavilion.

Here is, again, the kindness of Mr. Disney; he was so wonderful. About two days, or maybe a week, after we had done this little bit for him, there were two envelopes in our office, and they were 16 millimeter prints of the thing that you love, that piece of footage of us doing this thing together. And the note said, 'This is a little souvenir of the other day. I know that your grandchildren will enjoy seeing this one day.' And that was him. That's Walt. He gave that spoonful of sugar... and I'm going to start crying now. He was incredible.

Lou: You know, that just adds to—and I think that's why I love the piece so much—just a beautiful story that surrounds it, because you were unprepared and there's Walt Disney singing one of the true anthems of him and his career and everything he's done, and what you've done. And then he tells you to go back to work so he can finish talking to the GE people, but then does that—that small little gesture that, obviously, so many years later still means so much to you.

Richard: It certainly does. I'm telling you, there were many, many, many times he did these wonderful gestures. The main thing, I think, is he recognized in Bob and myself—these two pop songwriters—he recognized that we had more to offer than just writing pop songs. And I think this was one of the greatest things of all because he recognized we were telling a story within the songs, we were saying more than just 'I love you, I need you, I want you, I lost you, forgive me,' I mean, the typical stuff that songs are written about. And we were writing about something off the wall, something you don't expect. And he liked that, he liked that idea, that we sort of painted pictures.

Lou: And you did the same with the song that, for some time, replaced "Great Big Beautiful Tomorrow," you wrote "Best Time of Your Life," again, a happy, inspirational song.

Richard: Again, they wanted… the GE people had a new president, and they wanted a new statement. He wanted to say "NOW" is the greatest time, not just tomorrow. And so we were given an assignment, can you give us another inspiring song about today (laughs). And so we wrote "Now is the time, now is the best time, now is the best time of your life." And so we wrote that song, they loved that. I think for about ten, twelve years Disney in Florida, Disney World, that was the theme song. But then they've gone back to "Great Big Beautiful Tomorrow," I'm happy to say.

Lou: I figured you probably liked the original. But for me, and for so many people of my generation, I grew up with so many years of "Best Time of Your Life." But both songs I enjoy.

And one of the other favorite songs of mine that I remember from a kid, that I think a lot of people don't remember, was the "Little Orange Bird Song," that you wrote for Disney ...

Richard: (Singing) "Oh Little Orange Bird in the Yellow Tree..." Yeah, yeah, I remember that. That was the Orange Growers of Florida, or something, were sponsoring a pavilion or something, and we wrote a song for it. Anita Bryant sang it. Anita Bryant, lovely singer. Yeah.

Lou: It's funny, because there you were: you were writing for characters and people like Julie Andrews and Dick Van Dyke, now you're writing for singing tikis and flowers and a little orange bird who is singing his thoughts.

Richard: Well, you know, each one is a challenge, and each one is a kind of an opportunity. I always liked the idea of just sort of, like, letting myself become whatever it is I am singing. I like to think of myself as sort of malleable that way. I don't just write about what I think, I write about what that character thinks. So, in a way, you're an actor. I know Bob and I both sort of throw ourselves into a time period or a time frame or a situation — and not just writing what our viewpoint is, but what that character's viewpoint is. And it's a trick, but, again, it's part of storytelling.

Lou: It's brilliant. And it actually leads me to where I'm going next, because you wrote some songs for Epcot before it opened, specifically — again, you talk about this intangible thing that you try and define, which is the Imagination Pavilion — and you wrote "Magic Journeys," and you've also written "Makin' Memories" — but "One Little Spark..."

Richard: "One Little Spark," again—that wonderful thing that the human mind has, and that is inspiration. How do you explain it? It's the combination of everything you've lived, everything you've experienced, everything you've read and heard… and, to a moment, a split second of time when you fuse it into an idea. And ideas are remarkable things, and that's what that one little spark is: Inspiration, it's at the heart of all creation," (laughing)—I'm reciting my lyrics, but—"One little spark of inspiration is at the heart of all creation. Right at the start of anything that's new, one little spark lights up for you. Imagination. Imagination." That's what it's all about. Yep.

Basically, it was, again, a statement sort of culminating our thoughts about Walt Disney. He used to throw so many ideas at his staff and his creative people, and then that "one little spark" would either light up for you or it wouldn't, but many times it did, and that's what the birth of these songs came out of.

Lou: Yeah, I think "One Little Spark" for so many people is not just Epcot's sort-of unofficial theme song, it really is their sort-of personal anthem because of the message that it conveys.

Richard: See, within every human being there's something wonderful, you just have to find it and recognize it. You know, go with it, use it. And we, as human beings, have a wonderful thing over the animal kingdom because we can take those ideas. 'Cause who knows if an ape has an idea? It has a reaction, it has a pattern, but it doesn't have an idea, necessarily. But the human being has an idea, and he can work with an idea. And so it's a blessing to be a human being, it's a great blessing. And we use those little sparks, that's what makes us human.

Lou: Speaking of the theme park songs, after the attractions opened did you get a chance to go and see them? Or even now do you get a chance to go and visit the parks and hear some of your songs?

Richard: Oh, sure, I love it! I love to be there when they're singing along with it (laughs). I've always enjoyed that.

I feel blessed that I had the opportunity to write these things. There are a tremendous amount of very gifted people. I'm sure the people that are listening to this — there are a lot of people out there that have a lot to say and are dying to say it. And you've gotta keep trying and putting your foot in that door and making yourself available. Because one day, something good can happen, it can happen. I can't guarantee it, nobody can. Who knows? If Walt Disney didn't like Annette Funicello, would I be talking to you today? I don't know. But there it is.

Lou: I have to ask you — and I know maybe it's an unfair question — about a personal favorite song or accomplishment. One that's a personal favorite for you, or one you are most proud of, or maybe one that has the most meaning for you. What song or songs would those be.

Richard: Well, I think it's so difficult when you have five hundred children to pick your personal favorite, you know. Each child, or each song in this case, has a special story, a special meaning. I'm very, dearly fond of the score to Poppins, I think it's very special because it was our giant step forward. But how can I forget the fact that there was a little rock n' roll ditty called "Tall Paul" that started the whole ball of wax out? You know what I'm saying. And "it's a small world," which everybody in the world knows this song; and a lot of people want to kill us or kiss us for it, I know (Lou laughs). There you go. How can I say 'What is THE favorite?' It's an impossibility. I can only say I'm very grateful for the fact that I worked for Walt Disney. I'm grateful for all those opportunities he gave me.

I think, maybe, closest and nearest to my heart would have to be "Feed the Birds," because that was Walt's favorite. So it's mine, too.

Lou: Like I said, I kind of knew it would be hard to pick one, but...

Richard: Yeah, but it's not my FAVORITE, it's just one of my favorites … yeah.

Lou: Obviously, since you worked for Disney during that time, you did come back, you wrote some new music for Disneyland's new Tomorrowland, you came back and you wrote for the" Tigger Movie." I assume that, since then, you've been doing so much more with your work on the stage shows. Give us a little bit about what you have been doing since your work for Disney.

Richard: We did some twenty-five films for other producers. I won't run a list down for you, but we had the joy of writing some wonderful, wonderful books, adding music and lyrics to some wonderful stories. For example, we worked with Charles Schulz on "Snoopy Come Home." We worked at Paramount with the Hanna-Barbera people on "Charlotte's Web," a beautiful, beautiful book that we wrote music for. And for United Artists we did two pictures: Mark Twain's "Tom Sawyer" and then we did Mark Twain's "Huckleberry Finn," two musicalizations of those classic American stories.

We've done a lot of songs. And then we went to England and we did "The Slipper and the Rose," which was a retelling of Cinderella from the prince's point of view. A wonderful, elegant picture with Richard Chamberlain as our prince.

We had a lot of great, great experiences writing for other people. But the highlights of our life, I must say, have to be centered around the Disney product. Having worked for Disney on recent things, as well, it's kind of lovely that we have this wonderful relationship. I know that I've done a lot of interviews for the DVD sections of reissues of some of the films that we worked on, and that's a lot of fun — reminiscing. We did a thing with Julie Andrews and Dick Van Dyke sitting around a piano with me reminiscing about Poppins for the Disney DVD Special Edition that just came out a few years ago. This is the kind of thing that I've been enjoying doing. I never cease to be amazed at how I remember everything, because it's so vivid in my mind, it's like yesterday.

Lou: Well I definitely want to direct people—and I'll put a link in this week's show notes where they can find it—to go and pick up a copy of your book called "Walt's Time." It's more than just a very beautiful scrapbook of your professional career with your brother, but what I enjoyed about the book was it gives a very personal look at you and your family and, especially, the relationship that you had—and the love that you had—with your father and Walt, as well as now with your wife and children.

Richard: Well, thank you. It's a lovely thing. That book came out about ten years ago. I believe it's still available. I think you have to go to one of these dot-com situations to get it. I don't know; I'm not involved in the publishing of it, but it's a lovely book called "Walt's Time," by Robert and Richard Sherman. And it's a lovely thing.

By the way, my son, Greg Sherman, and my brother's son, Jeff Sherman, and doing a beautiful documentary on the life of Bob and myself. It's called "The Boys: the Story of the Sherman Brothers," and Disney is behind it, they're helping them put it together, and it's going to be wonderful. It's going to tell our whole life story, not just the Disney part of it, but from soup to nuts. And it's kind of a wonderful story, different. People will be surprised and, I think, amazed and enjoy it, I think, because there are a lot of things about it that—I don't want to give away anything about it—it resumes the resume of our existence.

Lou: I am personally looking forward to seeing this, really finding out about the growth of the professional and personal relationship with your brother, and just the personal aspects that were so formative for you and, obviously, led to the both of you creating so many beautiful songs for so many generations.

Richard: Well you have been very kind in saying these nice things about my brother Bob and myself. On behalf of my brother and myself, I thank you very, very much.

Lou: Well, you have to indulge me, if you can, just for a second because I need to just — you know, this is a rare occasion for me, so — on a personal note I have to say that I'm not just in awe of your work, but the music that you and your brother created have honestly helped to define me as a person. The songs that you wrote for your films are so much a part of my childhood, and they were so uplifting and put smiles on my face so many more times than I can count... I remember singing these songs with my parents. And the songs have truly touched me, they continue to do so, and now that I have children, I'm able to pass them along and see how they enjoy them. And, so, to that I really give you my most sincere thanks for bringing me and my family so much happiness for so many years.

Richard: Well I give you my most sincere thanks, that's very, very sweet. I appreciate that.

Lou: It has truly been a privilege to speak with you today. I hope you will always know how important and influential and meaningful your work continues to be to countless millions of families across the world.

This is where I would normally say, "To learn more about my guest So-and-So, go here-and-here," but to learn more about Richard Sherman and the Sherman Brothers, visit a Disney Theme Park or watch a classic Disney film with your family. And when you start to smile, you can silently thank my very, very special guest, Richard M. Sherman.

I want to thank you so much for taking the time to speak with me today. Please give my best to your wife, and thank you so, so much. I hope I have the honor of meeting you in person and shaking your hand some day.

Richard: I do, too. Thank you.

Richard Sherman handprints

Charles Ridgway

Not all Disney Legends were faces on movie screens, voices on the radio, "celebrities," or even front-facing executives. Some Legends are recognized for the remarkable work they have done "backstage," and "behind the curtain."

Journalist-turned-publicist Charlie Ridgway is one of those Disney Legends. He joined Disneyland's publicity office in 1963 to not only promote the parks, but plan hundreds of press events and celebrity visits through the years.

Charlie was born in Chicago, Illinois on July 20, 1923, and during World War II, enlisted with the United States Army. After the war, Charlie earned his bachelor's degree in journalism from the University of Missouri and in 1952, moved to Los Angeles, where he joined the staff of the Los Angeles Mirror-News. Just a few years later, he began promoting Disneyland as a news reporter, and even covered Disneyland's grand opening celebration on July 17, 1955.

Just a few years later, he joined Disneyland's publicity staff, and soon after was promoted to manager and then director of press and publicity for Walt Disney World in Orlando, Florida, which was still under construction. Charlie helped open the Walt Disney World Magic Kingdom park in 1971, EPCOT Center in 1982, and Disneyland Paris a decade later.

In 1994, Charlie retired after more than 30 years with Disney, yet continued to consult on special projects, including Disney's Animal Kingdom and the Disney Cruise Line.

In addition to a love of Disney, Charlie and I shared something else in common… our publisher.

EPCOT Center

My first book, the Walt Disney World Trivia Book (Volume I) was published by The Intrepid Traveler (to whom I owe everything that has come to me since... thank you, Sally and Kelly for taking a chance on me!!!). Charlie published his memoir, "Spinning Disney's World," with the same publisher, in 2007. Over the years, Charlie and I became friends, gathering for meals, book signings, and special events. In future podcast episodes, Charlie and I wandered Disney's Hollywood Studios to look back on its opening day, as well as Epcot during their 30th Anniversary celebration. Charlie was more than a Disney Legend to me... he was also my friend.

In 2013, on the occasion of Charlie's 90th birthday, Orlando City Mayor Buddy Dyer proclaimed July 26 as Charles Ridgway Day.

Charlie was inducted as a Disney Legend in 1999, and passed away on Christmas Eve, December 24, 2016.

Charlie's book, [Spinning Disney's World Memories of a Magic Kingdom Press Agent](), is available on Amazon.com

This interview is taken from my conversation with Dave on WDW Radio Show # 5, in March, 2007. You can listen to the interview at [WDWRadio.com/5]()

Lou Mongello: I am recording live from the Disney MGM studios and sitting here with a true Disney legend, and let me just say that it does not get any better than this. I must admit, out of all the interviews I've conducted, this was probably the most difficult to prepare for, and I mean it with the utmost respect and admiration for my very special guest. Because the difficulty lies really in trying to take a relatively short amount of time to interview the person who has seen and done so much, not only with the Disney Company but in his career. Knowing the stories he's able to tell and the opportunity to sit and chat with him is not just a pleasure, but it's honestly somewhat overwhelming. His extensive reputation and credits precede him having not only done work with Disney but as a travel writer as well. I am talking about none other than Disney legend Charles Ridgeway, who recently authored a new book entitled spinning Disney's World: Memories of a Magic Kingdom Press Agent. Charlie welcome and thank you for appearing on the WDW radio show.

Charles Ridgway: Well, thank you for having me. It's a real pleasure to see you again and I look forward to doing a lot of times in the future. We could have some good times together.

Lou: I hope so. We've had a chance to kind of sit and chat sometimes at dinner and the stories you've been able to tell have been fascinating and hopefully, we can share some of those with our listeners and introduce them to the new book that you just had that just came out because your book recount stories, not only that you as Walt Disney's press agent can tell, but you offer unique perspectives on Walt himself as well as the theme park and the entire company through so many years. Your first hand experience with Disneyland and Walt Disney World offers a truly unique look at the theme parks and you offer stories that nobody else to date has been able to tell outside the company. So I said, who better than a person with his own window on Main Street to tell stories about the opening of Disneyland and Walt Disney world as well as in his book offer quotes by Walt Disney that only you were privy to. So I've had a chance to read the book cover to cover. I have to say that it's definitely a must-read for any fan of Walt Disney or the theme parks. So I'm really honored to be able to have this interview with you.

Let's just give our readers a little bit of background before you begin. Your career in journalism began in 1947 when you wrote and edited for radio and newspapers, 1952 Charlie moved to Los Angeles where he joined the staff of the Los Angeles mirror news. A few years later, he obviously realized what was going to be a historic event and phenomenon that it would become and you covered the grand opening celebrations for a little place out of the way known as Disneyland. So, as I said before you started with Disney, you actually covered Disneyland's opening day as a travel writer. And the first question that comes to mind is, are the horror stories that we hear about some of the problems that Disney faced on opening day, are they really true or are they kind of a little exaggerated?

Charles: No, they were certainly there, although I claimed to be perhaps the only guy around who was there and remembers it with great fondness, and as far as I was concerned, I had a great time. I may be the only one who did. Yes, there were all kinds of things that hadn't been finished. Actually, I went out about three months before the park opened to do the first feature story I think of any metropolitan paper had done and I borrowed a neighbor kid to take with me to tie the story to it and to get the pictures up. So the idea was that he was taking in for a state preview. Well, it was only about half done, we posed pictures, they were David Podas and he was a real pistol. He was a neighbor kid, I borrowed him for the day and we put him on the stagecoach, no horses. Of course, we had him fishing in the river, but in front of frontier land, but there was no river and we had him posing in front of the castle in seven-league boots with an old cowboy hat on.

And the castle was about halfway up with scaffolding, still up the side. Of the course the street was dusty and it was a very pleasant day in April. And the story actually appeared on May 4, 1955. Exactly 50 years to the day when I went back for the beginning of the 50th anniversary of Disneyland which of course began three months before it should have but that's the way things are. But it was a great time and David, we had a ball with him and he was obviously having fun. And the only problem was he went back to school on Monday and Monday afternoon his mother gets a call from the teacher that says would you come in for a conference? And when she got there, they said, well, you know, we encouraged the kids to have imagination and so forth but David came in today with this wild story and he wouldn't admit that he was lying, but it was about three months later when I went out for the grand opening well, actually it's the press premier or preview, it was obviously going to be a big occasion, all the celebrities of Hollywood were invited, all of Walt's friends as well as the press from all over Los Angeles and a few from out of town and they were going to do a live television show that day, which complicated things no end I'm sure. I got there at nine o'clock in the morning.

I took my wife with me and we both got dressed up. She had a brand new dress, shoes to match, and so forth. And as we arrived, we were virtually the first ones to do so. And I think the PR people were probably really ticked off as about it. But as we walked up, Walt was up out of the train station platform telling some painter that they missed a spot on the ceiling. And later I walked down the street as Walt was rehearsing his commercials in front of the castle with a swan swing around beside him. He was nervous as a cat. I tell you, he was really having trouble and he was flubbing the lines a little bit.

And I didn't dare approach him and talk to him at the time because he was obviously too busy for that. And after a little while, I went back up to the press room and I gathered up some press releases and pictures and so forth in preparation for the day and watched a little bit of the preparations of the TV people. And finally about 10:30 or so, I walked out on the street with my wife and the crowd was beginning to come and it was, I guess around 11 and we, I said, we'd better go get something to eat before this crowd. So we went down to the Red Wagon, which was the premier restaurant, and then we had a wonderful prime rib, a luncheon.

We sat just across the way from Debbie Reynolds and Eddie Fisher when they were just in love. They joked that they were late getting there because Debbie had to change a flat tire.

And there were several other movie stars there as well. And we had a great lunch, as we came out, down off the porch of the restaurant, we saw the street was just totally loaded with people. And my wife said, "Well, we can come anytime, I'm going home… it's too big a crowd for me." And it was, it was hot. People had been in a traffic jam coming down, what was later, the Santa Ana freeway was probably Manchester Avenue still at that point, and so they were hot and tired by the time they got there. The street was blacktop and it was so soft that the women's high heels were sinking into it and they were losing their shoes. There was a gas leak behind the castle really, where they had to move everybody out of the way while they got that plugged up.

One of my, what became a friend later was escorting a state Senator around and they were riding on the riverboat, the Mark Twain, around and enjoying it very much until a window frame fell out and fell down over the top of the head of this official and sort of spoiled the day for them. I stayed in the press room off and on for a while and went out at I think about one o'clock when they had the dedication ceremony in the town square with governor Knight and his wife and the head of the Santa Fe railroad and his wife and Walt. I'm not sure Lily was out there. I never did see her in that picture, but I went out to watch it and that's about all I did was watch and then because other people were there to cover things, I went back and started watching things on television as they did this over television show, which was hilarious in many respects because it was done live and they had cables all up and down the street, people were tripping on with those all the time.

And the master of ceremonies would transfer to reporter Art Linkletter in Tomorrowland, only he would go to Robert Cummings in Frontierland. It was certainly an exciting show. And after the show was over, not very long, I went out on the street, it's probably five o'clock and the place is almost empty. Everybody had gotten tired, the kids were crying and they'd gone home and I called Gretta and I said, come on back. We're going to go on some rides. So we rode everything in the park. Almost everything was operating during the day, many of the rides broke down and people were waiting in line forever so it was a catastrophe as far as they were concerned.

But I thought it was just wonderful. All of the notes that I sent in were a lot of theories. I just thought it was an amazing new place. Well, I looked at our paper on Monday morning, and this was on Sunday, the next morning I went down and all the other columnists and people like that had written in all these terrible stories about how awful Disneyland was. Don't go, it's too crowded, they haven't finished it, they don't even have drinking fountains, and they're trying to make you drink Coca Cola. Well, that wasn't the case at all, Walt had a choice of having drinking fountains or toilets working… he made the obvious choice. But they were complaining about everything they could and four months ahead of time, of course, they were predicting that this was going to be a huge failure.

Why would anybody go out there in the middle of nowhere in Anaheim to build this thing when they could build it where the people are? Well, Walt had a lot of vision on those things. And he was right, obviously, and they were wrong. They asked him at the time this isn't, it's obviously not finished, so when will it be done? He said, well, it's never going to be done as long as there's imagination of the world. Of course, that quote has been carried for all the years since. So I had a great time. I was sorry to see the results from a PR standpoint if I had been in PR at the time, but actually, it turned out that people ignored the advice to stay away and rushed out to see what it was all about.

And so they had about 10,000 people, which was a lot in those days, for the next day was the first day that the public could get in; one of the problems that caused the problems on Sunday was that they had invited what they expected to amount to about 15,000 people and 30,000 showed up. There was a mix up in tickets and I have my own explanation for that. Because what they did was they sent out invitations that said you and your family are invited to come to Disneyland for the openings and send us back the cards and tell me how many people are in the family. So they would send back a card saying that we have five people. So they would send them out five cards, which said, you and your family are invited to come to Disney World. So, they, I think, handed them out to their favorite neighbor or their plumber or whoever. And so, they had all these people that showed up, but anyway it was far more than they were prepared to handle and far more than they had for a long time to come. And yet in the first six weeks, they had a million visitors, which was obviously phenomenal except that when the summer came to the end the kids went back to school and all of a sudden the place was virtually empty.

So Walt put in the Mickey Mouse Circus, Mouseketeers Circus and brought the kids down for that and so forth and did lots of things to try to attract people during the offseason. But it was tough, even when I went to work there, eight years later, we had many Friday afternoons where it was a little rainy or something when we had a total of 2,500 people in the park, you have that many people on the street corner too. But it was certainly a phenomenon; it wasn't long before it became internationally famous. It was eight years later before I went to work there and I probably wouldn't have lasted more than a couple of weeks if anybody had any sense. The second day I was there, I had this little office in the City Hall or right next to City Hall. It was about 12 by 12, but it was at least 30 feet high and we had shelves up the side of the office where we'd store our pictures, contact sheets, and so forth.

And I was standing on the desk reaching up for a shelf with my back to the door and the door opened, somebody walked in and said may we come in? And I said, sure, it's not my damn place. And it was Walt and several of the directors. And if I survived that, I guess I could survive anything. But it was a wonderful time for the next four years Walt was still around, I got to work with him a lot. When he was down at the park, I certainly wasn't a confidante or advisor in any way, I was just the publicity guy and I had a boss named Eddie Mack who taught me everything I know about publicity and carried me through the many years after that. Actually, I began in 1963 and have still done a few things for him in the last year or so. So it's been well over 40 years that I've been involved in trying to publicize the part.

Lou: When people talk to people that have worked with Walt Disney, so often they talk with such respect and such reverence to him. What was it like working with somebody that is such an iconic figure and legend?

Charles: Well, he was not anybody that bowled you over yet when you finished talking with him you knew you'd talked to somebody really unusual. He was inspirational. I remember one night we sat and listened to him talk about what he was going to build called Pirates of the Caribbean. And he talked for an hour and a half on it and I swear it was more exciting to hear him and just listen… It was so exciting as it has now been in both parks. Because it's here in Florida, it originally was in California and now it's in Paris as well. So it's been one of the premier attractions and one of my favorites.

But it was certainly a pleasure to listen to him talk about it. He, and he, I think those who worked with him were inspired by his total dedication to what he was doing. And that could be hard on you, he expected people around him to be as dedicated as he was and as some people just couldn't take that. But for those of us who were really enthralled with being there, it was a treat to work there. And it's something we'll remember forever.

Lou: Six years after you were hired, you were promoted to publicity manager and then later to director of press and publicity for Walt Disney World, which at the time was under construction. Tell us a little bit about that, when he moved over towards the Florida project.

Charles: Well, it's funny, if I can take a minute to talk about this. In 1969, they decided to have a press conference down here and this was three years after Walt died to explain what we were going to build in the first phase on this 33,000… Well actually it was about 28,000 acres at that point, we added to it later. And so we had a press conference out on the edge of town. We had a theater we hired and we had models up and so forth. And I was sent down to help out with the publicity on that.

And I had never been down here before. And it was a real eye-opener and I had no idea that I might be coming back a few years later. But the thing I wanted to tell you is I probably am as responsible as anybody and letting the cat out of the bag about the whole idea of Disney World because in 1965, we were having a 10th anniversary at Disneyland and we called it the Tencennial and we were inviting press from various parts of the country. We'd bring them out on Walt's plane. Walt gave us his plane after he got through using it to go to the world's fair and back, and he said, use it to bring some press down. And he said "Well, bring their wives with them. Iif the wives like the guys won't dare write anything bad about us." We invited the Miami Herald and the Daily News and the Atlanta Journal-Constitution and many of those didn't accept.

So we did get somebody from the news, a Fort Lauderdale paper and a couple of papers in Alabama and we needed some others and somebody said, well, what about Orlando? And I said, what's Orlando? Which is pretty dumb, but I just had never been in this part of the country before, so you sure could see how much I knew about it. Anyway three years later after Walt had died and I've gone through some training and a few things, we moved down here. I came down when the place was just a pile of dirt really, they had dug out what's now the Seven Seas Lagoon and moved about seven million cubic yards of earth around. They had stacked the earth up where the Magic Kingdom is now, so it could compress over a couple of years. And then they started digging a tunnel down through the middle where the tunnel is now and down under main street going down to the castle.

Then came the October of 197, we decided instead of doing what they had done at Disneyland, have everybody come out all that big day and be all involved with it, with the TV show and all that, we would plan to have it on the lightest day of the year so we planned on October. Traditionally the lightest day of the week is Friday, so we had it on a Friday in October, first Friday in October, and we hoped to have maybe 10,000 people for that day. Well, the newspapers in the area started to have sort of a contest among them to who could guess how many people we're going to have for opening and somebody said 20,000 and then another paper said 50,000 and other papers had 100,000. Finally, the Cocoa Beach Paper, which had been used to the big space program crowds predicted, we were going to have 200,000 people on opening day, which was sort of ridiculous, but even worse, one of the correspondents over there picked up that story and transmitted it over wire services in Europe and added a zero in the process. So in Europe, they said, we're going to have two million people on opening day. But when it came around, we did wind up with a little less than 10,000 people on opening day. And we had reporters; we had not invited any press to come for that opening.

But a lot of them turned out including Time Magazine, The New York Times and so forth, all the important publications around here. And we had a briefing from the night before at the Hilton and then told them what we could do and we agreed to come out at six o'clock the next morning and take them on a walk-through so they could see the last painters going out. And that was the way it was because we were still not totally done by any means. But on opening day we wound up with 10,000 people and the New York Times said it was a disappointing crowd turnout. But it was sort of mild then... we had just a fair number of people that came in for the next few weeks until we got to Thanksgiving. Well, this was the first weekend that people, particularly in the Southern part of the country could drive in and bring their families and so forth.

So on that Thanksgiving Day or the night before, we had people every hotel from here to Georgia was filled up; people were parked all up and down the roads. I had just heard this story yesterday that one of our top guys was telling me that afternoon we had to close the parking lot at about 12 o'clock in order to hold the crowd down in the park to a workable level and even then it was way overcrowded. And so there were people parked all up and down the North-South road for 10 or 15 miles away and they were out on the side of the road playing ball and throwing a volleyball around and so forth for three or four hours and kept asking, when are you going to open? When are you going to open again?

And later in the day, along about five or six o'clock, as is frequently the case, we were able to open and Friday it was a similar crowd. The whole weekend was just a jam and we knew that it was a success. Tragically though, Roy Disney who had been worried up to that point because that turn-out, had not been up to what was needed, they were able to call him on that Thursday and tell him that it was a huge turnout and unfortunately he died of a heart attack that next night. So, he was here to see his dream come true because he'd promised Walt on his deathbed that he would see this new place open and he did.

Lou: Your work at Walt Disney world obviously didn't end with the Magic Kingdom because you also helped open up EPCOT Center; I still call it EPCOT Center, and in 1982 how was the opening of Epcot different from the opening of the Magic Kingdom?

Charles: Well, long as we're on that EPCOT Center business, it was my idea among others that we call it EPCOT Center because it was not the experimental prototype community of tomorrow that Walt talked about. He talked about a city where people could live and people could come and see how they lived and try out all the new technologies. When we got to thinking about it, that didn't work well. To think about having a whole crowd of people come in and look at your new refrigerator didn't sound so attractive. So we began adapting, and Walt himself said when he saw the initial drawings on EPCOT, he said, this isn't exactly what I have in mind, but it would give people an idea of the kind of future that I'm looking at. So we think that in many ways what's now called EPCOT is a lot like what he might have done if he'd been around long enough.

EPCOT was an amazing amalgamation of the new and the international at which Walt had an idea that was, we would have the future world, but we'd have a kind of international... at least the shopping area and so forth. So we took those two and carried forward with them. And for the opening of EPCOT from my standpoint, was the most unusual thing. We sort of discovered for the first time the availability of satellites as a means of publicity. That place looks so intrigued to people that the switchboards in the stations back home lit up like a Christmas tree, general managers are called down, say, Hey, stay over and do another piece the next night. So from then on, we use satellite live feeds as major publicity. At various times we had as many as 13 satellite uplinks in place and well over a hundred television stations going live out of here in addition to the networks and people like that, that would come on their own and do their own thing.

Lou: It's funny because not only have you seen, you know, such probably amazing advances in technology to do what you do and to broadcast and allow people to report from Walt Disney World. But one thing that you had talked about was that Disney never paid for advertising. Disney prided itself on never paying for ads and you tell a story about the person that suggested taking out a full-page paid ad in the Orlando Sentinel?

Charles: As we were coming up to EPCOT this was a big unknown thing. Disneyland was known now around the world and Disney world partly because of that was also well known internationally and as well as certainly across this country. But we weren't sure about EPCOT yet so my boss suggested to his bosses that they take out a full-page ad in 25 papers across the country just saying EPCOT is open. Well, he almost got fired over that one because our people at that point, their background had been in motion pictures and they were used to co-op advertising where they would go into a town to advertise a new film and the local theaters would help pay for the advertising.

So co-op advertising was something they understood and with the participants that we had with us, like General Motors or General Electric or Exxon or various companies that have been associated with us, they would do various promotional programs with us and we would share costs and so forth. So we understood that, but when it came to direct advertising, our advertising budget compared to a company even the size of it at that point was minuscule. But despite that, we didn't do the television or the newspaper advertising, those television programs and the newspaper people that came to that opening day and so forth resulted in a survey show the next day that 95% of the people in the United States knew that EPCOT was open. I don't know that you could do it these days without that kind of thing. Obviously, over the years, the Disney television show, beginning with the one that started even before Disneyland opened, was a part of a huge part of the success of the parks in addition to word of mouth, which is always the best publicity.

Lou: Well, it's funny you say that because you know, with the advent of even newer technologies and new media like the internet, podcasting, blogging you know, internet fan community, how do you think that changes or affects public relations and that kind of PR for Disney?

Charles: Well, it certainly does affect it hugely. There are many things that we did in those days that would be very difficult to do today. There are a lot of rules about what newspaper or news reporters ought to do and ought not to do that have changed over the years. So it's the place that tells itself and that's really the basis of our whole publicity effort, it is to get people, the writers to come and see it for themselves and report it and of course the new media and in large as the scope of that, those opportunities and measurably and it, does complicate things I think because it means that there are a lot of people coming in doing reports and so forth of great importance that we don't know where they come from or anything along those lines. But so it did change and still changing and changing very rapidly and it's amazing to see it, it's wonderful to see. But I don't know, it was awful good in those old days too.

Lou: Yeah. I mean, you're right about the internet. It is still kind of the Wild West out there because anybody can publish, anybody can podcast. But I think the one good thing is, for the most part, it's driven by people who share a common love and passion for Disney, so they do it because they really do enjoy it and they want to help kind of spread what they enjoy about it and their feelings about it to other people.

Charles: Yeah, sure. Certain passion is what it's all about. And for that reason, if we were not the kind of place we are, we'd be in trouble because people wouldn't like us. But people come and fall in love with the place and they have to go out and tell somebody about it and now they have a way of doing it. So yeah, it certainly has broadened our field and I'm sure it's been of great help in seeing the company expand.

I remember in the year that Mary Poppins came out; actually, it was a year after Mary Poppins came out, and Disneyland actually made more money than the movies did. And that was a shock to those people who made movies in Hollywood who had really told Walt, quit fiddling around with that funny little plaything down in Anaheim.

I want to tell you one thing that when Walt was around it was an exciting time, it was the inspirational time and all those kinds of things. But when Michael Eisner and Frank Wells came on board in 1984, all of a sudden it was like Walt was back. The inspiration, the willingness to take chances, new things, was just an exciting time to be around. At that time they started… we held back on building more hotels for years and years when we had this huge demand at one time you had to wait a year to get a reservation here.

And so they decided to go ahead and build a few hotels, well, they built 30 more hotels in the next few years, they built two water parks, and they expanded in all directions. They built downtown Disney, which has turned out to be a huge entertainment dining area of great consequence and a great help to the parks because, in the wintertime off-season, when the parks close early, there's not a whole lot to do... there didn't use to be a whole lot to do. So downtown Disney helps to fill that void and we try to make sure that people who come find what they want to do, that they are able to have fun and particularly to have fun together as groups, whether they're families or school groups or bands or whatever they are. It's a place that you need to have somebody that you love to share with.

Lou: I've said it for a long time, and that's something I often write when I inscribe a book and I say the real magic is in making the memories here with your family and friends because that's really what it's all about.

Charles: Well, and I guess that's what my book is all about too. Spinning Disney's Magic is much more about the memories that I have, which are all favorable. I have to tell you, I can't remember any place that I could have been or anything that I could have done that would have been as much fun. We did crazy things. There was a Donald Duck's 50th birthday, we decided, wouldn't it be fun if we could get 50 white ducks to follow Donald down the street?

None of us knew whether that could happen or not. So we called an expert and they said, yeah, you can do it, but you've had to have Donald bond with the ducks from the time they're born. So we sent Donald down to Miami to the hatchery, and he was there when they hatched out and got down on the floor and played around with them when they were little yellow balls and fur, and then we brought them back up and put them out at Fort Wilderness. And as they grew up Donald, go out every day or two and throw out some lettuce and get them to follow him around. And when they got old enough, we made a little pond out behind my office in city hall, brought them over there and we decided, well, as long as they're going to a party, they ought to have party hats on.

So we made some little cone-shaped hats and we found a way of sticking them onto the top of their heads, and we put some ribbons around their neck with their names on them and we named them after Disney characters. So you had Dopey Duck and Goofy Duck and Donald Duck and Alice in Wonderland Duck and so on. The problem we ran into was, we started to put a hat on a duck and immediately all the other ducks attacked him, they were jealous. So we figured it out. We put a divider in the middle and we'd put the hat on the duck, put him over there on the other side. As long as everybody had the hat on, they were fine.

And it obviously was going to be a huge success, but you couldn't have them march that whole parade length of a day after day, so we built a float for them and added a little picket fence around it. They were put up on there and they were the head of the whole parade. The funny part was when they get warm ducks pant, they opened and closed their mouth and there was a duck song being played at the time, quack, quack, quack and it looked like they were singing with the song.

Lou: That's great and you led me into talking about the book itself because that's exactly what it's all about. We've talked about wanting to share our love and passion for something that we enjoyed so much and that's what you do in the book, again, its Spinning Disney's World: Memories of a Magic Kingdom Press Agent, on a personal note as a completist and somebody that loves the place so much, the book is definitely a true must-have. I read it cover to cover probably faster than I read any of the books and it's because of some of those stories that you share stories that we've never heard before, even for some of us that have read so much. Part of what I enjoyed was the fact that you had a chance to meet and host and entertain innumerable celebrities. And the names in the book are a true "who's who" of Hollywood celebrities and politics and international affairs. What is your favorite celebrity story or celebrity episode?

Charles: Well, that's a tough one; there were a lot of them that I enjoyed knowing. Actually, the stories in the book are the stories that I told over the dinner table or something with a lot of these people, most of them, of course, were newspaper or radio or television people that visited us or when I was visiting them and we'd start talking about Disneyland or Disney World, and I'd tell them about stories in the old days. So that's what these stories are all about. So there were many that became, I felt were good friends even though we didn't see each other very often. Helen Hayes was one of my favorite people. I remember I'll never forget one night we were up in the contemporary hotel looking out over the Seven Seas Lagoon and the lights of the Magic Kingdom, the Polynesian Village and the Grand Floridian across the way.

And she looked out over and she said, I have been all over the world and there's no sight like this at all. Another one was Bob Hope who for some reason got my name and I was the one he called usually when he wanted to visit. And he came down in this area frequently and he'd call up and say, Hey, I want to come over and see the park. Well, there were two occasions, one was we were having a new parade, and I said, Hey, how would you like to come and be the Grand Marshall of our parade? So he did. He came in, just volunteered. And then when we did the groundbreaking for the Disney-MGM Studios here, out in the middle of the swamp, we built a billboard with a sort of a Hollywood look to it and so forth.

And we were going to do a little ceremony with some fireworks and so forth. And Michael Eisner and Frank Wells were coming down for it. And two days ahead of time, Bob called us, said, well, I'm going to be in town and I wanted to come by and see what's new. And I said why don't you come and take part in our service? So he did. And everybody said how'd you get him to do that?

Lou: And again, it's a who's who, you not only work with, but you befriended people like William F. Buckley and Lowell Thomas, David Brinkley, Tom Brokaw, Peter Jennings, Charlie Gibson. One of the other stories that I liked, there was a story about Supreme Court Justice, Warren Burger, and his commemoration for the constitution's 200th anniversary.

Charles: Yeah. I actually, I was talking to Walter Cronkite and I used to drop in and see him in his office now and again just to chat.

Lou: Yeah, you don't know how impressive that sounds... "I just dropped in on Walter Cronkite...." (laughs)

Charles: That sounds to kind of being egotistical and it is, I guess, because I'm not in the same league with Walter by any stretched imagination, but you have to get with Warren Burger, he's looking for some way to promote this 200th anniversary of the constitution, you'd think that's so important that he's having a sort of a dull response. So I say, so I said, Hey, that's like us. So he put us together and we talked to him and he agreed to come down and do an appearance and we kept it a secret. We started our parade in honor of the constitution, so forth, and announced where we were going to start it.

And in conjunction with the whole area, it was a civic function really at the new convention center. We had a gathering of all the press that came down to cover this. And we had invited several hundred and so on. And so we had not announced this ahead of time and when Warren Burger walked out on the stage and associated with Mickey Mouse it was a surprise. I have to tell you but it's something, I'm not sure this is in the book and I haven't researched it so I haven't got any names for you, but at the time, there was a famous I think associated press you will probably recall reporter who had been captured in Iraq and held prisoner for some time and was released just like three days before this event. And a friend who was one of my other friends, who was the editor of Newsweek Magazine... the reporter was with Newsweek magazine.

I called him and say, how about having him come down and take part in this event playing tribute to the troops and all that sort of thing. So he did. And he came down and his was also even more of a surprise when this celebrity newsman walked out on the stage. So that event turned out to be memorable in many ways that I'm not sure how much news way, certainly had gotten television exposure and newspaper exposure the following day. It did certainly let people know that there was an appreciation for what America was all about.

Lou: And speaking of appreciation, you focus not only stories about Hollywood celebrities and some of these international dignitaries, but you do stop to reminisce and you talk about the cast members in the parks and you really evidence your true appreciation and admiration for them. How important do you feel the role of the cast member is here at the theme parks?

Charles: Well, none more so and Walt realizes that very early on, and of course, so much of this goes back to Walt. When they first started to hire people the managers, the guys who are going to run the park said, well, we're going to go to the carnivals and the amusement parks around and hire people that really know how to run these things and whatnot, Walt said oh no, we're going to hire young people that are willing to learn and we'll train him to do things the Disney way. And so over the next few months, and I think it perhaps took a year or so to do it, develop a program in which the employees were not employees, they were cast members, they were playing a part on a vast outdoor stage and their job was as a host or hostess, the people who came in are guests.

And that need to be treated as guests, not as customers that you exchange a friendly smile with them, you talk with them, you get to know them and whatever way you can to be helpful. It certainly affects the guests, but I think it affects the whole attitude of the employees and the fact that it makes it more fun to work here than the average country place. No, I think I have had so many friends, but one of the great joys of working here as I got older was the fact that I had young people to work with because we have a lot of young people here who come and work for us. And Walt said, however, when they talked about closing the park during the winter, that was suggested because you remember that first fall with things was getting pretty light.

And the people said, well, there's nobody coming, so we'll just close up for the winter as most amusement parks around the world did. And Walt said, no, I don't want to have a staff of gypsies. I want people who are here to stay and who can carry on the tradition from year to year. And so that's where it began it's what continues to today. Many of those people, of course, stayed on to go on to be in executive positions. Dick Nunez who started out as a trainer just out of college Disneyland opened was director of operations at Disneyland when I got there and went on to become president and then chairman of all of the Disney Parks for a number of years.

Bob Mattheson that I saw for the first time in a couple of years last night, started out not long before I went there as a park announcer. And he went up to be vice president of operation before it was done and one of the key people in the growth of the company. And we were talking about, I guess maybe it's something it shouldn't be talked about, I didn't think about mentioning in the book, but when, when Walt died the family asked me not to let any press come into the park and interview people about how sad they were that Walt was dead, because we didn't announce it, and the only time I think we did I think at the end of the day when we had our retreat ceremony, we announced that Walt Disney had died but only to those people in the town square.

And we did not lower the flag to half-staff as we certainly might have because all of this was because they said, Walt wouldn't have wanted people to be saddened by his death when they were there to have a good time in the park. So it was an emotional time for us and an emotional time for the nation in many ways but we didn't want to have the flag flying at half-staff to remind people about it every day of the week. We tried to follow that policy even on national occasions where in the park we didn't lower the flag as many parts of the nation did. And some people took that as being disrespectful and we finally have changed to some extent and did lower the main flag to half-staff when the nation is in mourning for saying, I'm not sure that there's any disrespect shown about it. Bob and I talked a little bit about it last night. And there are people who would argue that one with us, but it's a part of the Disney philosophy that we created another world where people can leave their everyday cares behind and forget about all the troubles and all the Wars and all the rest of this stuff.

Lou: Let me ask you a couple of questions on a personal level. You've opened, at quick count, probably seven of the theme parks. What do you think is your favorite, whether it is for sentimental reasons or just favorite of the parks to visit?

Charles: Well, I guess I'm like Walt. I really don't have a favorite attraction. He used to say the people were the favorites. And I think it's the feeling you get when you're in, I think all of the Disney Parks. I guess sentimentally, I have to say Disneyland is still kind of my favorite. It has a special charm about it.

The others are the one here, the one in Paris, which I helped open and the one in Tokyo all are much bigger, much grander, but Disneyland still has a special charm and I kind of liked the idea when I went to help out with the opening of Hong Kong Disneyland a year or so ago, that it's exactly the same size that Disneyland was when I first knew it in 1955. It has the same number of attractions. The castle is a lot smaller than the one here, but it has that special charm and I hope that it will continue to grow in popularity among a culture that is very different from ours and is not anywhere near as aligned with a Disney culture as Europe and even South America. But it's doing very well, I think, and I hope it even does better.

Lou: You know, as we're sitting here talking about your career, I'm an avid collector of Walt Disney World and theme park merchandise. I could only imagine what your personal collection must include. What do you think the one item is that you really look upon most fondly, as your most treasured and collectible?

Charles: I guess unlike you I'm not, I'm not a packrat, to put it bluntly. And I did not collect many of the things that I could easily have collected over the years. I have the statues or plaques or whatever that they give out at 10 or 15 or 25 or whatever number of years of service that are very special to me. One, in particular, is the Disney legends award, which is a small; I mean a rather large statuary kind of thing.

But I guess maybe the favorite is four little pictures. They were original cels from Donald Duck is one of them, and Chippendale and can't think what the other is at this point, but they were part of a rather special happening at Disneyland. Years back, Jack Olson, who was then head of merchandising, went up to the studio one day and saw a guy hauling a bunch of original Disney cels across the lot in a wheelbarrow. He said where are you going with us? He went, we'd have to throw them out, we don't have room for them. Can you imagine? Cels had not been sold at all up to this point. And Jack said; well let me have those I think maybe we could do something. So the first thing he did was totally destroy their value in a way, they were 12 by 15 size, he cut them down to five by seven so they would fit in a nice little paper frame.

And so they put them on sale at Disneyland for a buck 75 and I bought three or four of them. And we framed them and put them up in my children's room when they were babies and they outgrew that stage. And so we took them down and took them out of the frames and I put them in a drawer somewhere. And years later when the cels were selling for $100.00 or $5,000.00 or $100,000.00,

I went looking for him and I couldn't find him anywhere. And we moved to Florida and as we were making another move, I looked into the bottom of a drawer and one of our dressers, and there was this envelope and sure enough, inside where these original parts of cels, so I had them framed and they're on my wall and they are a favorite memento of mine.

So I don't have much of a souvenir. I have a sign that went on the back of the railroad train in Disney World in the Magic Kingdom. On the final car of the train, there's a round sign that goes into the back. They were getting ready to throw one of those out at the paint shop one day. So I still have that, but nothing very unusual.

Lou: People at home are shaking their heads and grabbing their heads much like I just did saying, oh, these people don't know the value of what they had to people who are collectors and just love the parks as we do. You retired in the middle of the air in 1994 but you actually continue to consult on special events including the launch of Disney's Animal Kingdom, the Disney Cruise Line, you helped prepare media for the opening of Hong Kong Disneyland like you mentioned, but in 1999 you received what I think you and I know me as a fan would probably be the ultimate honor. You were named the Disney Legend. You were honored with a window on Main Street over the arcade. Tell us about that experience and that award and what it really means to you.

Charles: Well, it certainly was a crowning achievement. Those two events were certainly a capping and a wonderful way to sort of end to a career. I didn't quite call it quits at that point, but it came close I guess. My old boss, Eddie Mac at Disneyland, when he was getting ready to retire shortly after I moved to Florida, they gave him a window on Main Street and I said, I want one of those one day. So that was quite rewarding as well. And several of my friends who have had their names up on the windows for a long time were involved very heavily in the construction or the design whatever. They were high up the ladder at that point. They got their names up there. So to join them is a real special treat for me.

Lou: Well, much like that this is actually a very special treat for me to be able to sit and talk and share stories with somebody whose work I respect and whose name I get to see every time I go down Main Street really is a thrill. And I know for the people who go out and purchase the book, again, its Spinning Disney's World: Memories of a Magic Kingdom Press Agent, we know we just scratched the surface of some of the great stories that you have there to share. Charles Ridgway, thank you so much for coming on. Again, your book is available at local bookstores; it's also available at the Intrepid Traveler website. I think you'll be appearing this summer at the NFC convention in Anaheim.

Charles: Yes. I'll be there. Probably also believe there's a convention here at Disney World in September. I'll try to be at both of those and I'll bring the book a lot. But it's something that I didn't anticipate. In fact, I didn't decide to write the book for a long time. All these people have been talking about it when I would sit over the dinner table, that's what this is, a bunch of dinner stories would say, hey, you ought to write a book. And I'd say, well, I've tried, but it seemed kind of dull to me. So finally one of my friends who's a very good writer who has written for National Geographic, one of my travel writer friends, in fact, I didn't do travel writing until I got to the retirement stage.

Anyway, he said you have to write a book. And I said, well, I've tried it didn't work. So he said, well, sit down with a tape recorder and talk it like you've been telling me over the dinner table. And so that got me started, and the first chapter or two got done that way and then from then on it started to flow. It was more fun doing than anything I've done in a long time. And bringing back the memories, many of which had escaped me was really as rewarding as anything I've ever done and I'm most pleased to share it with whoever wants to have a peak in my soul.

Lou: Well, it's a fun read, it's fascinating. Again, the stories are stories that I had never heard and I'd never seen elsewhere. But you could also find out more information about Charlie and some his other work at his website, which is travelphotoridgeway.com and again, you can also go to intrepidtraveler.com and I'll put links up on the website in the show notes to where you can get Charlie's book, where you can see Charlie, we'll keep in touch and you can tell me we're going to be making some appearances and I'll help you get the word on that because if you have the opportunity like I do to sit and talk to Charlie and have him meet him face to face and, and hear him and see him talk about some of these stories, it really is a true treat for any Disney fan. Charlie I can't thank you enough to sit and share this with me.

Charles: It's been fun.

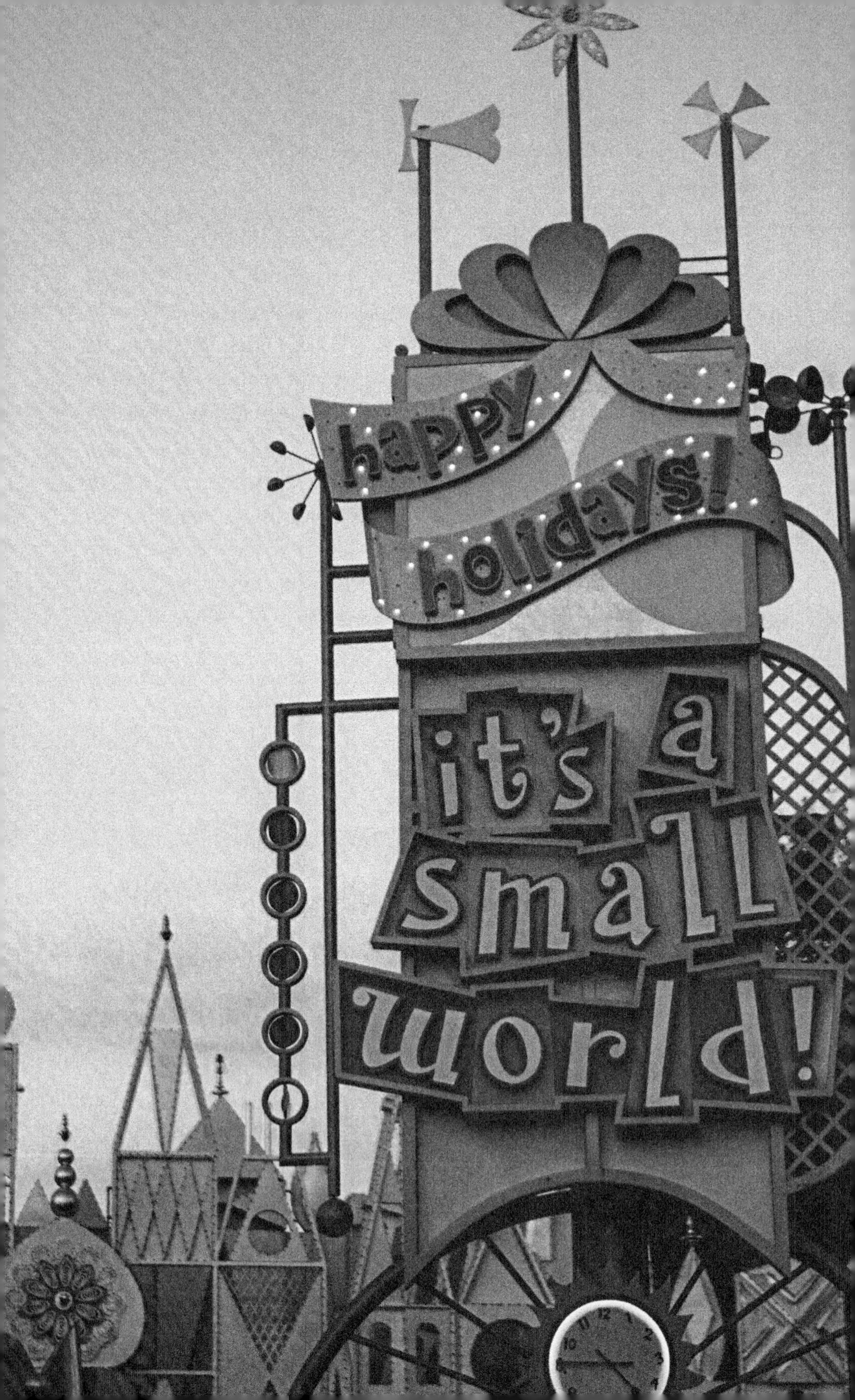
happy holidays!
it's a small world!

Marty Sklar

Marty Sklar was more than a former vice chairman and principal creative executive of Walt Disney Imagineering (WDI). He was more than a Cast Member who first joined the Disney Company just a month before Disneyland opened in 1955. Marty Sklar was far more than a scriptwriter, construction developer, creative director, and President of Walt Disney Imagineering.

To say that Marty was an international ambassador for Walt Disney Imagineering and The Walt Disney Company as a whole would be an understatement.

Born in New Brunswick, New Jersey (not far from where I grew up!), Sklar was a student at UCLA and editor of the school newspaper when he was recruited to create a retro-style newspaper for Walt Disney's new theme park. Under Skalr's direction, the first Disneyland News was published just weeks before the park opened. After graduating college, Marty joined Disneyland full-time to handle the park's publicity and marketing materials.

In 1961, Marty joined WED Enterprises (renamed Walt Disney Imagineering in the mid 1980s), where he worked on attractions for the 1964 New York World's Fair, including it's a small world. For nearly a decade, he crafted personal material for Walt Disney for use in presentations, documents, television, and movies. He later helped guide the creative development of EPCOT Center at Walt Disney World, and during his illustrious time with the Company, helped open each of the Disney Parks around the world.

Sklar also helped not only express, but preserve the vision and legacy of Walt Disney and his guiding principles and philosophies. Marty not only learned from Walt (he said that "...working with Walt Disney was the greatest 'training by fire' anyone could ever experience."), but processed his philosophies and knowledge into materials he wrote for Walt, and education he passed on to the Disney Cast Members.

His final role was that of international ambassador for Walt Disney Imagineering, which afforded Skalr the opportunity to travel the globe as both evangelist and recruiter for the Company. After more than 50 years of service to The Walt Disney Company and Walt Disney Imagineering, Sklar retired on Disneyland's 54th anniversary, July 17, 2009, where he was honored with a window on Main Street, U.S.A.

His window above City Hall in Disneyland (where he once had his office) reads: ID SOMNIATE ID FACITE — Main Street College of Arts & Sciences — EST 1852 — Martin A Sklar — Dean — Inspiring the Dreamers and Doers of Tomorrow (ID SOMNIATE ID FACITE means "Dream It Do It."

Sklar's autobiography, Dream It! Do It!: My Half-Century Creating Disney's Magic Kingdoms is available on Amazon.com

Named a Disney Legend in 2001, Skalr was later awarded the Diane Disney Miller Lifetime Achievement Award from The Walt Disney Family Museum.

Martin A. "Marty" Sklar passed away on Thursday July 27, 2017.

This interview is taken from my conversation with Marty on WDW Radio Show # 293, in September, 2012. You can listen to the complete interview at WDWRadio.com/293.

Lou Mongello: In all the years I have been a Disney enthusiast and been covering Disney, the company and Walt Disney World. One of the people, whose work I have admired most and who I had always wanted to meet and interview has been my next guest. And he is of course, Marty Sklar, a man who needs no introduction, but I'll tell you, Mr. Sklar, what a true privilege and honor it is to finally get a chance to sit down with you.

Marty Sklar: As long as you don't call me Mr. we're okay.

Lou: You know, we're, we're, we're unfortunately battling the clock today because we certainly can't cover such a storied career in a limited amount of time. But I do want to sort of go back a little bit to the beginning and share with us how you go from, you know, being sort of the, the, the, the news reporter in school to, you know, working at and for Disneyland and, and obviously Walt Disney.

Marty: Well, I was quite fortunate actually. There was a man by the name of Johnny Jackson who was the executive secretary of the alumni association at UCLA. And I had gotten a small scholarship. It's kind of a laugh when I think about it today. $50 a semester, which was my tuition at UCLA in 1952. And Mr. Jackson left UCLA and went to work for Disney and when Walt decided that he wanted to have a tabloid newspaper to be sold on Main Street, when Disneyland opened, Johnny recommended me and I went into an interview with Card Walker and who was then the head of marketing later the CEO of the company. And they hired me to do this. And I had just finished my junior year and it was about to be the editor of the Daily Bruin at UCLA. So I had to come up with the concept and I went to work a month before Disneyland opened and two weeks later I had to present the concept to Walt Disney, the Walt Disney, and I was 21 years old and never worked professionally. And believe me, I was scared as hell.

Lou: I was going to say that the pressure of not only taking on that kind of responsibility, but it's the Disney company, it's Uncle Walt, the person we had seen on TV. I can't imagine the pressure and the preparation and what that first day when that meeting finally took place was like.

Marty: Well, the real pressure was on him because this was two weeks before Disneyland opened. And in those days you know, it was a, it was a mess from a construction standpoint. And you know, the stories about the plumbers strike and he had to decide whether to finish the toilets or the drinking fountains. That's all true. And it was, you know, the first time doing that kind of thing. And I never, you know, I was taken aback by the fact that he had time for my little thing. You know, in the big picture, my newspaper didn't mean anything. But finally, you know, I finally figured out why it was important. For Walt, Main Street was a real place, real town. And every town in the 1880's, 1890's, 1900's had at least one newspaper. A lot of them had more than one. And so having a newspaper was part of the story. And once I got that, you know, this is all about the story right from the beginning, then you know, it all fell into place for me. But it took me a while to understand that.

Lou: And did you have any idea, you know, Disneyland was, just a new concept right, the idea of a theme park, like this was just a new concept. Did you have any sense before opening what it was going to be like, what this was going to eventually represent? Or when did that moment finally hit for you?

Marty: Well, it was... it was a mess right from the beginning because so many things didn't work and those stories about all the counterfeit tickets and everything. There were 30,000 people there when they expected 10,000. And so nobody had a good time. And then if you go back and look at the media at that time, Walt was really criticized and a lot of negative. And so he right away, he was, he, he said, we're going to fix all of this. And for example, Bob Gurr told me these stories about the Autopia cars, not one of them was running at the end of the first day. So they had to figure out, well, you know, you're in the business, it's 16 hours a day now in many cases. So you had to figure out ways to design things, ways to build things that are going to last.

Marty: But in those days it was all off the shelf one way or another. And so we, even in the media, which I was a part of, I was in the division, was called the public relations department. And we started from the next week inviting all the media back every night, to see Disneyland and see it without all those bodies that were there. That mad black Sunday as it was called. And so it was quite an education for me actually because we had Bob Thomas from the AP and Vernon Scott from UPI and all the editors in those days were four daily newspapers in LA. The Times, The Herald, The Examiner, The Mirror and The Herald and The Examiner two different, anyway, there were four papers. So there were, there was a lot of media to, to get back and get them to see the park the way Walt really wanted them to see it. So we were busy as heck.

Lou: So you go from the quote and quote editor of a fictional Disneyland main street newspaper to writing to be sort of the, the voice of the Disneyland brand to eventually at some point you are not just writing for Disneyland. But you're writing for Walt, you know, where you're writing speeches, you're helping to try and give a voice to the vision and to the legacy of Walt Disney. How does that come about? And again, now you are sort of tasked with giving a voice to a person who is speaking to, you know, generations of people about his company.

Marty: Well, Walt didn't really make speeches. He made one I think that I know of and that was when he was early in 1966 when he was the Cedar Owners of America made him the showman of the world. And he did make a speech and I didn't write it, but I did all the things that related to the park. And it came about very early on when I went back, I finished, I had gone back to school, finished my last year at UCLA and then came back to Disneyland. And very quickly Walt wanted to, to communicate to sponsors. And because so much of what we've done over the years has been as a result of getting sponsors to pay for a lot of the attractions and put their name on things, et cetera. And so Walt wanted a brochure about Disneyland.

Marty: There wasn't one to take to sponsors. So I did that. And then I did one about Edison Square because he wanted to actually do a street of 1890 Edison. And, and I did one on, on the hall of presidents Liberty Street. And of course the Edison Square later became the Carousel Progress and Liberty Street was finally done in the Magic Kingdom at Walt Disney World. But I did those brochures and then 59 came along. And that was a big opportunity for me because we did a lot of special publications that are inserted in the LA Times and other newspapers. And I wrote all of Walt's things for that. And pretty soon he came to accept me as a ghost writer, if you will. And we didn't use those words, but, certainly that's what I was.

Marty: And I wrote all of this almost everything that came out under his name for souvenir guides or annual reports. In fact, some of the best writing I did, I think was for those special additions, one in 59, one in 65 at Disneyland's 10th anniversary and material for Walt. And then the one I was really proud of was when we went to Walt Disney to announce Walt Disney World. We did, did two presentations. One was about the impact of Disneyland on Anaheim and Orange County, California, and the other was called the Disney Image. And, this was all about Walt's impact on the world. And I still think of that. I mean, I've done so much writing over the years. This was 1965, and I think that's the best thing I ever wrote. I really do.

Lou: So you found that you wrote better for Walt Disney than you'd wrote for Marty Sklar?

Marty: Well, after a while there was nothing to write for Marty's Sklar. It was all for Walt Disney. And he was wonderful because I, the first thing I did was I looked back at things that had been published under his signature. I found them very stilted and not Walt. And as I got to know Walt, so I really worked at simplifying it. Then I find things that he said. And for example, this didn't come across in print, but if it was going to be filmed in those days, if it was going to be filmed. He used the word things in a very interesting way. For example, he'd say, now the pirates are going to sack and burn the town.

Marty: And he said, and then we're going to do some interesting things and he'd just kind of throw it away. So I said, wait a minute, if you, if I wrote that into something for him, he's going to make a picture that is going to be beyond what we're talking about every time. So I started using that word and you'll find it in different places quite often. And so I really tried to understand how he wanted to be presented to the public. And it was very, it was very straightforward and very understandable by anybody and not a lot of highfalutin stuff that had been written in the thirties for him. And I didn't like that stuff at all. I, I, I even rewrote some things that were done. For example, there's a great, great quotation, he called the four CS, curiosity, confidence. I forget what the other two are at the moment, but constancy and courage. And he explained what those were and I found it very interesting, but not something that I wanted to read all the time. So I rewrote it and I got him to use it. So now it's become the accepted way of what he said, accepted quote. So there were, you know, you, you don't write for you about yourself. You're talking, you're talking about somebody who's one of the best known people in the world. And you had to think, try to think. I, you know, when, when my father died, I thought, you know what, I, I didn't have to think like my father did, but, but when Walt died, I had, I remember I had this thought, I, I said, you know, I had to think like he did. I had to try to think like he did so I could write the way he thought.

Lou: So when Walt passed, obviously you know, the impact was so profound was the goal for you to try and continue to have the message be spoken as if it was sort of from Walt? Or does that message have to sort of change over time and evolve? Or just sort of try and keep the legacy of how Walt spoke?

Marty: Well, I tried to keep it, you know that was one of the things I really worked hard. In fact, Dick Irvine, who was my boss at Imagineering when we started the Florida project and I still have this book, Dick, how do we get everybody on the same page? And I said, why don't, we put out a booklet just for internal use that has a whole bunch of different things about the way Walt thought. And the way people wrote about Walt from the outside. And so I put this collection together, probably 16 or 20 different items that went way back to something Bill Walsh wrote for which was even before Disneyland. It was about Disneyland, but it was from that piece that Bill Walsh wrote, came the dedication plaque for Disneyland. So I took all those and I put them in a book and we put it out October, 1967 to everybody at Imagineering to say, look, read this book. That'll give you an idea of a real solid foundation for how the way Walt wanted to be the things that Walt wanted to do for the public. And you know, when I wrote the Epcot film in 1966, which was the last thing he did on film, October, 1966, I have seven pages of notes from meetings with him about that. And, and one of them in more than one page is the expression, meet the needs of people, meet the needs of people. He was focused on that. So those are the kinds of things that I tried to pass on as I became more, more and more the creative leader of Imagineering.

Lou: So especially now with Epcot, 30th coming up and just a couple of, so let's talk for a minute about Epcot. Because obviously Walt's vision and what Epcot is today seem to be two very different sorts of concepts.

Marty: Well, in a way they are. But on the other hand, everything at Walt Disney World was related to that, particularly early on when, you know, we did all kinds of experimentation and energy and growing different things on the project, on the property. And how do we handle waste... everything there was done under the Epcot building code. It was called the Epcot Building Code. And I wrote the preface to it and there are two particular things in that preface that came right out of that Epcot film about encouraging American industry to participate in... not only participate but to think about new things that would affect how people live and how people enjoy things. And so we really tried to keep the Epcot philosophy right from the beginning of Walt Disney World.

Marty: A lot of things done environmentally et cetera. And you know, if you go to Walt Disney World today, there's 300,000 people on that property on a peak day between the cast members and the public, about 250,000 public. And that's a whole city. You got every kind of need, transportation, food, energy, everything else. I think there's a lot that's been done that has really related to the philosophy that Walt laid, laid down. And you know, when we started to figure out how to do that, I mean, it kind of laid dormant for about seven years while we put Walt Disney World together and opened it. But nineteen, it was 1974 and Card Walker called me and said, okay, what are we going to do about Epcot? And that was the beginning of eight years, eight years.

Marty: The first thing we did was, was, create what we called the Epcot Forums. And we invited people from academia, from, from, industry, from, just great people that we found in literature. And, you couldn't Google all these things at that. It would have been a lot easier. You really had to search to find who's doing what around the world. And we had these meetings and what they, what, all these people kept saying to us that the public doesn't trust what industry tells them. The public doesn't trust what the government tells them, but they trust Mickey Mouse. So you people have a role to play. And that's how we tried to define so much of what Epcot opened with particularly.

Lou: So it was less about the creation of the city and the urban planning specific issues of a city in the multiple layers of transportation. As it was the spirit of what each of those things represented the spirit of achievement and working together and future technology.

Marty: Well, I used to tell our staff that what we were doing was creating turn-ons and getting people to want to know more about these subjects so they could be better citizens. And I think a lot of Epcot, particularly when it opened and still today is that way. And there's certain things that I wish we hadn't lost over time. For example, we had a great teacher center where you could come in and learn about different things to take materials back. And in those days, I mean, if we had the communication that you have today, it would be so much easier. But, and in those days we wanted people to know more about different subjects, energy, transportation, et cetera. So we went, we researched and, and found companies that were doing leading edge things. And, and we made a brochure about each of the subjects, subject that followed the pavilions. And the deal was that if we use your name in it, you had to agree to respond within a week when somebody contacted you with information. And so we had a lot of people around the country and around the world that were participating in this.

Lou: And I think I actually have some of the brochures, the agriculture brochures are the ones that you speak of. And that as a kid always fascinated me about Epcot was it was such a very different experience than Magic Kingdom was. It was about this idea of the joy of discovery and learning and new technologies and you know, Epcot obviously evolved and it's changed a lot over the years. As you sort of look back on, on 30 years of Epcot. Do you think that that's still sort of the message or how do you think it's changed?

Marty: Well, I think it still is the message and I think because I know some things that are going on right now that it will, that there's another thrust to bring a lot of that more to the fore in the future. I think Imagineers are particularly anxious to be able to continue that kind of inspiration that you found in the original Epcot. And not that, I mean, it's still a fabulous experience. And, and meeting people from around the world. I mean to say this is you know, in Europe now, the World Showcase fellowship students, they still meet once a year. And then, we always said that one of our goals was that someday there was going to be a problem in the world. And two leaders of different countries were going to get together and solve the problem because they were friends from the time they were in the world showcase. And you know, I still think Epcot is inspirational, you know the space things that are there. And, and so many of the Innoventions area, which changes all the time and tries to keep up with things that are happening and, and that corporations are doing. And you know, right from the beginning, Walt said, no one company can do this by itself. And so the more companies, the more people from around the world that are involved I think it's, it really makes Epcot what it is.

Lou: You know, you made an allusion to something about almost, you know, in order to look forward; you almost have to look into the past a little bit. And there almost seems to be in the parks and resorts, a renewed sense of nostalgia, whether it's a simple thing like the return of the Tiki Room or the Orange Bird to maybe even something more on a grander scale saying, yeah, and making sure that we keep an eye on some of those very original philosophies and make sure we carry those forward.

Marty: Well, guess who that came from? Walt used to say, I loved nostalgia and I always, you know, when I did a piece for a film that was done about Walt TV shows done about him. I said Walt had one foot in the past and one foot in the future because he loved the nostalgia. And he loved the new things that were being done. That's what motivated him about doing an Epcot. And that was he, he used to go around to the laboratories, all these great companies, GE and DuPont and RCA and IBM and, and they, when Walt Disney came, they used to try it out, all the new things that we're working on. And he said, when can I buy that? When can I have something like that? And they said, well, we don't know if the public is interested. And he didn't have any doubt that he could communicate that and the New York World's Fair was a big piece of that because he showed right there that he, the King of that kind of communication and entertainment. And so Epcot really came out of a lot of those, those, opportunities that he had to go around to see what was going on in the great laboratories.

Lou: And so to that point, you know, in, during your tenure with the Disney company, you saw, you know, you saw everything, you saw the opening of Disneyland, you saw the world's fair, the Florida project to becoming Walt Disney World and Epcot center and the additional parks and, you know, 11 theme parks around the world. Again, you know, you wonder what Walt saw on the horizon could have ever have seen such global and exponential growth in a relatively short period of time.

Marty: Well, you'll have to read my book when it comes out next year. Disney Editions is publishing my book probably July or August of 2013. I've got a lot of the story in that book and it's called Dream It, Do It My Half-Century, Creating, Creating Disney's Magic Kingdom. I'm sorry.

Lou: That's okay. I was, if your ring tone would have been one little spark. Oh, so yeah. So, so going back to your book, you know, again, we're talking a lot about you with Walt and speaking, you know, working so closely with him and, and speaking for and with him. But you know, personally in what you've seen during that time frame and then even after you left as the head of, of Imagineering, you were, and I believe still, are the, the sort of the ambassador. And I have to tell you, it fascinates me and it thrills me because even just a about a month ago, I was there for the opening of Cars Land and as I was hooting and hollering on to Mater's Junkyard Jamboree, I look off on the side and there's Marty Sklar… and you were, you were peering over the fence. And I don't know why that had such a profound impact on me watching you look at that next step in the evolution of the Disney parks.

Marty: Yeah, I just walked through from the tower of terror and my good fortune was right after that I ran into George Kalogridis, who's the president of Disney and I said, George, you only have one park bench in this long distance between these two. You know, you gotta keep them on their toes.

Lou: And that's good because you're still bringing, you know, the simple things like where the benches should be, where you know, a garbage can should be.

Marty: Well, you know, all those things are important. And, and the detail, the parks are really about detail and story detail and every other thing. Because if, if the details are wrong, then you take people out of the story. And out of the time that you're that the, and the theme of that particular area. So all those things are vital. And as I get older, you know, my wife and I we, we like to sit, you know, a lot of times and that's where the benches are coming from. That was one of the things I told them about Cars Land there was no place to sit. And you know, we take our grandkids who were running all over of course they're 14 to 21. And so we don't worry about them anymore, but we like to sit down and wait for them. And so, things like that are important. And, as I say, I think when you, if you cut through everything else that the parks are about detail and, if the details are wrong, you get taken out of the story. You get taken out of the experience. And so those are important.

Lou: And so not to use the, the clichéd word, like immersive experience and interactive experience, when you look sort of from the top down out of Cars Land. That the expansion of Fantasy Land, at what James Cameron is potentially going to bring with Avatar and the Land of Pandora and the continued growth overseas. You know, how do you feel when you see some of those things and sort of the direction that it's going in terms of story?

Marty: Oh, I think they're fabulous. You know, Kevin Rafferty came up with the idea of doing Cars Land two years before they even started the Cars movie in 2004. And that cars were the natural thing for the California car culture. We should have done it earlier. But fortunately, cars came along and gave a real shot in the arm and getting John Lasseter involved. But it's like my, my grandson 14 years old said, I said, what do you think Jake? And he said, "It's just like stepping into the movie!", you know, and, and, in fact, somebody told me a story, they were walking in and they saw this little kid, you know, five or six years old. And he said, Oh, this must be where they shot the movie. And that's...

Lou: That's the greatest testament. That's right.

Marty: Absolutely. What a compliment that is. But I think about the people because of the talent that was involved in that project. I mean, my good friend, Zsolt Hormay who did all the rock work I mean supervise the rock work, that's brilliant. And you know, so these are the kind of things that you, that I know from the inside, he studied that from the way the sun was going to hit it at different times a day and, and, and factored that into his sculpting. And, and the way it was lit at night, I mean, not only, the neon on the street, which is beautiful, but also the way that the mountains are lit up. I mean, they're just, it's exquisite. And that is, you know, somebody really cared a lot of people really cared and that's what the Imagineers do.

Lou: You forget what's on the opposite side of that facade. You forget, you know, you forget that there's Denny's, you know, across the street and is it Zsolt? Was it he who also did the carvings on the Tree of Life?.

Marty: Yeah. And I complained to him. I say, my, my grandparents on my mother's side were Hungarian and Zsolt is Hungarian. We found him in Paris and he did Big Thunder and Paris, all the rock work. And so I said, Zsolt where's the Hungarian animal? And he said, well, they're not very interesting. And I said, come on, Zsolt you've got to find something. And he did. He found a nondescript animal and sculpted it in there. But that is brilliant. You know, all that, all those carvings had to be done right there out of cement. And just, you know, when you work with world class people, it's such a pleasure because you don't have to explain everything that has to be done. They know what, what, what to do. And all they have to know is what is the story and what do you want to accomplish out of this? And boy they start running.

Lou: My feeling is to sort of bring things full circle and wrap up is that I feel that that now it's such a great time to be a Disney enthusiast because I think what the company is doing is carrying on that legacy of Walt Disney, which is, he was the, you know, the graduate tool of master planning and, he surrounded himself like the company does now with the people who are the very best at what they do. They understand it, they know the importance of story, they know the importance of the guest experience.

Marty: Yeah. I like to say that, that these were all my kids at one time, you know. And all my kids have grown up and, and they become so professional and so caring and so knowledgeable. And, you know, they, a lot of them had the tail end of the John Henches and the Marc Davis's and the Claude Coats and Fred Joerger and all of those Blaine Gibson who taught us, you know, they really did. I mean, they taught me, they were my mentors. I was the kid. And they were so giving and they were fabulous teachers. And I think this group is like that. You know, you take the Joe Rohdes and the Tony Baxters and the Tom Fitzgeralds and Joe Lanzisero and so many of them, they're really great. I mean stars, you know, and, if they were in the movie business, they would be carrying them into the park on, on their shoulders. You know, they're that good. And I, I really appreciate the fact that they have become so professional and their teachers too, they're teaching a new generation and it's wonderful to see.

Lou: And for us at Disney enthusiasts. It's great that we're able to now start hearing from those people, hearing their voices, hearing them tell their stories. And you, you know, continue to come out. This event is a perfect example where you get a chance, whether it's here, Destination D, the D23 Expo to share those stories and let us sort of get, you know, an up close and personal look into your career at the company. I can't tell you how excited I am not just to be sitting here with you today, but for your book when it comes out. Hopefully, when it does, we'll get a chance to, to talk more again and again as a fan first on behalf of myself and you know, my little kids who, you know, who still enjoy what you and the team over those decades have done. I am so very grateful for what you and the Company have done to change my and my family's lives.

Marty: Well, thank you very much. I've really enjoyed this and I do hope we talk again.

Lou: Thanks very much.

Lou and Marty Sklar

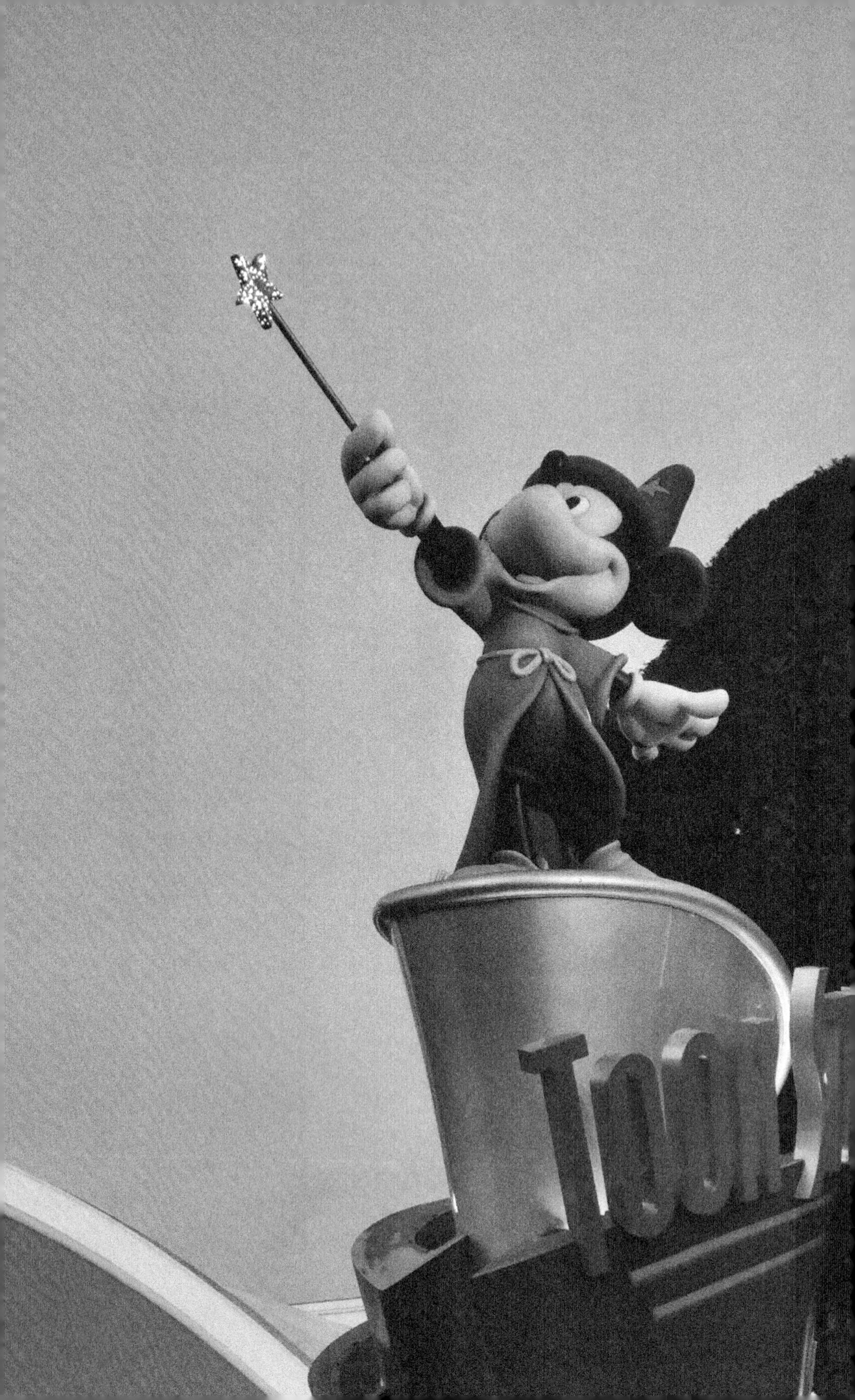

Bill "Sully" Sullivan

One decision can change your life forever... in ways you may have never imagined. Just ask William "Sully" Sullivan, who, on Sunday, July 17, 1955, was watching the opening ceremonies for Disneyland. The following Saturday, he went down to Disneyland and applied for a job, and by Tuesday, the 19 year old Sullivan was taking tickets at the Jungle Cruise. He graduated to ride operator to operations supervisor, and before he knew it, his "summer job" turned into a lifelong career.

That one decision eventually brought Sullivan to Squaw One decision can change your life forever... in ways you may have never imagined. Just ask William "Sully" Sullivan, who, on Sunday, July 17, 1955, was watching the opening ceremonies for Disneyland. The following Saturday, he went down to Disneyland and applied for a job, and by Tuesday, the 19 year old Sullivan was taking tickets at the Jungle Cruise. He graduated to ride operator to operations supervisor, and before he knew it, his "summer job" turned into a lifelong career.

Sully was later sent to SquawValley in Lake Tahoe to assist in the opening and operating of the Winter Olympics in 1960, where Disney was in charge of Pageantry. He later served as assistant manager for the attractions designed by Disney at the 1964-65 New York World's Fair in Flushing Meadows—Corona Park in Queens, New York.

His operations work in the parks led Sullivan to bring those talents and experience to movie premieres for such films as Mary Poppins at Grauman's Chinese Theatre and The Happiest Millionaire at the Hollywood Pantages Theatre before relocating to Florida for the opening of Walt Disney World in 1971. There, he moved from installations to operations, and later, vice president of the Magic Kingdom.

After nearly four decades with the Disney Company, Sully retired in 1993 and was inducted as a Disney Legend in 2005.

This interview is taken from my conversation with Sully on WDW Radio Show # 39, in November, 2007. You can listen to the complete interview at WDWRadio.com/39.

Lou Mongello: Some of us have either had or know of the dream of starting out at a company and moving on and up the ladder to eventually achieving something special on a completely different level. Well, my next special guest did just that while working for the Walt Disney Company. He is someone who has truly lived the dream by taking on a summer job as a ticket taker in Disneyland to eventually working for the company for 38 years in a number of different roles, including many at Walt Disney World. Those accomplishments led to him receiving Disney's highest honor: the naming of him as a Disney Legend. So I'm pleased to welcome Bill "Sully" Sullivan to the WDW Radio Show.

Bill "Sully" Sullivan: Hello! And thank you for that beautiful introduction!

Lou: Well, thank you for coming on and taking a few minutes to chat with me today.

Sully: My pleasure.

Lou: Like I said during your introduction, you really lived the dream of starting out as a young man who took on a summer job to somebody with his own window on Main Street! (Sully laughs.) Tell us how you started with the company.

Sully: Well, it was interesting because I was working in Anaheim, California in the aircraft industry at the … I can't remember the name of the place now… but the guy that interviewed me at Disneyland, Chuck Whalen, had just left there the weekend before. And so they hired me. And it gave the Wardrobe Mistress a little bit of a problem because I'm only 5-foot-eight and I had a thirty-four inch waist, and I didn't fit the pattern that was turned out, but thank God for Lou, she took care of me and she always adjusted my pants and stuff like that, but it was interesting because I got to start at the Jungle Cruise. And, yeah, the Jungle Cruise are all, indeed, guys. And you had to be somewhat of an extrovert, and a nut, to work on the Jungle Cruise because we took three trips an hour, or three trips and then take one off—the trips lasted 7 minutes at that time—and so we'd get a quick break and then back on the boats! It was fun because we never knew what was going to happen and we had the opportunity to help build the place. Like, they gave us… when we started, we didn't have much of a script, so the guys all got together and kinda wrote our own script. Then they brought in a professional and he tried to change it all and we stayed with our own scripts because we liked them better. But you had to be somewhat of a rogue to be there, too.

But, we had some real characters that worked on the Jungle Cruise; we had a gentleman that had spent 15 years in Marrakesh working in the oil fields; we had a gentleman, Don Ware, who was the first one to grow a beard, and he came in one morning and he had chameleons tied around his neck on a little wire. And we had Tex, who was just a jockey: a normal trip was seven minutes, and his trips would last four minutes. Just stuff like that. And there was a bunch of nuts working there, really.

Lou: And this was very early on in the opening of Disney. As the story goes, from what I understand, you basically on Sunday night watched the opening ceremonies for Disneyland. Less than a week later, you go down and apply for a job.

Sully: Disneyland opened on the 17th. I went and worked there on the 27th. I spent two and a half years in the Jungle, as a Jungle Bunny and then I had the opportunity to move around the park and work a lot of the different attractions. Then I was promoted to what we used to refer to as a Yo-Yo Supervisor; we'd be promoted and go on salary in the peak periods because we couldn't afford to keep me up year round, and there was about half a dozen of us like that. Today we'd be a Supervisor wearing a suit and tie and tomorrow we'd be back in costume! And we did that for a couple years, and finally, in '59, when we did the re-dedication and opened the Matterhorn and the Subs and the Monorail, I was promoted on a permanent basis on Main Street as an Assistant Supervisor.

Fortunately, I was in the right place at the right time. I guess I had the personality and the drive and the initiative to get promoted up, up and away. In the meantime, going up, I got picked to go and do a couple of premiers up in Hollywood and crowd control and working with the press. We got to tour John Kennedy and

Bobby Kennedy and a lot of the dignitaries Walt would come down and host. Unfortunately, we didn't get to see our Russian friend, but that's alright — Khrushchev.

We got picked for Squaw Valley, there were three of us that went up to Squaw Valley and worked up there for six weeks in security of the valley, because they forgot to hire any security people, so we had to put together a team. And we did that.

Lou: And that was for the Winter Olympics?

Sully: The 1960 Winter Olympics in Squaw Valley, up in Northern California. Great time, great time. Learned a lot; met some great people. It's where we met Willy Schaeffler, when we were talking about doing the program up in the mountains that Walt wanted to build, but the Sierra Club shot us down and we couldn't do that. So we went on from there.

But, then we got to go back to the World's Fair; spent a year back there. I'd never been east of the Mississippi, and I got a phone call up from my boss one day and he said, "Sully! Sell your house, both your cars, and be ready to go in 30 days." I says, "Where am I going?" He says, "You're going back to the World's Fair. And you're going to be an Assistant Manager at the four Disney World's Fair Shows back there." So we went back, with my family; my kids were clean for nine months because we lived in an apartment; my oldest daughter started kindergarten in PS99 in New York, in Queens. And that was a great experience. Again, we met some great people, made some good friends, and learned a lot.

Lou: I can only imagine, like you said, about the experience that you had, not only working at the parks, but being able to go outside the parks to things like the Olympics and to the World's Fair that obviously would have long lasting effects on the Theme Parks worldwide because of what Walt put there.

Speaking of Walt, how closely, if at all, did you work with Walt? What was it like to work for him and with him?

Sully: Well, we always knew when Walt was around and gained a lot of knowledge just through osmosis and from what we heard and what we saw. In the early days of Disneyland, our operating hours were from 9 to 9, and we worked 7 day shifts. It was interesting because those foggy California nights would come aboard, and you couldn't see across Main Street. And Walt would be just down walking the park and seeing what was going on. We'd be sitting around there, and there'd be nobody in the park hardly. And so Walt would come down and sit on the boats and shoot the breeze with the guys and just see what our attitudes were and what our opinions were. And he got to look at us. We were kind of the reprobates of Disneyland. We helped start — the guys on the Jungle Cruise — helped start the grooming standards down there because he didn't like our haircuts and our beards and our moustaches (Lou laughs).

But he was a neat guy. He knew what he wanted and he talked to people. It was interesting to watch him because he didn't want people to do special things for him. He would just want to walk the park. If he was just up in his blue suit and his Smoke Tree Ranch tie, he was just out visiting the guests. And if he had his blue pinstripe pants on and his old leather jacket and his boondockers and his straw hat, he was working. He went over to Tom Sawyer Island and he'd go out on the painted desert, and look things over, and then go back to his designers and design something new.

But it was interesting. You always knew when he was around, though, because the guys in security would call in and a word would go out over the radio that there was a Code W — and that meant Walt was in the park. Or a Code R, that meant Roy was in the park. But the Studios would always call us and say "He's on his way down." And about 35 to 40 minutes later he'd be arriving at the Harbor Gate, or at the West Street Gate. And we always knew when he was around.

And it was interesting because he would pop in and talk, and it was interesting because people would see him in his blue seat and they'd crowd around him for autographs and stuff like that. And we'd walk up and say "Mr. Disney, this way, please." And then he'd correct us and say, "My name's Walt, not Mr. Disney. There's only one Mister at Disneyland, and that's Mr. Toad." And, later on, Mr. Lincoln, too. But he was a good guy, and he would appreciate it, and we would walk him out the back and he'd come out another gate and go see the park someplace else.

He'd wander the park at night. I worked graveyards for eight months, graveyard security — I'm rambling a lot, but it just popped into my mind — I get this call over the radio, I'm sitting in the office by the dispatcher, and there was a Security Host out in the park who says "Hey, there's some guy here says he's Walt Disney." He's a brand new guy. This was, like, after midnight, like two o'clock in the morning. And I said "Oh, oh." So I jumped on my bike and I ran out there where he was, and, sure enough, it was Walt. And Walt looked at me and said "Oh, God, Sully! Thank God it's you... this guy's about to arrest me!" (Laughter) So, we walked him up to his apartment on Main Street up above the Fire Station and said Good Night.

He's a great guy. He was a very warm individual person like that.

Lou: And everybody that I ever have spoken to that knew Walt described him exactly the same way. He wasn't what you might perceive as being your boss or an executive. He was very warm, and he didn't look down on anybody. He cared about what everybody thought and their opinions and treated everybody with respect.

Sully: It's interesting you say that, because when he would come and see us and when it was slower and nothing was going on, he would say "What do you think about this?" But he did that at the Studio, also. There was one guy that he worked with, we heard, that was a janitor in the Animation Building. And Walt would go up to him and say, "What do you think about this, Rufus? What do you think about these?" And he'd say, "Well, I was looking at some films, and some of the boys are doing pretty good work." It was funny, but he would talk to everybody and get opinions.

Lou: It's wonderful. Like you said, he knew what he was doing, and being able to draw from people that had the first hand experience in the parks or at the Studios...

Sully: Not only that, but he would walk the park and he would stand and he would smoke a cigarette and lean on a trash can. And people would walk up to him and say "Hi, Mr. Disney." And he'd sign their autographs and he'd say "Did you have a good time today?" He'd strike up a conversation with them: "Well, what can we do to make it better? How can I make you happy?" He'd talk to the guests and said, you know, how can we make it better for you? Not for him, but for you. And that was important. Like he always said: take care of the guests, they'll take care of you.

Lou: You know, as you tell that story a smile was coming on my face, and I'm sure on listeners as well, because you can't fathom seeing Walt Disney in the park and not only walking up to him and getting his autograph, but him saying "Well, what do YOU think? Are you having a good time? And what do you think about this?" Walt obviously cared and took your opinion and it had an impact on what he did in the future.

Sully: Absolutely, absolutely.

Lou: But after the World's Fair in '64 and '65, you were once again relocated, and this time to Florida. When and why did the company move you down there?

Sully: Well, the word got out at the World's Fair that something was happening on the East Coast. Nobody knew what it was, and that was when Walt Disney World was called Project X. And Bob Foster was down there buying properties. And it was announced that we were going to do something in Florida, and I told the bosses I'd like to be one of the first guys down there. "Nah," he said, "you've got too much to learn."

So I went back to Disneyland, and that was in '65. I got moved around a lot, and I got a lot of training. And I got a lot of exposure, and it came one day that I was moved over from Manager of Fantasyland to Project Development. And that's where we started providing input into WDI—or at that time it was called WED, short for Walter Elias Disney—input for operating input into WED for Walt Disney World, and for the Magic Kingdom particularly. And I got to work on the design and the layout of Fantasyland, because that was my area. Unfortunately, we had it—Rolly Krump and I, we had it laid out beautifully—we were starting to run out of money so we had to shrink things down some, so that's how we got that little narrow passageway over there. I doubt it was shrunk too much.

I was sent down here to do different jobs—my title was Senior Staff Assistant to the Vice President. That meant I was a high priced gofer, so I did a little bit of everything. I came down and set up the Post Office down here for Walt Disney World and for Joe Pharr and the construction. I came down and I went to work for the hotel company for a while, and we took over the Hilton in Southland on International Drive to get some exposure to the guests who were here and the purchasing and marketing of different stuff. I came down and helped open up the Preview Center with Holscher and just, you know, varied and sundried things! And I did the first legislators weekend; I did that for Jack Lindquist. So I just did a lot of different stuff, and that was fun because I got to get exposed to a lot of different people and a lot of different things, and got to do a lot of different stuff.

Lou: Right, and you clearly had a hand in so many of the different elements that ended up becoming Walt Disney World, and, like you said, you mentioned Fantasyland. I didn't realize you had such a hand in the design and the layout of Fantasyland.

Sully: Well, I designed the Main Gate, the Main Entrance of the park. Not only of the park, but for the ticket sales. And like the width of Main Street: the Main Street is twelve feet wider than the one at Disneyland because we wanted to do bigger and better parades and wanted to have more sidewalk. So we added a few feet here and a few feet there and made it easier for our guests to get up and down the street and still do our parades.

Yeah, I got to do a lot of different stuff. You see, I was on that three, four years, something like that. Then when I was assigned to the hotel company and moved down here, then about six months later I was assigned to Security and Fire Prevention, and we hired the first 75 Security Hosts that we had and set up security. And set up a liaison with the Fire Department and the local Sheriff's Department, and just different stuff like that. I had fun, I learned a lot.

Lou: I've gotta just go off on a tangent for just a little bit because, going back to when you first started with the company, you were nineteen or so, correct?

Sully: I was nineteen years old.

Lou: Now, you've done all these different things, you have all these different roles in the company from Ticket Taker to everything else that you've described. Was your background in anything that may have given you a leg up? Or did you get, basically, all of your experience and training while you worked for the company?

Sully: When I was in high school, my major was Architecture. I worked at my Uncle's chicken ranch for four years during high school and for a year after I got out of high school. Finally, he said, "go get a real job." So I went to work in the aircraft industry. And

I did that for six, eight months, a year or something like that. You know, I was used to working outside and enjoying the sun. I was in a building all day, and you worked from 7 to 3:30 and you got a break in the morning and one in the afternoon and lunch and if you wanted to go to the restroom you had to ask your boss. I didn't like that.

So, I found me another job. And I went to interview with Chuck Whalen, and he hired me. And 39-and-a-half years later, I retired.

Lou: I'd say, clearly it worked out pretty well for you! (Lou and Sully laugh).

Sully: Yeah, we had a good time! We worked hard, and played hard!

Lou: You stayed down in Florida, and you were there for, not only the opening of Walt Disney World and the Magic Kingdom, you were also there for the opening of Epcot, and, obviously, we were just celebrating the twenty-fifth anniversary a couple of weeks ago, so this is something that...

Sully: Yeah, they invited me out for that, and I went out for that.

I worked on EPCOT Center for four years prior to its opening, and, again, I was back providing operational input into the attractions and all that. We started developing an inventory system for the show installation, and I was in charge of people also, and I had a couple guys working for me — they'd be promoted later on. At the opening of EPCOT Center, I was in charge of all of the operations. That was fun, and anything that happened or any of the other divisions that wanted to do something for EPCOT went through me.

We went to WDI, or WED at the time, and we gave them this input. The boss said, you know, it's your baby and you're gonna run it, so you make it right! And so that's why I got involved doing that. We got to know a lot of good people in their divisions and we assigned each division, which there was nine of, somebody to give me the input, and we'd go together to WDI and we'd give them that kind of input. I didn't approve any of the designs. You know, if I didn't like it or it didn't work with the operating areas, we would make some changes.

I did that for four years, and I ran it for two years, and I went back to the Magic Kingdom and spent ten years in the Magic Kingdom. Primarily running the Magic Kingdom and doing a lot of training. And that was one of my main thrusts at the end was training our new people.

Lou: And that was back in 1987, right, you became Vice President of the Magic Kingdom?

Sully: Yes.

Lou: One question: I want to go back to the opening of Epcot real quick.

Sully: OK.

Lou: I had heard that — and this is something that I had never seen before, I've never heard it — but that an interview was conducted during the opening ceremonies with Walt's widow, Lillian, who normally did not give interviews. But you were the person who made that happen, is that right?

Sully: That's correct. I got thinking that the boss isn't around, and that, you know, Mrs. Disney had a great influence on what took place in the company in the early days, how she'd keep Walt straight — just like all wives do to their husbands — and so, I says, I talked to Bob Allen, Jr. and said let's do a film with Mrs. Disney. And he said, you know, she's never been interviewed; we don't have any interviews with her. I said, well, all she can say is no! And so Diane was there, Lillian was there, and their oldest granddaughter was there. And I said to Diane, "What would your mom think about doing an interview with us?" And she says, "Well, what's it for?" And I said, "Well, for posterity, and we'd show it to our people so they'd get to know your mom!" And she said let's go ask. So, she was in a golf cart touring before opening, and she said, "Sully! Ask Mom!" So, I said, "Mrs. Disney..." and I laid it on her, and she asked "Who is it for?" And I says, "Well, I'm asking ya, and it's for something I can show my people and my young guys and gals coming up!" And she said, "It's not for the press." And I says, "No, ma'am. I can guarantee you that." And she says, "OK." And so we set it up, and we did it at 8:00 one morning in the gardens of the English Pavilion, which were gorgeous, and Mrs. Disney was there, Diane was there, and her oldest granddaughter, Joanna. It was her oldest granddaughter, and she was a sweetheart.

And Bob Ollin conducted the interviews, and I finally found the tape. I was talking to a guy at the NFFC Convention, and he says "well, I've got the tape." I says, "No." Now, this is going back, what, 25 years ago?

Lou: Right.

Sully: That we did that tape? I had never seen it in 25 years.

Lou: No kidding?

Sully: And he says, "Here it is." I went to a meeting the other night and he says here's that tape that you've been looking for. So I've got it on my desk, I'm going to review it and take a look at it.

Lou: Wow.

Sully: That's the only tape I know of that is of Mrs. Disney, and I've never seen it before.

Lou: I was going to say, that's never been shown to the public, has it?

Sully: Absolutely not.

Lou: Wow. You want to talk about not only a wonderful opportunity to set up the interview, but to now have what may be the only tape in existence of it is amazing.

Sully: I think we sent one to Diane. And probably Sharon, when she was alive. As far as I know, that's the only ones I know of. We checked with Dave Smith in the Archives: he didn't have one!

Lou: And I assume you won't be putting it up on eBay anytime soon...

Sully: (Strong laughter.) I don't think so!

Lou: In addition to working at Disney...

Sully: It's a good idea...

Lou: I promise that you will sell one. I would be the very first to purchase one. But, anyway, you almost opened Disneyland for all intents and purposes, and the Magic Kingdom at Disney World and Epcot and the World's Fair. You also worked overseas as well for Paris and Tokyo.

Sully: I did a lot of training for Jim for Tokyo. I was asked to go, and I said I didn't want to go. Jim Cora, who used to work for me at Disneyland, he was promoted as the Vice President over there, for Disneyland International: that's the outfit that handled all the overseas parks. And Jim called me one day prior to the opening of Paris—during the construction of Paris—and he says, "Sully, come help me open this park. You and I are the only ones who have ever opened a park before, and I don't have enough help." I said, "Nah, Jim. I don't want to go over there. I've got a good job." I was Mayor of Disneyland; I wanted them to make me King, but they wouldn't do that. So, I had a good job; I was Vice President of the Magic Kingdom at Walt Disney World. I had a GREAT job. And so, he says, "I'll tell you what. Come on over, spend a week, bring your wife, and just look at the project."

Lou: Famous last words.

Sully: I said "I'll do that for you." I got to Paris, and it was dark, and dreary, and rainy. And I said "It ain't for us, Jackie." And she says, Naah. But my wife would do any traveling that I asked her to do; because she never unpacked her bags.

He was rotten, because we walked down the gate from between Hills Brothers and the Balloon Shop, and turned the corner in front of the Kodak Shop looking down Main Street and saw the castle down there at the other end. It was absolutely gorgeous. That's the most beautiful castle we ever built, the one in Paris. And I said, "Ahh, shtuff." (Lou and Sully laugh).

I says, "You're rotten, Cora. (pause) I'll be here."

And so I called my boss, and we sat down and he said, "Well, I'll go ahead and make sure you'll be able to come back to the …" I said "He needs help. I'm more than happy to go with him." And we figured out who would take my spot and run the park while I was gone. And I said "You know, I'm only a phone call away…" And he says, "How long are you going to be gone." I said "Six, seven months. Maybe eight." And, he said… Bob, being a great company guy, knew that we needed the help. And he said OK. And he told Nunis, who was my Big Boss, what we wanted to do, and he says OK.

So, on January 1st I jumped on the airplane and flew to Paris, and spent seven months in Paris opening that up. That was an interesting experience. It was cold, rainy, snowy, cold. Ugh! I've never been so cold in my life. Come to find out Marne-la-Vallée, where the park is, is called the Refrigerator of Paris. But, it's a gorgeous park, and it's beautifully done. The designers did a magnificent job, went way overboard on it. But, Hey! That's what Michael and Frank wanted, and they got it, and it's absolutely gorgeous! And I haven't been over there in 15 years, so I hope it's as good, if not better, than it was.

The landscaping… Luc Behar, who came over and studied under Katie Warner, who was my horticulturist at Walt Disney World. Luc Barre is French-Canadian and was hired to be their landscaper over there. So Luc came over and studied with us and worked with us for about six months and went over to Paris and did a magnificent job in landscaping that park. And maintaining it, too.

Lou: And, like you said, I've heard as well all that; the castle just being absolutely magnificent and the park really coming into its own and being a very beautiful place to kind of walk through. When you start talking about other parks that are beautiful and accomplishments that Disney has done with their parks, Tokyo comes to mind because everybody I know that has gone over to Tokyo has come back just awestruck at how beautiful Tokyo is.

Sully: It's beautiful because it's got its own little personality. And it's got all these neat Japanese guys and gals walking around taking care of the place. And Main Street is covered over, like an arcade. Which gives it a different feel. And the food is phenomenal over there. And the merchandise... they've done an interesting thing with their merchandise.

Each one of the parks has its own personality, and they were designed that way. And people say, you know, which park do you like the best? You know, of course I love the Magic Kingdom. And of course I love the Jungle Cruise at Disneyland. I'm closer to Disneyland and the Magic Kingdom at Walt Disney World and Paris, so, you know.

Let's face it. Walt touched Disneyland. And that made it what it was, and what it is.

Lou: Very true.

I can only imagine, in the 38-year plus career that you had at the company, the amount of amazing stories you can — and probably can't — tell. If you had to pick one of the most memorable stories, or moments, or funny things that have happened to you in your career, what do you think that would be?

Sully: Well, it's very simple as far as I'm concerned. There was a young lady working across from the Jungle Cruise, this cute little blonde. And she was wearing a Hawaiian skirt. And, well, let's see... on the 11th of October we celebrated our 49th anniversary. I married my wife out of Disneyland. And it was the greatest thing that ever happened to me.

But there was a lot of stuff. We flew Tinkerbell at Walt Disney World, which we'd always wanted to do but could never figure out how to do it. But, me and Arnold Lindberg and Hank Danes, we bootlegged it and it worked! (Laughter).

And just being affiliated with the opening in '59, and being affiliated with the opening of Epcot Center and Walt Disney World—you put them all in one big basket. I had a 39 year great run. As far as I'm concerned, we had the Golden Years of the Disney Parks.

There's not one particular thing I can say that was the greatest thing that ever happened to me, except marrying my wife out of there.

Lou: I was going to say, you talk about living the dream... not only are you working at Disneyland, but you meet your wife there. So, it doesn't get any better than that.

Sully: Yeah, and four beautiful kids later!

Lou: There you go! And it gets even better, because you retire in 1993 and in 2005 you are inducted as a Disney Legend — I have to believe the highest honor the company can give to any of its cast members.

Now, more importantly, you hold the very, very rare distinction of having not one, but two windows on Main Street USA. Tell me how you were able to swing that one, because you have Sully's Safaris and Guide Service, where you are the chief guide, and the Windermere Fraternal Hall, which I'm going to ask you about.

Sully: I think they were trying to fill up windows on Main Street when they did the first one, with the Windermere guys. But I was really pleased when I retired when they gave me my own window, with Sully's Safaris, because I'm a hunter and a fisherman and good stuff like that. And I was honored that way with my own two windows on Main Street.

I was always envious of the guys that were Disney Legends, but I respected those that were because that's a pretty strong group: with the Nine Old Men, with the John Hench's, and all those good guys that really started the whole company!

When Michael called me and said, "Sully, you're going to be receiving a letter in the mail. We want to honor you as being a Disney Legend." I just fell right through it. My wife said "I've never seen you speechless. And, when you read that letter, you were speechless."

I didn't give a big speech at my reception because I didn't know what to say. I was so awestruck with being made a Disney Legend. It's really a great honor, as far as I'm concerned.

Lou: And very well deserved, obviously.

Sully: Thank you.

Lou: But I want to ask you about the other window that says "Windermere Fraternal Hall, Lodge Meetings every Friday" and the Charter Members are Bob Allen, Pete Crimmings, Dick Evans, Bill Hoelscher, Bob Mathieson, and you, Bill Sullivan.

Sully: What happened to Jack Olson?

Lou: Oh, you're right. I missed him.

Sully: Those are just a bunch of fun loving guys who were just "Us." You know, they guys who have been with the company for a long time. And we all lived in Windermere. And I think they just filled a window.

Lou: I have tried researching to find out what the Windermere Fraternal Hall reference was, I said "Did these guys get together? Did they meet up every Friday for a drink after work?"

Sully: Well, a lot of us used to fish together and party together and work together. Our families grew up together, and all that good stuff, so... They're just a bunch of good guys.

Lou: Do you still live in Florida? Do you get a chance to get out to the parks at all?

Sully: I do go out to the parks occasionally, but it's been quite a while. You know, I don't work there anymore. I know if I go out there I'd get upset and start raising hell with somebody, and I don't there anymore! I agree with some of the things they do, and I disagree with some of the things they do. But, it's not my park anymore! It belongs to Philip, and McFee, and Mike, so I don't go out there. But the parks are beautiful.

Lou: We actually met on the eve of Epcot's 25th up in the Canada Pavilion. Having just celebrated the anniversary, and you having such close ties to the park, how do you think it compares today to what it was in 1982?

Sully: Like I said... they run their parks the way they want to, I ran my parks the way I wanted to.

Lou: (Laughing) Very diplomatic answer!

Finally, Mr. Sullivan, my last question is what do you think — again, your history with the company is so storied and so remarkable and such a variety of different roles and positions that you had — what do you think you're really most proud of, looking back?

Sully: As part of the crew that I had, because people ask me today: What do you miss out there? You know, I miss my park, but I don't miss the meetings, I don't miss the politics, I don't miss the infighting, and I miss my people. Because I had 7,500 of the greatest employees that any guy could have! And, you know I had almost 400 salaried people; a great bunch of people that worked hard, played hard, and they were just good people. And they carried on the Disney tradition the way it should have been. The way we trained them how to do it. And I was very proud of them. So, my people.

Lou: Everything that you've said is the same theme that resonates through everyone that I speak to, because the first thing they do is give credit to the people that worked with them and around them. You talk about tradition, I guess that's kind of carrying on the tradition of what Walt did: Walt was a genius in the fact that he knew to surround himself with people that were incredibly talented and people from whom he could pull even more talent than they knew they had.

Sully: Walt had a philosophy, and Walt would say "We can design, build and create the greatest park in the world, but without the people they're nothing." And that's absolutely right.

The people make the magic. The people are the ones who take care of the guest. When a kid falls down, they pick him up. When a kid gets lost, they grab him, they pick him up and find their mama and daddy again. The ushers that run the attractions and helps them. It's the people that make it work.

Lou: I whole-heartedly agree with you a hundred percent. The cast members are what make Walt Disney World and everything that Disney does so truly magical.

Mr. Sullivan, I want to thank you so much for taking the time to speak with me today. It's always an honor to have the opportunity to chat with somebody who, like I said, is truly a Disney Legend. On behalf of myself and every other guest that continues to enjoy what you helped create, I want to say thank you very much.

Sully: Thank you. I appreciate the honor.

Lou: Take care.

Sully: Thank you.

Tom Nabbe

Tom Nabbe has one of the most interesting, unique, and intriguing Disney stories, as he went from a 12 year old Disneyland Day One Guest, to a Disneyland Day Two Cast Member. A boy whose looks landed him the role of his lifetime as a classic literary figure in the park.

Tom went from helping to influence Walt Disney, to a man who managed the monorail in Walt Disney World, and helped open Disneyland Paris. Tom's journey from boy with a dream to Disney Legend is both fascinating and inspiring, and I had an opportunity to sit down with Tom to talk about his unique career path, from stories of working with Walt, to his window on Main Street, USA, being the last working member of the elite "Club 55," and more.

Tom was inducted as a Disney Legend in 2005.

This interview is taken from my conversation with Tom on WDW Radio Show # 511, in February, 2018. You can listen to the complete interview at WDWRadio.com/511.

Lou Mongello: Sitting here in the lobby of Disney's Polynesian Village Resort, I am reminded of a quote from a very, very wise man who talked about how you can design and create the most magical place on Earth, but it really does take people to make those dreams a reality. I believe that whole heartedly, and I am so incredibly honored and thrilled to be sitting with someone who I have known for years and whose story I'm excited to share with you in his own words. He is a former Disneyland and Walt Disney World Cast Member, more importantly, he is a Disney legend. He is Mr. Tom Nabbe. Tom, welcome to the show.

Tom Nabbe: Lou. Thank you very much. So looking forward to it. We've been planning this for all those four years, I think, of getting together after a couple of the events that we've had. And he said, "Oh, you need to get together so I can do an interview." And I think we played tag on several occasions. I guess we have to go back and start a little bit at the beginning. I was born in Santa Barbara, California and we lived there for a while. My mother married a gentleman by the name of Eddie Maura and in turn, we moved from Santa Barbara to Anaheim just in the late forties and fifty time frame. I was just starting elementary school and I had dreams of grandeur, of having a paper route. And I found a way that I could ride the bus up to the Coliseum in LA for the football season, selling newspapers and I was able to earn enough money selling the newspapers at the Coliseum to buy a bicycle. And once I bought a bicycle, then I could have a paper route. And so I ended up getting a paper route there in LA.

I grew up in Florence, Los Angeles, which is right downtown, Slauson and Alameda area. If some people know just right around the block from Watts, so right in that area. During this time frame, it was when Disneyland came on television on Wednesday evenings. And television was relatively a new, new thing. Had a little black and white TV with the big fish tank in front of it to magnify it. My mother was a little bit of a starlet wannabe, and she used to go up to all the premier openings up in Hollywood. And she's that lady that you see standing behind the barricades with the autograph book, looking for everybody to get autographs. She used to take us to anything that she could get into, TV, new TV shows, premier openings, anything along that line. And she got very enamored with Walt's discussion of Disneyland and where it was being built in Anaheim. And she sort of looked at it and my stepfather was a GI and eligible to get a GI home loan. And so she went down to Anaheim and checked it out and found a place in Anaheim, about seven tenths of a mile from Disneyland. She could qualify to buy the house on the GI bill.

So in December of 1954, we relocated from LA to Anaheim. And when it got to Anaheim, the problem that I found is Anaheim was a very rural community during this time frame, and I couldn't get a newspaper route. Okay? I had my bicycle, but I couldn't get a newspaper route. You had to have a driver's license, and I was only 12 years old, so I wasn't able to drive a car, but I could get a Sunday paper out. And so I developed around the neighborhood, I had about 20 to 25 people that deliver to the Sunday Herald Examiner too. And I had a deal with the manager, the newspaper manager that any papers that he had left over, he couldn't drop off. And what I did is, I tried to get over to Disneyland and they were working three shifts, the construction people. And I'd get over there early on Sunday morning, and sell to the third shift people that were going home, Sunday papers.

And I met a gentleman by the name of Ray Ahmet. Joe and Ray Ahmet Joe had the concession on Main Street called Castle News. And they also were going to do a publication called the Disneyland

News, which was going to be a monthly newspaper that told the history of Disneyland, a little bit of a coming event and what was going on in that month, and all the leases that had businesses in Disneyland would advertise in this paper. When Disneyland first opened up, there's only about 600 people that actually worked for Walt. There were the people in the Administration, the people that are in the Rides and Attractions Area on the people in Maintenance. But all the food locations and all the merchandise locations and everything were run by these leases and Joe's had the concession. He also had a wheelchair and stroller rentals to go along with that. And it was one of those where you could get your name put in the headline as a paper gay, or they did wanted posters and that type thing.

So he had a very lucrative business going at that time for him, but he would show up every morning after the park opened. I am getting a little ahead of it. I watch Disneyland grow out of nowhere. When we moved to Anaheim, they were just starting to build the Santa Ana Freeway, still was Manchester Boulevard, and they had just finished building the overpass for Harbor Boulevard over the Santa Ana Freeway. And they were working on the overpass for ball road that went over to the Santa Ana freeway. So you could get up on the top of the overpass and actually looked down into the construction site at Disneyland, and you're looking in on the backside or Tomorrowland. You see some of Fantasy Land and you could see the back of the buildings on Main Street, and you could see the train station and the castle.

Lou: So you literally watched Disneyland being built from the outside end?

Tom Nabbe: Oh yeah, yeah. Well, especially every Sunday morning when I'm riding up there, stop on the top and sit. And then as it progressed, then they built the Berm and that restricted a little bit of the view, and then they landscaped the berm and that blocked a little bit more of that view, but it was able to watch it. I remember myself and a couple other guys chasing the TWA rocket down Harvard Boulevard. It was on a flatbed truck and we were sure we chased it all the way to the Harbor gate. And then it went inside the park and so we rode back up to the top of the overpass because we were sure they stood that rocket right up. Well, it took about a week, week and a half before they stood up the rocket in Tomorrowland.

So once the park opened up, Ray told me, he says, "Come over every morning. I'll be in front of the gate. And if you sell a hundred newspapers outside the gate, then you can continue to sell papers through the day, just come to the office and pick them up." Okay, so that was a pretty good deal. So on July 17th, guess where we were? We were at Disneyland and my mother had her autograph book and that was the press out slate. So all those celebrities were there and she's getting those autographs. And I was down around the corner staring through the fence was an Autopia, because I wanted to drive them Autopia cars. Now realize I'm 12, okay? So I really wanted to drive those Autopia cars. And back during this timeframe, 'Highway Patrol' was a very popular TV show, and they had six cars on the Autopia were done in black and white and looked like the highway patrol. And they have flashy red lights and a siren, and they didn't have any governor on him. And I'll talk about that a little bit later here.

So I ran over there. Well what happened is Danny Thomas was coming out. My mother asked Danny Thomas for an autograph and he very cordially gave her an autograph and he sort of leaned forward and he says, "Have you been in the park?" And my mother said, "Oh no, we weren't invited." He says, "Well, I got a couple extra tickets." Okay. And so he gave my mother two tickets and sure enough, she come call me and we went into the park as guests of Danny Thomas on the press opening of Disneyland. Now I have my tickets still and if you look at the ticket, there's no serial number on the ticket. So if anybody ever asks you, Tom Nabbe has ticket number one to the press opening of Disneyland. Now they were sort of broke down in timeframes. My tickets say 5:30PM, I think on them. And the ones in the archives say 2:30PM, so there were some stagger people coming in. And you can sort of go back and say, they didn't number the tickets, they probably didn't know how many tickets they have that gets back to that. Black Sunday analogy of working at Disneyland.

So we got inside and I remember we did ride the carousel. And I know we went to Carnation Gardens and we got a soda Carnation Gardens, not Carnation Gardens but Carnation on Main Street. But I think that's the dirtiest or trashiest, I think would be a better word. The trashiest I've ever seen a Disney park in my 50 year career. And I think Walt saw the same thing because from that point forward, cleanliness was right on top of the list. And that's something he preached to everybody. And if you ever walked the park with Walt, he'd bend over and he was picking up trash as he went through. And that's something you learned. My wife threatened to divorce me one time because I was picking up trash in the Florida Mall, but it's just one of those things that you can get conditioned of.

Lou: My wife says I pick up more garbage at Disney World than I do at my house.

Tom Nabbe: Yeah, yeah, yeah. It's funny how you get conditioned on those things. So, on the 18th, my neighbor across the street, Doug Harmon and I, we went over and stood in line. And bought tickets to go in the park, it costs us 50 cents and that was a child's admission at that time frame. The next day, on the 19th of July, I went to work as a newsie. So, I met Ray Ahmet out in front of the gate and got my a hundred papers... sold those. That was a slam dunk. All those people standing in line waiting to buy tickets and they wanted, needed one... and people read newspapers back at that time frame. So I sell those a hundred papers and then I was able to get inside the park. Well, those of us that sold all our papers out early, we get inside the park and we'd run over to Tomorrowland. Because what they needed was to get all the cars driven around and lined up for when the guests would come in on the Autopia. So we'd all run over there to drive the cars around to get them lined up. And every once in awhile you get to drive them police cars. So that was sort of neat.

Lou: You had dreams coming true literally on day one. Like you were in Disneyland working at Disneyland and you've got to drive the car that you wanted to, that you were looking at 48 hours earlier through the fence.

Tom Nabbe: Yes. It was the end of the first summer and I don't remember who, but somebody mentioned to me that, Walt was going to build Tom Sawyer's Island on the Rivers of America and that "you look just like Tom Sawyer and you should ask Walt for a job."

Lou: Now, had anybody told you that before that you looked like Tom Sawyer? Or was it only because this was going to be coming to the park?

Tom Nabbe: No. Well, my mother would. The star wannabe would dress me up in a costume, anyways, so I had cut off Levis and a straw hat... because of my complexion, I had a straw hat and she puts his suspenders and I had a blue and white checkered shirt and that was the costume that I wore to sell newspapers. And people would say, "Oh, you look like Huck Finn, or you look like cops or that black thing. So it wasn't unusual for this person to tell me that you look like Tom Sawyer and say ask Walt for a job. So Walt was in the park quite frequently back during that time. I think everybody was aware he only had the apartment above the fire station. He'd drive down on Friday evenings from the studio and spend Friday evening, Saturday, Sunday morning, and then he'd drive back up to the studio on their side. So he was pretty available. Walt used to walk around the park quite a bit, and he didn't look anything like the Walt Disney that you saw on TV. He usually had a couple of day's growth of beard, he had a white Panama hat and a pair of gray trousers and a blue jacket and he sort of walked around. So if you didn't really know it was Walt Disney, you wouldn't recognize Walt Disney.

But I interned, I recognized well, and I approached him and introduced myself and told him that I had heard that he was going to build Tom Sawyer and I looked just like Tom Sawyer, and he should hire me. Well, he didn't because if he had said no, we wouldn't be here talking. But what he said is, "I'll think about it." And I sort of reflect a little bit back on that and sort of realize that he may not have thought he was going to have a Tom Sawyer. He was going to build Tom Sawyer's Island, but sort of that the guests that went there was going to be Tom Sawyer sort of like the people went on Snow White. That you were actually Snow White. You didn't see Snow White in the attraction. So I think I convinced them into hiring a Tom Sawyer, so he said he'd think about it. And so for almost the next year, anytime I could find Walt and I asked him if he was still thinking about hiring me as Tom Sawyer. I remember one conversation that we had that he told me that he could probably put a dummy or mannequin, I think it was a mannequin over on the Island that wouldn't be leaving and every five minutes for a hamburger or a hot dog or a Coke… or that type thing.

Lou: I want to stop you for a second because I think there's something really interesting and profound about what you said was, on day one you approached Walt and throughout the year you approached Walt. I think the fact that not only was he present, but that he was approachable and that you as a young boy didn't look at him as somebody who was on TV that you felt comfortable enough to approach him. I think it says a lot, not only about you, but I think about Walt himself in that he allowed himself to not be removed from the Cast Members, but to be accessible.

Tom Nabbe: Well, would you look at this whole time frame. Yeah, we know Walt had a lot of child actors and actresses. Mickey Mouse Club was very strong. He had two daughters, okay, so he was fairly comfortable talking with kids. The other thing is he would listen to you, okay. He wouldn't cut you off, he wouldn't boohoo you, shoo you away or what? He'd listen to what you had to say and then he addressed what you said. That's like I say, when I asked him to hire me as Tom Sawyer, he said, "No, but I'll think about it." It's not one of those.

Lou: And so was that something that was in, like you woke up in the morning and like today I'm going to find Walt and I'm going to ask him to hire me, or was that something that sort of came to you on the spot?

Tom Nabbe: I don't remember waking up with it and then having that strike me as something that I needed to do that day. It just materialized. I was in the park and Walt was in the park and I pretty much had a goal. I accomplished one of those just recently when I was made a Disney legend. That's the same time that Peter Jennings passed away and Bob Iger went to Peter Jennings' funeral and Marty Scholar hosted the Legends Program and so I didn't get a photo op with him. But I have it on my bucket list and it took me 12 years, but this last D23 at Disneyland, I got my photo op with Bob Iger again. And we were walking up to the Legends' luncheon, and I saw Bob and I said, "Bob, you know, I didn't get my picture with you back when I was made a legend, would you pose with me now? He said, "Absolutely." And so I ended up getting, so I'm sort of tenacious along that line. I've been that way all my life. And maybe it isn't a good thing this week, in two weeks from now, it's a good thing. So yeah, I always keep those things in the back of your mind so you can then turn, inject those in a while. I think we talked over lunch about a couple of things that we did that back in the fifties or whenever.

Lou: So you go to Walt and you sort of plant this seed in his head that it wasn't an idea that he had, you really came up with a concept. How does it go from seeing him in the park and planting that idea one day to? How does it go to you actually becoming?

Tom Nabbe: Well, I was in the Penny Arcade, I remember this vividly, spending my hard earned paper money, playing the baseball machine in the Penny Arcade because I absolutely loved that baseball machine. And a gentleman by the name of Dick Nunez came up and tapped me on the shoulder and Dick at that time frame was a supervisor of Frontier Land. And Dick said, I know you know Walt but when Dick says, come with me, you don't argue with Dick, you go with Dick. So, Dick says, "Come with me, Tom." And so I went with Dick.

Lou: And you're probably not thinking this is something good at this point when Dick Nunez says…

Tom Nabbe: Just to throw me out of the park. He usually accuses me of sneaking in. I didn't sneak in, but I got down there legally. But in turn, so I'm walking with Dick and we were going over to Frontier land and this is when the Chicken Plantation was still there in the Indian village. She walked over to this little bridge and the Frontierland train station was there, Chicken Plantation and in the Indian Village was all compacted backed in that area. And Walt and Morgan Evans, Bill Evans, the landscape architect for Disneyland and Walt Disney World, were coming off the Island on the route. And Walt said, when he got to the dock and he says, "It's obvious you still want to be Tom Sawyer?" And I said, "Absolutely, Mr. Disney, I do. And he says, "Well, super. You need to get to work permit and a social security card." And I said, "Okay." And he says, "Once you do that, I'll put you to work as Tom Sawyer." So getting a social security card wasn't any problem. I just went to the office at Santa Ana and filled out the form and got the social security card.

Now the work permit was a little bit more of a challenge. I had to go to school and I had to get a form and then I had to take that form to the employment office and then the employment office had to fill out the form and answer all the questions. And then I had to return that form back to school and then in turn they would issue me a work permit. So, in turn I got my form and I went in, the employment office for Disneyland was in an old house on West Street, just opposite of the Disneyland hotel, and that was the employment office. I went inside and lay there and I told her my story that Walt had hired me to be Tom Sawyer and she gave me one of these nods, "Oh yeah, okay." And asked me to have a seat. And this side of the story I hear from Dick is that she went in and told Chuck Waylon, who is the Manager of Employment that, "I have this kid out here and that Dick Nunez knows all about it. And so Chuck picked up the phone and called Dick and said, "Dick, I got this kid over here that says Walt hired to be Tom Sawyer." And Dick said, "Yeah", took a little bit of a deep breath and told Chuck, "Chuck, Walt did hire him. Let your conscience be your guide."

And at that point, all my paperwork got filled out and I went to work as Tom Sawyer. Now, what did Tom Sawyer do? Okay. Well, first of all, they assigned me to entertainment to work for Tommy Walker, who is the Director of Entertainment back at that time. And only lasted about two weeks because they didn't know what the hell to do with me. So they gave me back to the Rides and Attraction side, back to Dick Nunez. So under him, one of the conditions of employment was, I had to bring him my report card. And if I didn't maintain a C average, I was no longer employed. And I know Dick reviewed my, I think, Walt assigned Dick to review my report card. So in turn, I pose for a lot of pictures. We had to stock the Rivers of America with Bluegill, and catfish and sun-perch and had the area. There were two piers right across from the landing for the Mark Twain, and they had that area netted off, and that's where the fish were stocked in that area.

Lou: And people could, you could actually fish at that point and it wasn't catching release right?

Tom Nabbe: Oh no. At this point, it was catch and clean. And part of Tom Sawyer's job was to clean the fish if the guests wanted to clean. And I had some plastic bags, and in turn I cleaned the fish. Well, that didn't last very long either. Maybe two months if it lasted that long, from June, July, by August, old smelly fish had showed up in places where he didn't want old, smelly fish. So we went from a catching clean to a catch and release. And I went through and debarked all the hooks. But there were two fishing piers, I'd have 25 fishing poles on each of the piers. Had worms for bait and little cans sailed up around the railing and would put top soil in the cans. And I'd put the worms, they actually came packaged and smart pails, rabbit poop. So you had to take them from there and put them into the...

Lou: So you would do a little bit of procurement as well as sort of, you know, guest... Because really, what was your, what was your title? I mean, did you have a...?

Tom Nabbe: I'm what they called a Guest Aid sound?

Lou: They didn't know what else to call you, right?

Tom Nabbe: Sounds like a good job description and legacy. I posed for a lot of pictures, I baited a lot of fishing hooks, repaired a lot of fishing bolts. And I was either Tom Sawyer or Huckleberry Finn, whatever the guests wanted me to be. And when you really look at it, Huckleberry Finn had the fiery, red hair and freckles, Tom was certainly more of a sandy blonde kid.

Lou: So, while you're sitting there and you're de-boning fish in the middle of the summer.

Tom Nabbe: De-gutting.

Lou: I'm sorry de-gutting. When you are de-gutting these fish in Disneyland in the middle of the summer, are you like, "Yeah, this is exactly what I hoped I was going to be doing when I walked up to Walt."

Tom Nabbe: No, I don't think that ever went through my head. It was part of the job that was explained to me as part of the job. So that was acceptable. You know, back in those days, you did a lot of the things that you were just, that's the job, do it.

Lou: You want to pose for pictures, you're also going to clean some fish?

Tom Nabbe: Yeah. So, I would respond to either Huckleberry Finn or Tom Sawyer. I didn't respond to Becky Thatcher Indian Jones. And I did that all through Junior High School and High School. And I remember one time Walt came over to the park early one morning, and he said, "Tom, I'm going to rehab Tom Sawyer's Island. Let's walk the Island, and I want you to tell me what you think the Island needs." And I'm going, "Okay, that's pretty good." Now, later in my life, we were told, thou shall not art direct, but during this time I hadn't had that speech. So we were walking the Island, and I told Walt that we have a lookout point OK, and I told Walt, well we have the lookout point is we need a Treehouse. And then we have Fort Wilderness and we needed an escape tunnel from Fort Wilderness. And so when the Island came back up from, from rehab in 1958, we had an escape tunnel from Fort Wilderness. We had a Tree house up on the top of the Island. We also had Merry-go-round rock, Teeter-totter rock, Castle rock but those weren't part of my ideas. I think those were Walt's ideas. So in turn, I will take credit for art directing the tree house and the escape tunnel.

Lou: But did it sink into you then? I mean, obviously, certainly now that you, Walt didn't dismiss you as a 12 year old boy with silly ideas. He actually took your ideas and he executed on them. So when the Island reopens, you look at it, was it that sense of pride, like, "I did that, like that was all my idea"?

Tom Nabbe: I was very impressed that had a Treehouse and an escape tunnel. But I think Walt's philosophy all through his life has always been employee involvement. All the people that worked at Web was people that he'd go talk to and say, "What would you like to do?" And then he'd say, "Okay, well, you're going to go to work for WED. Then you can go do what you want to do." Like the Bob Gurrs and the Wathel Rogers and all those people out there and Walt listen to a lot of people. When he was in there in the morning, he was talking to the landscape people, he was talking to the security people. That's another one, when the park opened, security was a lessee, it was Burns Detective Agency and I hear the story, one of them from Walt. Got up at one, I'll walk in the park one night, out of the apartment, then one of the Burns Detective Agency guards approached him and said, "yo, who are you?" And he said, "Well, I'm Walt Disney." And he says, "I don't care who you are, you can't be out here at this time of night." And at that point, we no longer have Burns Detective Agency. We had Walt Disney Securities. So, those are those stories that go along that line. But Walt listens to the guests, Walt listens to the people. He was always asking, "How can we do it better? What do we need?" And trying to get a whole feel for what was going on during that time frame.

Lou: And I think just as a quick aside, like so much about the story you've told so far from a business and entrepreneurial perspective. So you were the young, consummate entrepreneur from a young age. You had that hustle, you had that drive, you certainly had the courage to be able to go for the thing that you wanted, whether it was the paper route to get to the bicycle, to get to Disneyland, to get to become Tom Sawyer / Huck Finn / Fish gutter, to being able to go to somebody who was the head of this company, who not just pacified you by listening, but actually paid attention and took the recommendations that you and others made to heart. I think there's a lesson to be taken away from there, not just as an employee, but certainly as an employer that you are not the end all or be all that. That sometimes the people who work for you and with you, are able to contribute in remarkable ways.

Tom Nabbe: Yeah. Well, I think part of what you have to understand this, I went and found Walt, but Walt came to me also. So it was one of those, it was sort of a two way street. So he was soliciting my input versus me soliciting him to hire me.

Lou: Which is even more impressive, right?

Tom Nabbe: Yeah. Sort of a mutual relationship there. The last time I remember seeing Walt was, one of the deals that you always look for is that if Walt got totally inundated with people wanting autographs and that type of thing, he wasn't that familiar with on how to get out or backstage in the park. And I remember it was in the early sixties, it was after Mary Poppins, it was in the early sixties, it was in Frontier Land, and he was sort of inundated, and we were in between the Oaks Tavern and the Malt Shop there where the silver banjos and so I helped Walt get backstage, and I told him, "I'm Tom Sawyer, you hired me to be Tom Sawyer." He said, "Oh yeah, I remember that." And so we talked for a little bit, but that was my last encounter with Walt, back in that timeframe.

Lou: As a kid, did the scope and the magnitude of who, not just who they were working for, but who you were able to have such personal contact with. Did it impact you then or it wasn't until maybe later on, that the importance and the magnitude of who he was and the relationship that you had with him kind of sunk in?

Tom Nabbe: Well, you saw Barry Night on Wednesday night on television, so he was very much a celebrity and understood my mother was enamored with celebrities.

Lou: Did she ask you for Walt's... did she ask you to get his autograph?

Tom Nabbe: She tried a couple of times. She didn't have that autograph. All those books ended up with my younger sister. So I that was one of the things that I really wanted, but that didn't materialize. A lot of it is being at the right place at the right time and knowing what the opportunity is and seizing that opportunity. I look at today's world and there's a lot of people out there that are very focused. I was very open to change. A lot of people have their entire goals laid out for them, and they know if they don't do it, or if I don't make Director in five years, I'm going to go someplace else and try it. Those are those things that you learn and, and dealing with the people, I think that's part of one of the things that I really feel so satisfied out of my years of employment is the folks that I've worked with, a hint that I've watched a mentored and watched them grow and mature into professions either within the Disney experience or outside in the real world. Back in the fifties, every day was a new record, a new learning curve, a new way of doing it. There wasn't a college of hospitality like there is today, you can't go to UCL and go to Rosen College of Hospitality. There wasn't a college of hospitality back there and you learned as you went forward and you had some great teachers and great mentors. One of my stepfathers took off when I was fairly young, so a lot of the people at Disneyland filled in that void for me and became my surrogate fathers and mentors through my life. That's how I ended up in Florida, is one of those guys that was going to be the Operations Manager for the transportation for the operation here in Florida and he wanted me to open the monorail system for him.

Lou: Because after being Tom in Disneyland, you stayed in Disneyland for a while. You had other roles and responsibilities there too, right?

Tom Nabbe: Oh yeah, yeah. That first summer was a slam dunk. I turned 18 in 1961, I was a raft operator and I had learned how to drive a raft long before I became a Raft Operator. I used to come in early in the morning and the guys would teach me how to drive and that type thing. So I was a very experienced raft operator before I was old enough to technically drive a raft. I started out very quickly on Tom Sawyer's Island and actually I was a working foreman four days a week, what they call relief foreman; the day foreman had two days off the night foreman had two days off, so I would fill and cover their shifts. I was in a leadership role fairly early. Disneyland was closed on Mondays and Tuesdays in the wintertime. So on a Sunday evening my supervisor at that time, Jim Hut and Jim came over and handed me a script and he says, memorize this, you go to work on the Jungle on Wednesday morning and so show up at the Jungle on Wednesday morning. I stopped by wardrobe and changed my Tom Sawyer's costume for a Jungle Cruise costume and showed up and made three or four trips and then from that point forward I was as Jungle skipper.

There were two attractions that you knew you were going to work as a male operator that had the largest manpower was the submarines and the jungle crews. Those two attractions had the most amounts of male employees. So you are going to work those as you worked up through the seniority lists, then you're able to work on other attractions. With Disneyland being closed on Monday and Tuesdays. So you had a schedule on Saturday, you had a schedule on Sunday. You had a schedule on Wednesdays. So it was usually eight hours, eight hours, and four hours and if Wednesday was busy, they would extend the shift down. So I was having trouble making my rent on 20 hours a week. So what I would do is I would come in on Thursday mornings and on Friday mornings and sit in the operations office and wait for people to call in sick. So in turn a lot of attractions I didn't know, because I was there, they went out and trained me. And so the next time somebody called in sick, I was trained and ready to go.

Lou: So you sort of made yourself the relief pitcher that just sat there on deck, whenever somebody was going to be sick, you were going to be the guy that went to.

Tom Nabbe: Well, yeah, yeah. Well, in order to get the dollars to do that too. And so I learned a lot of attractions that first year very quick and worked almost every attraction in the park with the exception of the monorail and steam trains and the reason being that those two attractions were run by Retlaw and Retlaw is Walter spelled backwards and Retlaw was a company that the Disney family owned and they actually ran the monorail and steam trains and the situation, in order to work on the monorail, they wanted this image and you had to be six foot tall. Well, I was never going to be six foot tall, so that's why I never worked on the monorail.

Lou: I feel your pain. Don't worry. So you were there for a number of years, so you meet your wife eventually at Disneyland?

Tom Nabbe: Well, yeah, right about that timeframe in 1965 all the lessee contracts started to expire. Some were five-year contracts, a good portion where were 10 year contracts and all the fast food operations at Disneyland was run by UPT, United Paramount Theaters, which was a subsidiary of ABC, how things go around and come around and their contract ran out and they took about 50 of us and trained us in management in fast food operations. And so I went to work in Frontierland and my wife to be was the counter lead there. Right at the same timeframe, I got an invite from my other uncle, not Uncle Walt, but Uncle Sam. Uncle Sam wanted me to participate in a little bit of a war in Vietnam and there was no way I was going to pass a physical. And so I sort of, we do some dumb things in our life, but I sort of said, if I'm going to go to Vietnam, in my mind I wanted to be the best grain and as far as I'm concerned, the Marine Corps is going to train me the best to survive.

So I went down and enlisted in the Marine Corps and I listed for a three year hitch. And the reason being a three-year hitch, I had no reserve time. It was three years active duty, three years in active duty because the people that were in active reserves weren't real high on the schedule lists because they had to go play soldier one weekend a month and they had to do a summer camp and then that type thing. So I didn't want that obligation. And so I ended up going in the Marine Corps and I had orders to Da Nang and I would have had everything all packed up and I had; they made an aviation radio repairman out of me. Somehow my aptitude was strong in electronics and I ended up going to sign up for a three year hitch. I was eligible for all the schooling their four year hitch would have. So I ended up going to radio repair school. The incentive to graduate from radio repair school was that if you failed, they made a radio operator out of you and the life expectancy of a radio operator was rather short, so you just didn't want to be a radio operator. So I passed and I ended up getting promoted to corporal out of school and I had orders to Da Nang and I had everything packed up and going home on... it was a St. Patrick's Day weekend. And I had to battle off highway 101, Pacific Coast Highway, a drunk hit me head on and tried to kill me and put me in the hospital for five months. And then from there I ended up going back to school.

This is the same time that Walt passed away; the New York world's fair and Walt's passing happened all during the time that I was in in the Marine Corps. I ended up getting mustered out of the Marine Corps went back to Cal State Fullerton; dreams of grandeur of being electrical engineer. About a year and a half into schooling at Cal State Fullerton, I realized I was a good to be a good electronical engineer and what I really wanted to be was a in rides and attractions at Disney. They started interviewing there for all the people that come to Florida. So I went through a round of interviews and I ended up getting promoted into management in

1970. Just prior to that I was home on leave and I ran into a mutual friend of my wife and she gave me Janice's number and I called her and we started dating and we got married in June in 1968.

Lou: The plane is literally in flight in terms of Walt Disney world coming into being. How does it come to pass that you; because I want you to tell a story of not just how you literally made your way out to Florida, but how did it come to pass that you were going to come out here and be part of the opening team for Walt Disney world?

Tom Nabbe: Well I only thought I was going to be in Florida for three years. I had the opportunity to interview to open a monorail system here with Pete Crimmins who I had worked for off and on through the years and was one of my mentors. The company was going to build a ski area in Mineral King, which was just south of Sequoia national forest, which is about halfway between Los Angeles and San Francisco. So that was my goal to go to work and transportation and to make a name for myself and transportation and then the whole concept of Mineral King was they were going to build a parking area in the village and everybody got transported from the parking area up to the village. So transportation was a very key element and role there.

So in turn I came down to Florida. I'd never been East of Phoenix. My mother tells me we went to Chicago on the train, but I don't remember that. But Janice and I made that decision and I had two Volkswagens at the time and so we decided to drive a Volkswagen and tow a Volkswagen; we had a dark blue convertible and had a yellow Volkswagen. In the back of the yellow Volkswagen had a sign put in... two more bugs for Florida. And so we drove country cross country. It took us about six days to drive here, it was rather interesting. It was like 30 miles an hour up the overpass and 70 miles an hour down the overpass. The one that was really scary was coming through the tunnel. So coming down in a tunnel, I'm staying up with traffic. Well coming up on the other side of the tunnel I'm brewing a little slow and I get over and clear and right there, there are toll booths and I got the brakes on, I got the emergency and we're sliding through and slow right through the tollbooth. I had to get out and go back and pay for both cars and go back to get it. But that was a little scary on that one.

Lou: Again, this dream of wanting to operate the monorail, it comes to fruition in a very, in a different time and a different way in a different place because it takes you coming out to what little there was of Orlando at that time to help sort of manage the monorail operations and part of the construction too?

Tom Nabbe: Yeah. Well, there's a whole concept that was developed during New York world's fair called PICO, project installation coordination and what they do is they take people out of the operating side and you get assigned into the construction and project side and your coordinators sort of gophers or whatever needed to help along that line. And then as you hire people, you train those people. And then when the attraction opens up, then you become the management group that operates the rides and attractions. So that was sort of the philosophy and the monorail is my attraction. We had the two beams, express beam and local beam, the contemporary and one we're sitting in here in the Polynesian where the two hotels on what we call the local beam and the express beam went from the TTC, ticket transportation center to the magic kingdom. So that was a concept behind the monorail system.

Lou: So if the stories that I've heard are true you very much were a hands on person when it comes to your monorail. And when I say hands on, I mean not boots on the ground, I mean boots on the beam. Is it true that you used to walk the beams?

Tom Nabbe: Well, US steel built the two hotels and the Golf Resort and also a complex called the Court of Flags down on I-4 and Sand Lake, right in that area. Well, they were very difficult to deal with. Thank God that Roy bought them out right after opening, but they were very difficult to go and it would take me sometimes as long as four hours just to get clearance to get into the hotel to check my stations. Past your security people because I didn't work for US Steel, I worked for Disney. So I've found the easiest way for me to check the stations was to walk the beam. To the Poly… no big deal… maybe two city blocks to the Polynesian. Now the beam is 30 inches wide. So it's wider than this table.

Lou: Okay. So 30 inches isn't a lot when you're 60 feet above the ground.

Tom Nabbe: Well, yeah and you don't do it in high winds and lightning and thunderstorms but in turn I could get up into the contemporary very quickly. The problem that we had was the two beams that were on the north end of the contemporary were all the beams that you look that have the curve bottom to them, those were fabricated in Tacoma, Washington, and shipped here by rail to tap and from tap they were crap over to property. Well, the two beams that were 110 foot long beams were on the north end of the contemporary hotel. The train went right and the beams went straight ahead and had a snow storm right after that. So we couldn't find the beams. So they had to in turn fabricate those beams. So we're about almost three months late and closing the loop on the monorail to have a closed loop. So we did a lot of training and a lot of shuttling going back and forth. But in turn I checked the stations out and in a very short period of time just like clicking up there and back when we originally opened a monorail system, the monorail, the parking lot, watercraft and the submarines were all on the same radio frequency.

What we didn't realize is that the batteries on the radios in the monorail had a very short transmit life on it. So you could only transmit maybe two, three minutes and you are out of boundaries, you can listen, but you couldn't transmit. I remember one breakdown I had, a young lady in the train and she did her transmission and then we couldn't talk to her. And so the easiest thing was to walk out on the parallel, because beams are parallel, walk out on the parallel beams, have her open up the door. I talked her through what she needed to do and had the work tractor come out and tow her train in and get the guests off that type thing. But it was one of those things that you did.

Lou: Without a harness, you're not safety rigged; you're just walking the beams?

Tom Nabbe: Yeah.

Lou: It was a different day and age.

Tom Nabbe: Right. It was a different world back in that time frame. I would say if the director knew that I was walking, he'd probably be a little upset with me. But those are things; we rode in cars without seat belts. We drank water out of the hose in the yard. There was a lot of stuff that we did back there that you wouldn't dare do in today's world.

Lou: And there actually were plans, because people still to this day talk about expanding the monorail; I mean there were plans at one point right, to expand the monorail out to like 192 like an industrial park, weren't there?

Tom Nabbe: Well, if you look at the entire project, the Magic Kingdom and what you see today, I think was in phase 35 or 37 or whatever. But in between the Magic Kingdom complex and what was proposed as the original Epcot project, there was a whole industrial park and an airport. So all of those things were in the master plan. Now, as you know, the master plan didn't get totally built, but yeah, talked about; the monorail is very costly and the advantage here was you have sort of very restricted group. Everybody's got to either ride the monorail back down or the Osceola's or the trams. Didn't have the bus fleet we have today, didn't have the ferries that we had today. Didn't have ten monorails as we have today. Ten six-car monorails versus six, five-car monorails. Yes. So, things have changed and going forward.

Lou: Your role in Walt Disney World changed... So again, it's interesting going from a very onstage presence as Tom/Huck to sort of more backstage with the monorails, but that was not your only role in Disney World you ended up doing more in terms of logistics and whatnot?

Tom Nabbe: Well, I sort of got tagged as a nuts and bolts guy and sort of got tagged as the guy that you wanted on your team's new construction and new openings. And so after we opened a monorail up, I ended up deciding to help build Tom Sawyer's Island in Frontierland, Liberty Square and the Richard F. Irvine. So I went on that project the minute we wrapped up that project in 1973 went on a project to rebuild Tomorrowland. When Tomorrowland opened up, it was pretty scarce of what was in the Tomorrowland area. We put in the Wed Way, the Star Jets, Carousel of Progress and Space Mountain. So '73 to '75 and then once we opened all that up, then the decision was to take 20,000 Leagues down and when we originally opened 20,000 Leagues, all the art directors that came out here went to Silver Springs and were enamored with the clarity of the water and everything and so the decision was to pump the water out of the aquifer through 20,000 Leagues that went into the moat and from the moat that went to the Jungle Cruise and from the Jungle Cruise that went into the Rivers of America... from the Rivers of America went down the light boat channel in the Seven Seas Lagoon and from the Seven Seas Lagoon, they got distributed over the 55 miles the drainage canals that are on property.

Well that was great. The only trouble is you didn't have the volume of water coming and being pumped through the 20K that you had coming out of the springs at Silver Springs. They started getting pockets and algae started growing. So it finally made the decision to enclose 20K and chlorinate it and filter it and so we did that in 1975. Once we wrapped that up and opened that back up and got that running, we had the opportunity to go back to Frontierland because we were going to build this little train over there called Big Thunder. We built Big Thunder and just right as we opened up Big Thunder there was another little project down the road that got funded and ready to go. If you remember when I said earlier, I only came to Florida to be here for three years. Well, we were going to build an area, a ski area in Mineral King. Well, that sort of got shut down by the Sierra Club because of the roadway that had to be built there and the sea/air club didn't want that roadway built and they petitioned, so that project moved to an area of above Truckee, California, which is just north of Lake Tahoe.

That clicked along quite well until there was a little conflict of people going on our board from in order to get the permits and everything going on there and Card Walker at that point, basically said no, we aren't going to build any ski areas and all the monies that we have, I'm going to focus on the Epcot project. So if you sort of look at it as Disneyland was Walt's park. Walt Disney World Magic Kingdom was sort of Roy's park. Walt's dreams and ideas and that type thing but Roy brought it into this world and Card decided that Epcot was going to be his park if you head a little farther down the road. Then the Studio and Animal Kingdom tie us into Eisner and in his parks. Shanghai is Eisner's park. So everybody, and I sort of look in a company, sort of has a 20 year cycle. So in the twenties this thing was developed. In the forties, went through World War II and it almost cost the company.

Again, in the sixties Walt passed away, in the eighties was the end of the Eisner era and the Iger era and we're getting ready for another one down the road, but I sort of look in the big 20 year cycles along that. Now I forgot where we were going in the conversation and then I went out into the Neverland.

Oh, I got a call and asked if I wanted to be involved in the Epcot project. And I said, oh, absolutely. Norm Dirges and Bill Sullivan we're going to be the guys out there and I thought I was going to be a pavilion coordinator, but in turn Norm wanted me to run a warehouse complex that they had. We were in the process of developing what we called an item tracking system for OFI. OFI stands for "owner-furnished items." So anything that we bought for show installation was basically going to be installed by Buena Vista Construction, okay, was called OFI and we would tag and label that. So all of the show set pieces, all the props, all the animation, all that stuff fell in that category. What was going to happen was there was going to be a warehouse that project was scheduled for later installation. Anything that came in could be installed, was directly to the site to be installed.

I had a crew of people that were working for me and that's what we did and so in turn went through the opening of Epcot that was that was a real; had gone through the opening of Disneyland as a child and went through the opening of Walt Disney World as a Magic Kingdom, as a young adult. Epcot now I had the chance to use all those skill sets to go forward and it just fit like a glove right in there and headed down the road. I adapted very quickly to the warehouse operation. I sort of took that in my mind and it's sort of almost like any ride or attraction or running a parking lot, you have to bring things in. You have to park it, you got to be able to get through it. It was real easy to equate to that. This owner furnished... we gave everything an item number. All his shows were built and bought off in California and they were built in Tujunga and our directors would buy them off and then they would just assemble them number and label them, load them on a truck and send them to Florida, either to be warehoused or to be installed.

They get to Florida, and a good portion of it is; we handle about $400 million toward the materials through the warehouse. You'd open the back of the truck and you look and you go, God, how did they get that in there? Then the next question is, how are we going to get it out of there and not break it? Understand this is a one of a kind item. You can't go to Home Depot and buy another one. So in turn, that was the challenge that went along that and we went all through that process and I think if you've read the Storming the Magic Kingdom or that type of thing that Epcot coming real close to bankrupting this company and did not hit the return on investment. And so all of us that went through that opening that processing, getting through that relief all of a sudden got into another or didn't know if you're going to have a job tomorrow.

But thank God that Walt Disney went out and did his thing and he got the best brothers on board and made the decision to hire Frank Wells and Michael Eisner and brought those people on and got everything coming out of it. Right at that time frame I made a major career change and went from being in rides and attractions and guests oriented to the support side of the business. I liked what I did in the warehouse portion of it during Epcot and I sort of enjoyed that and had a job opportunity to go into warehousing for Walt Disney World and I did that for the last 22 years of my career.

Lou: So your three year stint at Walt Disney World did not just take you from Anaheim to Orlando, but somehow your circuitous journey also took you to Paris, correct?

Tom Nabbe: Yes. After we went through that whole process of storming the Magic Kingdom, getting everything back online and this property just exploded with hotels and hotel rooms and the stock went from chunk change up into the hundreds again and the whole decision that Michael made was to build the park in Paris. In turn I had the director of distribution for Disneyland in Paris, let's say it was called Euro Disney back at that time frame over for almost a year of training with us and he felt pretty comfortable. I had gone over there for a couple of visits to warehouse operations, sitting through some planning and concept process. But I wasn't slotted to go to Paris. In the latter part of, well actually the 1st of January of 1992, I get a telephone call from my boss, Howard Roland and Howard Roland's in Paris and this is on a Friday morning and Howard says Tom, I want you to in Paris on Monday when I want you to meet with me in Bauma Lake. I said okay, he says, I got the travel company working on tickets and we'll see a Monday.

Sure enough, the tickets showed up, went to the airport, packed up a bag, and I got on an airplane and came to Paris and got off at in Orly airport and found a car and drove downtown Paris and met Paul and Howard and Howard said Paul; Paul Molay who was the director of purchasing who had run the warehouse system here, who I worked for. He says Tom what I want you to do is be a liaison and help John Louis get through opening and do pretty much what you did for Epcot here in Paris. And so that's what I did. So in turn we went; I finally left the end of April. April 12th is hard to believe it's only three, four weeks from now and we're going to go through a birthday for Paris. But being able to go through that process got back here went through monitor material handling, which is a publication associated with warehousing and that type thing, came to us from wanting to, and this was right at Walt Disney World's 25th anniversary came to us wanting to do a little short story on the 25th anniversary.

They came in and we showed them what we did and they got so involved in what we were doing then in turn this little two, three page article turned into a 20 page article and was their lead publication for that year, won the awards that they just didn't quite understand how we could handle a city of about 250,000 people back at that time on a daily basis. So if you take everybody to stand on property, everybody that's coming into property as a day guest and in all the food and all the merchandise and all the equipment to keep that going on a daily basis, it comes through the warehouse operation. So they were very impressed with that.

Lou: Even as a kid that was something that always impressed me how this place really is a real working city that operates 24/7/365 and the logistics of not just the manpower and the guests, but of the things that we don't think about as guests. All the things that need to populate the shelves and the stores and the restaurants is an incredible undertaking. But eventually your very long journey from 12 year old Tom Sawyer and Huck Finn to coming back to Walt Disney World, you decided it's time for it to come to an end and you retire what year?

Tom Nabbe: I retired in '03, I hired a financial advisor back when we did a living trust that, and he did very well, and so I asked him on my 60th birthday... was coming right around. June is a very active month for me. My birthday is in June. My company anniversary date is in June. My wedding day is in June. My retirement date is in June. Father's day is in June. So June was a very active month for me and I basically told him I'd like to retire in June. So if you ever retire from the Walt Disney Company, you want to retire from the last day of the month that way you get your pay for that week and then the first day of the next month you get your retirement check.

So I in turn made that decision and so told my boss that I had planned on retiring and he'd sort of said, well, Tom, what would you like as a retirement gift? And I told him, I said, if I qualify, what I'd really like is a window on Main Street at Disney and one at Walt Disney World. And so I thought that just sort of went this way. So about two, three weeks later, he comes back and he says, look couldn't do the Disneyland thing, but I got you a window on Main Street at Walt Disney World. So if you ever come into the Magic Kingdom at Walt Disney World, and you look at the Cinema, my window is right above it, on the right hand side.

Lou: And what does your window read?

Tom Nabbe: Sawyer Fence Painting and Proprietor, Tom Nabbe, Anaheim, California, Lake Buena Vista Florida. So yeah, super, it's one of those things. So I thought that was the height, the crème de la crème type thing and my goal every fifth anniversary of Disneyland is to be on Main Street at Disneyland on July 17th. We were out there for the 50th anniversary, a couple previous trips, the mouse paid for it, but most all the trips I've paid for it and so we are there and the Disneyland alumni club was having a dinner dance. We went to the dinner dance and we were there in our gentleman named Jim Cora. Jim Cora retired as the president of Disney international and they had worked with Jim on opening here at Walt Disney World and had worked a little bit alongside German in Paris. And he sort of said, hey Tom, I'll see you in September and anybody that ever worked with Jim Cora, he's one of these guys that'll sort of toss out and see if he had to hook you on something, if he could get it, he'll play it to the help. So I said, "No, Jim I'll be back here in five years, but I don't plan on being back here in September." He says, "Oh no, you and Sully and me are going to be inducted as Disney legends." I said, "Oh, okay" but I didn't bite on that.

So when I got back to the hotel room, I called my sister who was house sitting for us here in Florida. I said, "Is there a letter there from the studio?" And she said, "Yeah" and I said, "Would you open it up and tell me what it says." And she says, "Oh, it's something about you being inducted as a Disney Legend in September." And so Cora wasn't pulling my leg. It was a true thing. So in turn, the Disney Legend program was very much a Roy E. Disney's thing. He was just totally enamored in that and I think I mentioned earlier in the conversation that when I got inducted as a legend the same time Peter Jennings passed away and so Marty Sklar and Roy hosted the Legends luncheon and induction and I had the opportunity to talk with Roy a little bit. I'm a sailor and Roy is a sailor and so we talked about sailing and my boat's 16 foot long, his boat's a 116, but sailing is sailing. So in turn that one, and it's really nice to be a living legend, the alternative sucks. But had the opportunity, what they do is they have a clay mold there at the ceremony and you do your palm prints and you sign it and then they cast a bronze plaque and then that there's a Legends Plaza at the studio and it gets in the studio. So the next trip out for Disneyland 55th, I had called the Archives and because I hadn't seen my plaque and asked to borrow his Legends award and we went out to the gardens and took some photos out in that area of myself and my plaque. So that's sort of a thing.

Lou: You have seen so much, you have done so much from being there on opening day as a guest to 24 hours later, being there as a guest facing cast member in a role that you designed and had created for you. You knew Walt, you interacted with Walt, and you influenced Walt. You've done so much here in the world. You are in Paris. You are a legend, you are a member of the Disneyland, that club 55 you've seen and done so much. And of all the things, when you look back on your time with the company is there any one thing, any one moment that you look back on most vividly? I can't say favorite because I'm sure there's so many, but most vividly or most fondly and the one that sort of is most meaningful to you?

Tom Nabbe: Working for wed being Tom Sawyer, absolutely. But I had…

Lou: Because you are the only one right?

Tom Nabbe: No, they held a contest to replace me. So they had one replacement and after that, then there wasn't any more Tom Sawyer's. But working in wed watching things come from a storyboard concept to reality, to build it, to watch guests actually appreciate it and ride on it, that is phenomenal. That was probably the crème de la crème. Making the transition into warehousing, one of the things; the hardest thing was trying to get the people in the warehouse operation to feel part of the show. What I did there is I went to the Institute and we partnered with the Institute and we've brought people in to tour the warehouse operation because they had enamored with that, just like the people from modern material handling. So we would bring people in and tour them through the warehouse. Well, I didn't do the tour in the warehouse. I in turn had the warehouse people tour the people in the warehouse. I did do a Q and A on some of the things I do.

Once a month I do a Disney heritage thing for RCID, Reedy Creek improvement district. They decided to go through and retrain all their older employees along with new employees that were coming on board. And the manager of HR for them was a drinking buddy of mine asked me if I would come share my story with him. I said, yeah and that was three years ago. So every third Friday of the month, I get to do that. I do a lot of speaking for Disney events. I do the Disney Fan club several times, the college program; I do it for the ambassadors. I enjoy that. Now one of the questions I normally get at the end of my presentation and it's about an hour presentation, we're a little longer on this one, is have you ever thought about writing a book and so I did. So if you want to hear the real long version of the story of Tom Nabbe then you can pick up my book. It's available on amazon.com or you can go to my website, tomnabbe.com if you want it personalized and autographed.

Lou: I will link to that in the show notes. I have one last question for you because I want to sort of flip things a little bit because now you come to the parks, you come to Magic Kingdom with your young granddaughter. Give me your impression now coming to the parks as a guest versus when you were here as a Cast Member from sort of helping to create that magic that we talk about to experiencing it and sharing it with your own grandkid.

Tom Nabbe: Well it's phenomenal. She's just a little over two right now and I'm going, what is a two-year-old going to know, well, I tell you, she knows the characters. A character breakfast is on property. She just loves them, eats them up, all the experiences in the park. One time here and we went to Epcot and we went down and she's totally involved in Ana and Elsa and all off them from frozen and to watch her, the interaction of her and Anna and Elsa down there is just; and the kids that play those characters do an excellent job also, but I know now why I work where I work so I could get my main gate pass so I can get her in on a daily basis if I want to except for blackout dates.

Lou: Well, look at that, that happiness and that pride that you feel as a grandfather towards your granddaughter is the same thing that you, when you were being Tom Sawyer gave to those parents and grandparents back in 1955. So as a guest, as a parent I thank you for everything that you've done to contribute to this Disney magic that we know and love so much and I will tell you, Tom, you were worth the wait, you were worth waiting four years to get this interview done. Because I can listen to your stories all day again, your book is fascinating and filled with so many more and I appreciate you spending time today and certainly for everything that you've done for us.

Tom Nabbe: So very welcome and I'm sorry you had to wait four years but I've been practicing so you got the best of the best.

Lou: Excellent. Tom, thank you so much. I really appreciate it.

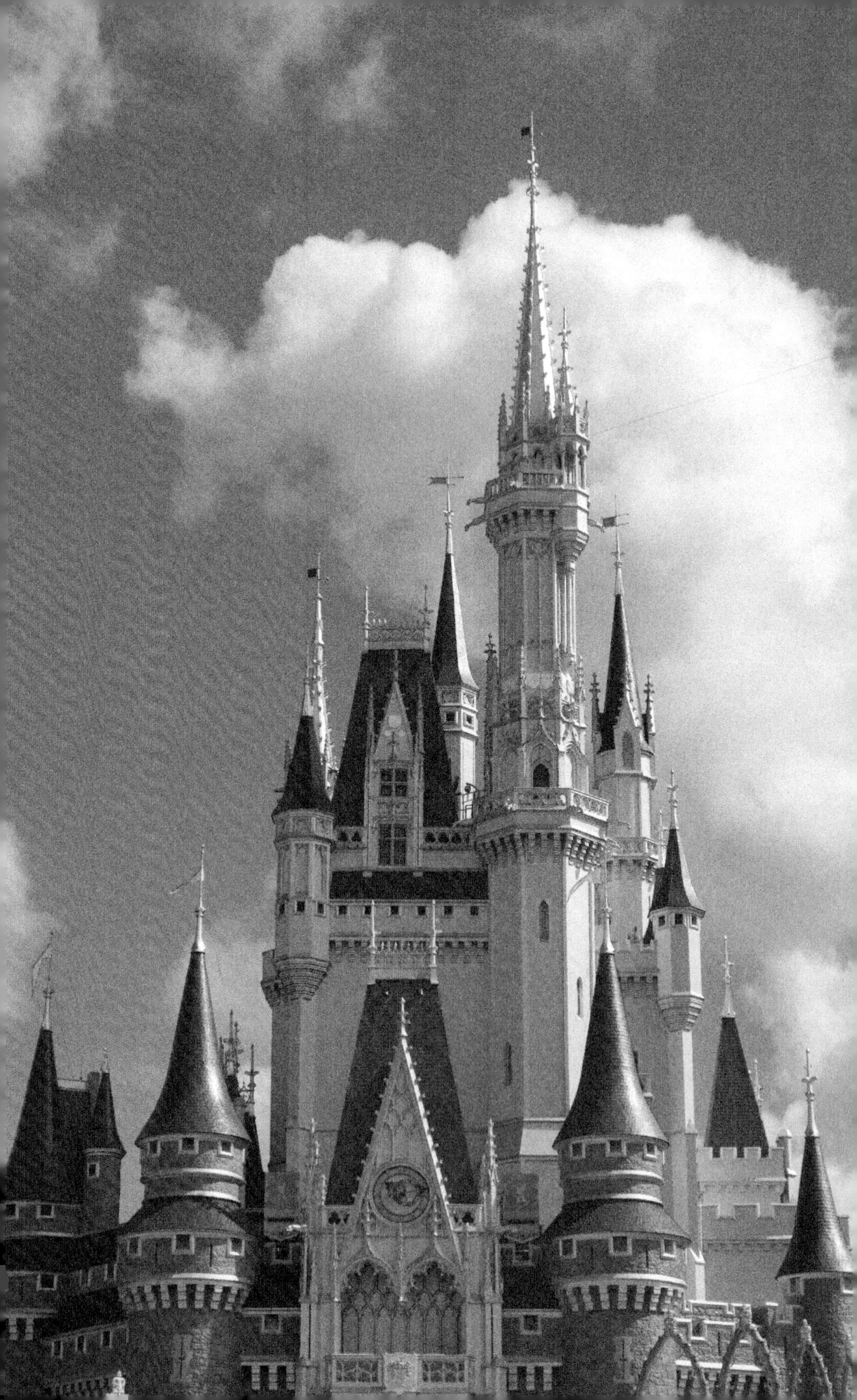

Al Konetzni

Affectionately known as the "Idea Man" by Walt Disney, Disney Legend Al Konetzni joined Walt Disney Productions in 1953 as an artist for the character merchandising division, based in New York City. In his nearly 30 years with The Walt Disney Company, he developed countless ideas for toys, clothing, stationery, greeting cards, jewelry and much more, including the famous Pez Mickey and highly collectible Mickey Mouse lunch box (more than nine million classic Disney lunch boxes were sold based on Al's original design!).

In our conversation, Al shares his personal journey, including working with Walt, why he considered himself a "salesman with a pencil," and shares advice for those looking to become an artist for Disney.

At his retirement party in 1981, Konetzni said fondly, "I'm still Disney… 'Working for Disney is like a religion. It gets in your blood and stays there… It was a thrill." When asked how he would like to be remembered, Al replied; "As the artist who drew for children around the world and made them happy."

Al was inducted as a Disney Legend in 1999, and passed away on Monday February 8, 2016, at the age of 100.

This interview is taken from my conversation with Al on WDW Radio Show # 511, in February, 2018. You can listen to the complete interview at WDWRadio.com/511.

Lou Mongello: Born in Brooklyn, New York in 1915, young Al Konetzni only wanted crayons and pencils from his parents for Christmas. And while Mickey Mouse always made him smile, little did they know that years later, he would work with Walt Disney and help bring smiles to the faces of millions and generations of other children as well. So it's my pleasure and honor today to meet and speak with Disney legend Al Konetzni. Al, welcome to the show.

Al Konetzni: Thank you. It's nice to be here. And I'm glad to meet you.

Lou: It is great to meet you as well too. And we had a chance to meet briefly yesterday and the first time I met you was during the Art of Animation opening a couple of months ago. But yesterday you gave a great presentation and I was fascinated by your story and by your journey. As a kid, you love to draw, and like I said in the intro all you wanted were crayons and pencils, from your parents as a kid.

Al: Let me add one thing, I wanted boxing gloves too. But I very seldom tell anybody that.

Lou: I think it's probably better that they gave you the crayons and pencils instead of boxing gloves.

Al: Isn't that amazing I haven't mentioned that in interviews... that's just kind of a secret to you.

Lou: I think that's really neat because obviously you chose the right path. You went to the very prestigious Pratt Institute, you ended up working in New York at the Gertz company and then at the Pal Persona Blade Company, where you actually helped create the Pal guy character.

Al: Oh, yes, I was the art director for Pal Persona Blade companies. And I'll tell you about the Pal man. It was a rounded head thing and with a lot of shaving cream on them. And when I first introduced it to them, my first year being an art director with them, it was turned down and that was funny. And I love to tell art students about this. I said wait a minute in about two years with them. I introduced it again and boy they went for. It appeared on their checks, on their stationery, on all their packages of razor blades. They were manufacturers of razor blades from someplace upstate New York.

And also speaking of that company, they told me I had a job for life. Every time I went for a raise, they said, you know you have a job here for life. And that was great because it lasted 16 years as an art director, but all of a sudden they sold the company. I think they sold it to the American safety razor company. And a decision had to be made. And I was shocked but anyway, what I decided to do, I had by that time I was married, the owners even were at my wedding. But then we had three children and I decided, well, I'm going to take a three-week vacation. And we went to Montauk Point, Long Island and had a ball but at the back of it all, I said, look, I don't have a job now I have to get a job.

So immediately when I got back, I went to a head agency. It is a headhunter, really. And I showed him my portfolio and he said, I got the perfect job for you. It's a promotion job. And you're a promotion, man. I said, wait a minute, I'm an artist. And he said, well, from all the work you're showing me in your portfolio, I have the right company for you. And it's the Walt Disney Company. And I must be honest, and frank with you I love Disney but Disney was not what it is today. I mean, they were struggling.

And I said, well, I would like to be interviewed anyway. So I was interviewed at Disney by a man by the name of Lou Lispy. I don't like to mention names much, but the guy was an art director for Disney for 40 years. And I got the job. And I said, well, I'm only going to stay maybe two years because I wanted to get into TV advertising and color was just starting to come in. And I'm glad the way it worked out. I stayed.

Lou: Well, they say everything happens for a reason. And sort of that path that you followed from artists to doing newspaper ads for the companies you work for, to this job with Disney. Again, it's one of those things where you thought you're an artist, and then they said, no, you're really a promotions guy.

Al: Yes. And not only that, but I was doing finished line drawings for Gertz department store before I showed him my portfolio and I had a load of stuff that I had done. And I was qualified for it. And I'm glad it happened the way it did.

Lou: And so do you remember when you were first hired and going to work for Disney on Madison Avenue in New York what was your first job? What was your first set of responsibilities?

Al: Well, let me tell you about that. First of all, we were not on Madison Avenue, to begin with, we were in Radio City. And I saw the old theater that most people will never remember, Roxy theater, I remember them tearing it down. And I was with Disney then in Radio City and that's where we started. And then we finally moved to Madison Avenue. And most of those years were made in Madison Avenue, so you're right about that.

Lou: And so when you were first hired, what was your first job at Disney?

Al: Well, when I was first hired, I spent two weeks drawing Mickey Mouse. And I guess Donald Duck too.

Lou: Well that's what I'm curious about. Because I saw some of your very early drawings and things that you did as a kid at home when you drew characters, and I'm showing my age, like Little Orphan Annie and Felix the Cat, when you go to Disney, how does that start where you're being taught to draw Mickey. Are the artists there, or do you go out to California?

Al: Well, I tell you what I love to draw and then I guess I was nine and a half or 10 years old. And I saw these comics in the newspaper and I could draw them. I didn't trace them, I drew them and that goes way back. I was fascinated by them. And a lot of them, people today wouldn't even recognize them because we're going back 75, 80 years, maybe longer. Anyway, I still have those drawings whether you believe it or not.

Lou: I saw and you know, at that age, obviously you're self-taught. And what's it like when the Mickey Mouse character is so iconic and the integrity of the character is so important to the Disney Company. When you're there and first brought in to New York, do they have artists there on staff who spend the first couple of weeks just teaching you how to draw the characters?

Al: Absolutely. You draw all angles and shapes and whatnot running, jumping, skipping, and whatnot. I'll tell you it was interesting... you fall in love with the guy. And well, that was a long time.

Lou: And so what did you actually do there? Because you are very well known for some of the products that you helped license and create. The quintessential one is that Mickey Mouse and characters school bus lunchbox. I remember the old metal lunch boxes as a kid, and 9 million lunchboxes later obviously that was one of your best selling items. But talk about some of the things that you created while you were there because you did toys and clothes and stationery.

Al: That's absolutely right. There was no end to it, anything that I could find where Mickey would have proved the product. I brought them in and I started to get into sales so I brought a whole bunch of companies in. Hasbro, the second-largest toy company in the world. And I just happened to think of Colgate Palmolive, which I don't talk much about, we signed them up. And US Time was already signed up. I didn't handle that one and I'm trying to think, and I also did not sign up National. They are in Nashville, the people who did my studio... school bus lunch kit.

And when I showed it, as a matter of fact, I lived in Pleasantville, New York, and I commuted for about an hour to my office in Madison Avenue in New York. And many times, oh, boy... Walt should have heard this... many times I spent a whole hour in a train, preparing for a nine o'clock meeting, and I could walk to my office from Grand Central Station. And I saw a school bus and I said, oh my God, what an idea for kids they are going to love to have a toy with a school bus. And then my second thought said, wait a minute, wait a minute, kids don't love school. Who am I kidding?

So I put it aside for a couple of days. But then when I got back to my office and started to make some sketches, we used to work in pastels and I made a beautiful sketch of a school bus with all the characters in each window and we presented it to National, I forget the name right now excuse me about that and they accepted it.

And they put it in the marketplace, I was in Chicago when I got an award for it, as a matter of fact, Chicago housewares show. And they sold 9 million of them, which is a pretty good number.

Lou: Well, and tell us about what that process is like, was it one where you would come up with a concept or an idea, you were an idea, man, right? So did you come up with an idea and then choose the appropriate company or did companies come to you and say we're looking for a product to license.

Al: In many cases, it works both ways. We searched them out. As soon as I had a secretary we found out who to talk to in these large companies, and we only dealt with nice companies. And I would work the other way where they came to us and we talked to them and we would get them in a conference room. And we would call all the artists in and we talk maybe to a president of a company or a vice president or an R&D man. And we throw all these ideas out for something that we knew they could make, we knew what kind of merchandise, how their machines would work and so forth, or packaging or whatnot. And as a matter of fact, many times we let them walk out with all these ideas and we did not get a contract. But I want to say most of the time we got them and I was very happy about that.

Lou: I have been reading about you, and was listening to you the other day... it seems like when you were going to pitch an idea you did it more with pictures than you did words. Your sketchbook was really your selling tool.

Al: Well, selling was easy, as a matter of fact, I got to say when they ask me, they said, we don't ever want you to stop creating stuff. But we would like you to be a contact man and that may be foreign to you, but it was foreign to me contact man. What is the contact man? Actually, to make it simple it's sales. And all of a sudden now I'm in sales and I did not know that I was a good salesman. I signed up some wonderful companies. As a matter of fact, one toy company I signed the contract and a woman signed the contract at the Waldorf Astoria and handed me the check and I brought it back to our office and things like that happened. It was wonderful.

Lou: And you worked with some famous watch companies and clock companies and made toothbrushes. Tell us a story about working with Pez?

Al: Oh Pez was interesting. The man in Pez. it was an Austrian company as you know and he was the head of The United States for Pez and he wanted a contract so bad it was unbelievable. And we got to be really good pals and friendly. And it took me a year and a half to get him in because my company and I'd say when my company Walt Disney, my boss, he was never excited about it. But finally, we got him in and we signed the contract and I can't tell you how they're doing today. But they were all over the country and they were all over the world, as a matter of fact, and I was very proud of it.

Lou: And when I think of your most notable companies that you brought in and a relationship that still exists today is with General Electric. Tell us a little bit the story of how General Electric the GE night light came to be.

Al: Oh, that's a very interesting story. GE, I was so happy with getting that contract. What happened is first Pez came and we did both Donald Duck and Mickey Mouse and they had a little night light for Donald duck and was never going to get one. They had a little night light with nothing, it was like a half a watt or two watts or something like that. So my secretary found out who we talked to at GE, and I'm in Providence, that division, and it was either he came up to see us, or I went down to Providence. But all these people always like to come to New York, they would bring their wives and they would go to shows or whatnot. So it was easy to bring him into our conference room and talk to them.

But anyway, Al Richardson his name was, and he came down to my office and I said excuse me, not Al, Mr. Richardson. And I said, I don't know if this will work, but I'm going to try it. So I had a Pez Donald duck and I broke the head off the top of the Pez and I clamped it on the top of their nightlight. And I said, I don't know I'm not sure maybe this will work but I want to try it. I pull down all the blinds at an office in Madison Avenue, they had five windows I think and they say if you have one window you're very important, but I did feel really important. So we put out the lights and they snapped it in the plug and my god there was. They signed a contract right away. And I want to tell you one thing they are still selling nightlights, children's nightlights

Lou: I know because my kids may still have some in their room and that's what's amazing and looking that's why you said, you're not an artist, you're not a salesman, you are an "Idea Man." And when you're able to, sort of, come up with an idea like that on the fly, thankfully it works, it sells itself.

Al: Oh, yes, it worked. I'm so grateful. I love that stuff. And it all starts from a rough sketch from the idea and then we'd make a comprehensive sketch, and sometimes even go further. And normally, we did get the contract. And I'm sure Disney is happy.

Lou: Well, I'm sure they're happy now and I'm sure they were happy at the time. And to that point, it was and always will be Walt's company. And as much as Walt was in California, he was very hands-on and I know, he made frequent trips, a few times out to New York. Tell us about the first time that you met Walt. When somebody says to you oh, by the way, Al Walt is coming here tomorrow. What that first meeting was like if I remember?

Al: It was fantastic. It was right before Disneyland opened an, of course then, Walt Disney World, later on. He came to see us about four times a year to find out what they were doing. Tell us what kind of movies they were going to make and what we had to work on. And he sat there on this big veranda thing and he says, you know, you fellows, he said, you're going to make me a million dollars this year. Well, I'm telling you, we made about 4 or 5 million for him. And we needed money for everything that he was doing. It was unbelievable. But what a man, charming man, he came over. He has a knack of remembering names too because he called me out by name a couple of times, and I was surprised at that but I'm very happy.

Lou: Were you nervous? Were you excited? Because, again, you're talking to like 1953, 1954 you know, Walters on TV. He's working on Disneyland. He's got all these movies out was there a lot of excitement or nerves or pressure when THE Walt Disney is coming to meet you?

Al: Absolutely. I mean, when you know the big boss is coming by, you get all nervous, he visits every bullpen to talk to us. And at that time I worked out of a bullpen. I wasn't a big, big salesperson at that time. But he was so wonderful, it was wonderful to meet him that way. And then I met him a few times after that when I went to California, to Burbank. So I've met him a few times.

Lou: Because during your tenure at the company, which spanned almost 30 years, you didn't only just work in consumer products for general characters like Mickey Mouse or household items, jewellery, clothing, but you also did some stuff which related to some of the movies like Mary Poppins and Zorro and Hundred and One Dalmatians, Davy Crockett.

Al: Absolutely, we worked on every movie that they came out with. Maybe we missed a few I don't know. But every single movie we had Burbank would send us prints of what the movie was about, and we would work on stuff for Mary Poppins products.

Mary Poppins, Zorro I can't remember them all. Mickey Mouse Club was very big and we worked on that one. We worked on Disney Land for merchandise. We were a pretty busy gang and we didn't have any more than maybe seven artists in New York and we have all the artwork for the United States and all our work. If a company that was signed to the contract had its own artist and they made artwork that artwork was supposed to be brought to this Mr. Lou Lispy, the Art Director for approval. But you know what would happen once in a while they would hit the market before giving us a chance to approve it and people thought some of that artwork was us but it wasn't.

Lou: Well look, Mickey Mouse, and the consumer products that were coming out, really changed licensing as far as what Disney was able to do and just how far the brand had reached into so many homes across the country and across the world. When we talk about things like Davy Crockett and the Coonskin hat I mean, they could not produce coonskin hats fast enough and that was the case with a lot of merchandise.

Al: That's an interesting thing you mentioned Davy Crockett. I forgot to mention Davy Crockett, because I know I designed the first box that contained the cap, the coonskin cap, and I still have pictures of it. It came in a beautiful box. I think it was done up in Connecticut somewhere. But that was one of the biggest things we had. Everything was going crazy. When I used to go down to toy fairs, everything was Davy Crockett. And it was funny what happened because that picture was shown on TV and the next day everybody was humming at Davy Crockett. It was exciting to know what was going on.

Lou: And everybody wanted a piece of merchandise. They wanted to be Davy Crockett.

Al: They bought everything and they even had Davy Crockett on diapers. I am not kidding, it was unbelievable.

Lou: Well, for you, it's got to be so rewarding to see your items go from concept to approval to production to store shelves, and people's homes, and now they're going to collector cases.

Al: It's very true. To get the idea, and I hope you don't ask me where you get your ideas because that's a tough question.

Lou: Now you know I'm going to ask you.

Al: Well, that's all right. But coming from a concept drawing to the finished product is very interesting. You write about that. That is unbelievable. And I remember one time, one company, I guess I could mention the name. Anyway, the ones that did the wristwatches and we had a few different companies that did it. But they missed the Mary Poppins. If they don't get at the workout right away, they have to be on the shows and be on display before the picture breaks. And if they're not there, they're going to miss it. And they miss Mary Poppins. And it was a beautifully designed watch. I suppose they made some but they missed the main market.

Lou: Well, just quickly going back to Walt, he asked you to make them a million, you probably made him a few million after that, and you had a chance to —

Al: I hope that's not a secret.

Lou: I don't think it's a secret anymore. And look, I'm sure, Walt was very happy and you saw him not only in New York but when he went out to Burbank. I need to ask you about the passing of Walt because I know what it certainly meant to the company. And I see from talking with people, what it meant to them personally to

Al: Well, it was very tough. I really don't like to talk about it, but I did yesterday at the big meeting. Actually, our office was on Madison Avenue, and with plenty of restaurants around there, but there was one favourite spot where a lot of our Disney executives dined. And I remember sitting at a round table and all Disney people for lunch. And I don't want to get too sad about this thing, but we were having lunch and somebody came down from the office, from our Disney office and whispered into the ear of the main guy that was at that table. And he walked away and then this fellow turned to us and he said, I just got word that Walt Disney passed away. It was sad.

We got up like, unbelievable, we all got up like it was the end of the world. We didn't know what was going to happen. Were we out of jobs or what, I don't think we were thinking of ourselves, we were thinking about him. And we all went back to our office. And my recollection is that the stock market went down, hit the bottom and then the following day, it went way up. And that was something that I do remember, but it was a sad thing. There were tears all over the office. And I'm sure all over the world that had connections with Walt Disney. So great man and it's still unbelievable what he's built here. And right now I'm speaking from Disney World, which was one of his dreams that he had when he was...

And I remember the stories I heard when he was not feeling well and maybe dying in the hospital. He told his brother, he was looking up at the ceiling and he said, and he was looking at the ceiling and saying, in his words, "I think we'll have a lake here and we'll have this there. We'll have this and that. And the automatic what he calls it the Skyway, the monorail...." and he was explaining that whole thing. Well, then, of course, he only lasted maybe another week or so after that. But he was so involved right up to the last minute for him.

Just remarkable, I just thought of something else that interests me. He put out a little book, it's a booklet, and everything in it is written by him. And I went through it one time. And this is very rewarding to me anyway, he said in this one paragraph, he says, I was really not a great artist. And he said, also, I wasn't a great animator, but he says, I was an idea man, and he knows how to promote. I almost fell over because I was hired as an idea man so I was very happy to read that.

Lou: It goes that you certainly follow in the legacy and the footsteps and the ideals and the visions of Walt Disney. And to that point, you were rewarded for that by being named a Disney legend a number of years ago and certainly, that is the highest honor that could be bestowed upon any cast member at the Disney Company. Can you tell us about what that was like when you learn about being a Disney legend and then going out for your legend ceremony?

Al: Oh, very excited. I was overwhelmed. I got the message, a beautiful letter from Roy Disney, I think it was. And my whole family who was from all parts of the United States came along with me. And they were there to see me get the award. And believe it or not, one of the things there was maybe four or five, maybe six awarded, and three of them were already deceased. And who has to come up first. And then we had different characters, bring them up to the podium. And they use Mickey Mouse and I was the first one to speak and I tell you, I was nervous, really nervous. It was Roy Disney and Michael Eisner, I guess at that time and I got the award, it was a great thing. Oh my god, I'm very happy about that.

Lou: Yes, you received your award the same year that Mary Costa and Tim Allen did and we have a photo of you over at Legends Plaza.

Al: Imagine that, but it was some pretty big people. Oh, you know, another very important person. He was the president of Walt Disney World and that's amazing, but he was a Dick Nunis. He was made a licensee too, I mean, a legend excuse me I get those two words mixed up.

Lou: And so tell me you know, yesterday we spent some time over at the Disney design group here at Walt Disney World where they create a lot of the hard and soft line goods for theme parks around the world. Tell me what it's like now coming here and seeing this new generation of artists and new generation of different types of merchandise, and new technology that's being used to help create it.

Al: Oh, it's so moody I can't even understand some of it. But one thing I did find out that they're all specialists. In other words, to come up with ideas for let's say, Disney and Christmas, that's one group. Another group might work on Mother's Day and we never had anything like that. I mean, we had to do all these different celebrity days. And that amazed me and some of the people that got hired, they're unbelievably artists, great artists. In fact, I had dinner with one of the best one last night. And you know who he is. It was interesting. I've seen so much artwork yesterday, I've seen more artwork and beautiful stuff than I have in my whole life, seeing these studios here,

Lou: And you see things that are even you know the legacy of Al Konetzni continues on because you see the Pezes are still being created and like you said the nightlight is still being created. And then obviously the scope and the breath of merchandise is just expanded exponentially.

Al: It's very true. The thing goes on and on and on and I guess you know, I'm 97 years old so I don't know how long I'm going to be around. My number hasn't been picked yet but we'll see what happens. You know for an old guy I'm doing all right. I still sketch, I do a lot of work for abused children and cancer people. And I've been doing that since I retired. Oh, as a matter of fact, when I did retire Disney was doing a deal with Ringling, Barnum, and Bailey and they grabbed me right away. And it was the best year I ever had financially working for them getting retirement and Social Security. That was my big year. But they couldn't keep me busy enough so I forgot about it after about two years, and went back to my own stuff.

Lou: What about those people who are listening or who are watching and are young artists like you who, you know, like my daughter who always has a pencil in her hand or even may be older and has dreams of working for the company or wanting to be an artist for Disney. What kind of advice would you have for them?

Al: I'm glad you asked that because that's one of the favourite things I have to talk to young artists who want to pursue a career. And the one thing that I want to leave with each one of them, and I try to do this, and that is that you have your samples and you're trying to get your placement and get interviewed by somebody, never forget to send them a message and thanks for the interview. I think that's very important. And I made sure that when I was interviewed by some top art director at Disney that I sent a letter of thanks. And I got to be really good friends with him many years later. And he said, yes, he said, that really had something to do with us picking you. So remember that. It's very important.

Lou: I think that's great advice. And at 97 years young, I can tell that, like you said early, Mickey Mouse still makes you smile. And I think you should know that what you've done and the stories you shared and the things that you've created years ago continue to live on and your legacy. So I want to thank you so much for sharing that with me and sharing that with my audience out there and there's the school bus.

Al: That's my big, big one.

Lou: Well, I think that's great Al. Thank you so much. Congratulations on everything that you've done and your Legend Award and thank you so much for your time today.

Al: Thank you very much for the interview. I appreciate it.

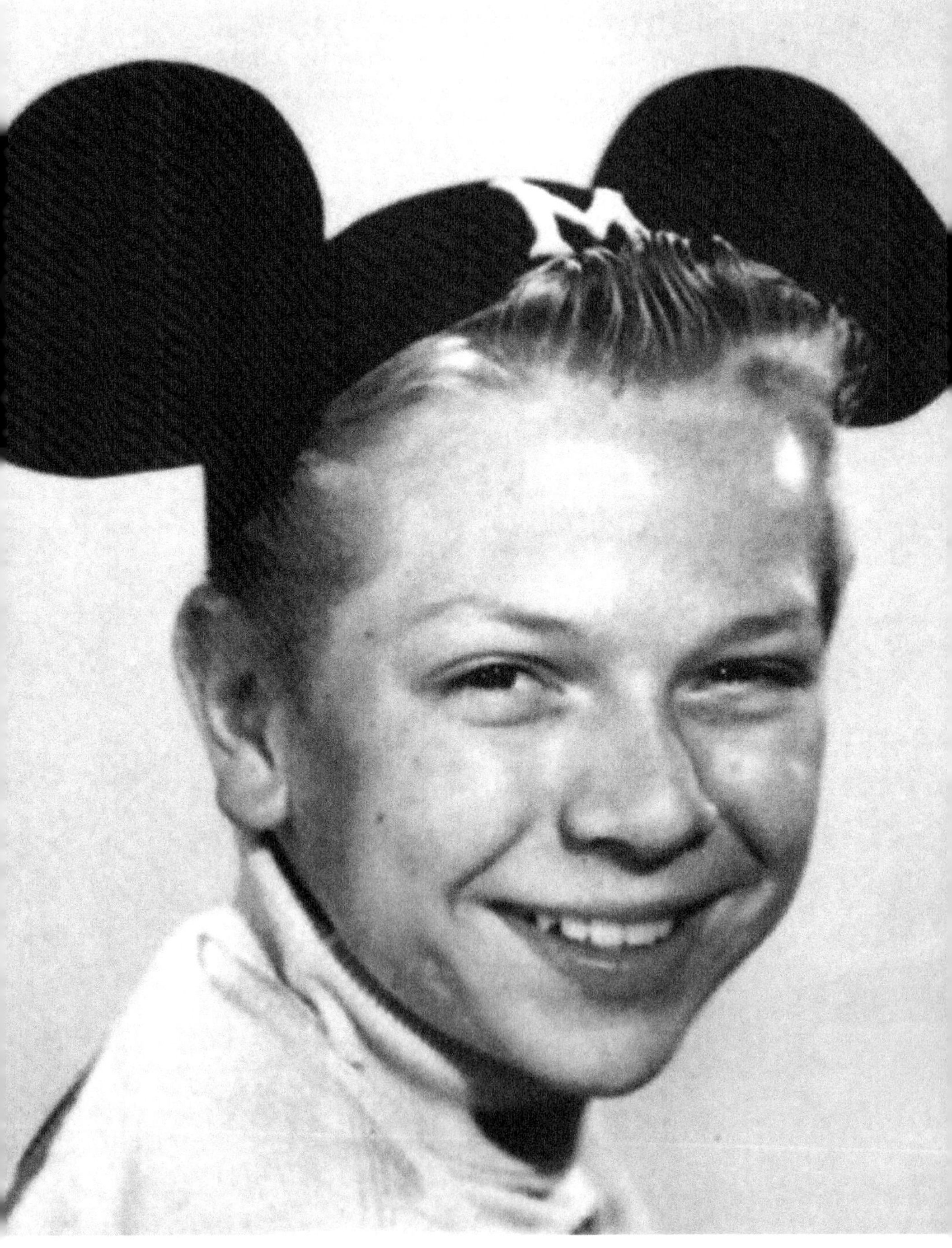

Lonnie Burr

Lonnie Burr was born on May 31, 1943, and is best known as one of the original Mouseketeers on Walt Disney's landmark children's television show, the Mickey Mouse Club. Lonnie was one of only nine of the original thirty-nine Mouseketeers who remained for the complete filming of the show, from 1955–1959. The original Mickey Mouse Club show was the first national television show to feature children who appeared primarily as themselves as well as acting as characters in scenes and musical numbers.

The original show aired in syndication in the 1960s, reran again in 1975, then was replayed on the Disney Channel from the 1980s through the early 2000s.

After his time on the show, Burr's career continued as both performer and writer. He went on to continue to act, dance, sing, and choreograph, and is also an author, playwright, lyricist, journalist, critic and poet.

His career spans six decades, and Lonnie has been in 25 films, more than 300 television shows, 49 plays and musicals including Broadway, off-Broadway, regional theatre and national tours, commercials, and heard on more than 100 radio shows and voice overs.

No matter where life has taken him, however, Burr reminds us that, "... I shall always be known as Mouseketeer Lonnie."

I had a chance to speak with Lonnie about his time on the Mickey Mouse Club, working with people like Annette Funicello and Walt Disney, and so much more.

You can purchase Lonnie's book, Confessions of an Accidental Mouseketeer, on Amazon.com

This interview is taken from my conversation with Lonnie on WDW Radio Show # 112, in March, 2009. You can listen to the complete interview at WDWRadio.com/112.

Lou Mongello: With the announcement of Disney's new community for Disney fans, D23,. I started thinking about the origins of Disney fandom and more specifically its roots in the Disney Company itself. And as Disney archivist, Dave Smith stated during the announcement of D23, Disney fan clubs originated as far back as the 1930s when unofficial Mickey Mouse Clubs gathered at theaters. But it wasn't until the 1950s that Disney began to not just reach out to its fans, but form an official club for them to be members of... The original Mickey Mouse Club television show let everybody know who was watching that they were a member and part of this club.

And I thought it would be interesting to take a look back, not just at the club itself, but what drew fans to it and created really a phenomenon unlike anything of its time and it's a legacy that continues to this day. And who better to talk about the Mickey Mouse Club than one of its original TV members? So, it is my pleasure to welcome someone who is literally part of Disney history, a member of the original club that was made for you and me.... Mouseketeer Lonnie Burr... Lonnie, welcome to the show. Thank you so very much for coming on.

Lonnie: Hi, how are you?

Lou: Oh, I'm great, and it's really a pleasure to talk to you.

Lonnie: Thank you.

Lou: You know, when the Mickey Mouse Club originally aired, maybe it was just a hair before my time yet I still was able to watch it in a number of places.

Lonnie: Youngster.

Lou: But tell me about how this got started for you. I know you were an actor from an early age, but how do you get the role of a Mouseketeer? And at the time, did you even know what a Mouseketeer was or was going to be?

Lonnie: Well, I talk about that in my book the Confessions of an Accidental Mouseketeer. No, nobody knew what it was going to be. Of course, it was Mr. Disney so you thought, well, it's probably going to be good, but nobody knew what a Mouseketeer was. Although Dave is correct, there was a Mickey Mouse Club in the thirties, before Mickey was a character, and then the title was loaned out to Warners and they did the cartoons with two characters, they were called the Mouseketeers. And then they decided to start our show, it's unique in TV history, I talked about that in the book too. The book is not just about the Mickey Mouse Club, although there are two chapters on it and then the longest of 18 chapters is on it.

But it talks about how seminal and innovative and different than everything else before it. It was just an amazing thing. We were the first human connection between all the great characters and ideas that Walt had had. So, kids could identify with these characters as their buddies did. And he said, anybody who watched the show, was a Mouseketeer and they saw us grow up as they were growing up. They grew up along with us, even though we weren't even on that long the first time. But we hit 18 countries, translated into five languages, and then we ran it in the sixties. Soon afterwards, the first run went off in '59 and started rerunning in '62. Then the seventies prompting the second new Mickey Mouse Club, and then the eighties and the Disney channel came on. And then in '89, they started what's called the "earless", the third version of the Mickey Mouse Club.

And then when they went off, we ran again from 1995 to September, 2002 and then we've covered two centuries and every decade since the fifties. But the show had elements of it that nobody else had done before. There were kids on TV, in characters, I was one of them, like on the Danny Thomas show. And these are kids playing characters. Then, Howdy Doody had kids on live with him, but they weren't focused on the kids. It was all on Howdy and Clarabelle. And by the way, Bob Keeshan, premiered the same days that we did on October 3rd, 1955, as Captain Kangaroo and he was the first Clarabelle, of three on Howdy Doody. And we had been on TV first when Disneyland opened on July 17th 1955.

But the show didn't premiere until later in October. But having the kids that you could sing along with and find out what they're doing and have them talk as themselves, not as a character, was unique. Another had been cartoons before, but they weren't Disney cartoons and that segment of the show, there were four segments and all these great cartoons with the Mouseketeers introduced. And then there were, what I call the didactic about learning things which Sesame Street particularly developed that have said what a debt they owed the Mickey Mouse Club… they took a longer way to learning but we had that too. And then we had what I have always called the teen soaps. There've been soap operas on radio and TV, but they were for adults. We had Spent a Marty and, Being that Serial and Quirky and White Shadow and Hardy Boys and these were really soaps for young people as opposed to for adults. So, the show was something that had never, never been thought of before.

Lou: Yeah. And that's one of the things, like you said, it was very unique. And again, this was sort of Walt's second foray into television out of the first one being, the Disneyland series.

Lonnie: So, 54. Yeah.

Lou: Right. And both sort of you know, were vehicles to help finance and promote the building of Disneyland. But you're right as far as what this did for and with children because it wasn't just the variety show with singing and dancing and what not. Again, you guys are now not characters but yourselves, but it really was, you know, you have like the newsreel and things like that.

Lonnie: Yeah, exactly, for the learning aspect of the show, like how children celebrated Christmas in Thailand, one of the first ones was, how to become a pilot or an airline stewardess. Now, given the timeframe we're in now, I apologize for airline stewardess, we don't call them any longer, but that's what it was then. But they learned about careers and are going to point out what it is to go to school in South America and all kinds of things like that, which again, there were no newsreels or things like that for kids. And the ones in theaters were all for adults.

Lou: Right, and in 1955, you were how old when you got the role of a Mouseketeer?

Lonnie: I was 11.

Lou: Okay.

Lonnie: Excuse me a second, I was 11 when we started and turned 12 midyear, May 31st and my girlfriend the first year and through the Mickey Mouse Club circus at Disneyland that November, December, January 56. And my girlfriend was Annette Funicello and she was a little older than me. She turned 13 later that year and she was very kind about that in her autobiography.

Lou: I'm going to touch on that in a little bit because you know, not only the fact that you're 11 dating an older woman who just happens to be Annette Funicello...

Lonnie: I started dating at 9 and in the 50's that was quite shocking. My mom and dad were a dance team at Wago and also nightclubs called Push-Button Grass. So, they would go out dancing and I liked to dance and I was a good dancer. I started dancing lessons when I was four. And I would take a girl along as a date and we dance and I'm on a day I would dance and so I started dating at nine. Now, that's not so unusual, but in the fifties, people would look and say, oh my goodness, what are those children doing?

Lou: See, my respect and envy of you are increasing the longer we keep on talking. But tell me about maybe, you know, when you called and I guess you auditioned for it?

Lonnie: No, that's why I call it, Confessions of an Accidental Mouseketeer now actually, if we get down to the facts, there were two accidental Mouseketeers. One was Annie, she was just in the ballet chorus, a ballet that Walt Disney happened to go to and he said, "I want her on the show." And she's the only person of 39 kids who were on our show the whole time that was chosen by Walt... Annette Funicello. And, my accident is that I was established in the business. I had done The Greatest Show on Earth for DeMille, I had done Hans Christian Anderson with Danny Kaye. I had been on like about a dozen Colgate Comedy Hours. I had had my first lead on TV and on stage at the same year on TV, it was the Range Rider as the title character, the Holy Terror on which I did my own riding because I'd had a force before that.

I had done a lot of work so I read for a much higher paying job as the actor Marty on Spin and Marty and I did not get that. Now what they were having was what they called then and now "cattle calls," which is hundreds of actors or singers or dancers or all three come out and audition. And this was massive for weeks and my agent didn't want me going on that because I had done leads, you know. So, one day my agent... I had other agents prior to that... but my mother became an agent later and she was my agent then, and she got a call from someone, another kid I had worked with professionally. They said they need a boy right away, Capital on Melrose, which is right by Paramount.

And she raced over from Glendale and I went in and sang on the record, all kids one adult, Jimmy Dodd. And afterwards he said, you also dance and act. And I said, really, I act and dance better than I sing. And I had a private audition for Hal Alquist and the executive producer, Bill Walsh and Jimmy in the animation building, right across from the theater on the Disney lot. And that's a lot different than a mass audition with the amateurs because Walt said he didn't want professional kids. And somehow of the twenty-nine, two of us slipped by because Sharon had done a lot of work as a dancer previous to the Mickey Mouse Club. But I was primarily an actor who also sang and danced. And I got in there as a fluke because I wasn't going to audition and go through that process, my agent just wouldn't let me do it. So, that's why I call it "Confessions of an Accidental Mouseketeer."

Lou: Right. And I actually know for people who visit Walt Disney World and go to the Walt Disney one man's dream exhibit, there's a huge exhibit there about the Mickey Mouse Club. And there's a quote from Walt there where he says, you know, he doesn't want any of these professional kids. He doesn't want kids, I think he said that tap dance and can play the trumpet and you know, and skip rope at the same time. But that's actually what you were able to do.

Lonnie: Yeah didn't play trumpet or couldn't or skip rope. I was a professional actor and dance singer and trained and had done a lot of work and I guess I was genuine or not. He was talking about a certain type of child actor I think, really and there was a little affected and a little too perfect. Sometimes people say it's the kids on the second version in the seventies, that's one of the reasons it didn't last very long. They were just too good, too perfect, you know, they weren't like real kids, they didn't make mistakes. But our shooting schedule was so difficult that sometimes we had to leave things in where somebody's singing you know, off key or they missed the lyric or they missed a step a little bit. We couldn't correct it, didn't have time for it and that helped the kids watching say, Hey, it's like real people, you know, it's not like whatever the child's children's version of Las Vegas was then where everything is perfect, you know?

Lou: Right, and they were able to obviously relate to you much better I think probably the cause of that.

Lonnie: Yeah. Well, because I'm one of the nine, only nine of us lasted the entire filming of the show of the 39 kids. There were two to run for two seasons, one made quite an impression and she unfortunately left us January 6th of this year. Cheryl, she did season two and three, but she was very talented and warm and it came through. She was very popular, got lots of mail and she died prematurely on January 6th, which bothered a lot of us... people talk a lot about her smile, which was wonderful. She had a grace that nobody else had. And she was the most successful after the show, except for Annie, Annette doing a lot of TV and film.

And she was on Leave it to Beaver for two seasons. I didn't watch The Beaver and we couldn't keep things then; she was with

Wally's or the beaver's girlfriend for two years. But then she married Lance Reventlo and she left show business and she was very involved with charities all of her life. She gave a lot of things and it was a real shock to all of us. I had my life and I just moved to Oregon, California. And things weren't hooked up then, I didn't find out until a day later that she had died and it was very unhappy for me. And then she's the fourth of the thirty-nine kids, two are no longer being with us, there were three earlier.

Lou: Now when the show first started, you were one of twenty-four, I guess, original.

Lonnie: Yeah. Well, the first season of twenty-four of them.

Lou: Right, Right.

Lonnie: They kept ten and then they hired back then they realized they didn't need as many. So, they hired seven more the second year and they kept, if I remember correctly, only one of those, which is Cheryl. And then they hired six more for the third season and people don't realize it, but we were only on for years and we only filmed three seasons. But like they're doing five shows a week and the seasons were longer than they now are. So, that's a lot of shows, the estimate from Disney or something like that, 340 shows somewhere around there.

Lou: Do you remember what that first day was like when you show up on the set for the first day of filming?

Lonnie: Well, even though you're a pro, as I was, you're nervous because you don't know what the heck is going on. So, you want to figure out what you don't know what the thing is. I mean, it's not a sitcom. It's not a variety show. They said that you had to sing and dance, but we didn't know what we were going to be doing, how it's going to work, where the other 23 kids were and all that stuff. So, it was like going to school for the first time in a way, except we were obviously older than kids who start the first grade, but it was very like that.

And then we would, you know, find people, like it was 12 boys, 12 girls and I looked around and I said that one and fell for Annie pretty quick. But I had mentioned about her before that she has something that died a long time ago, only not at the time when we were doing the show, but later and what I fell for, she has always said that she wasn't the best actress though the best thing or the best dancer. And although she was very talented, it was all free, but she had charisma and it's a misused term now almost, they say it about too many people and it's not true. But she came on screen or in a room or whatever and everybody noticed that it's there. They were compelled to, they had no choice. So, that's what Annie was... I keep in touch with Glen and Annie and go to her house and keep up what's going on and all that.

Lou: Yeah. I mean, she was very much, you know, instantly sort of America's sweetheart and she was, from what I understand, you know, Walt's sweetheart too. Was it something that just happened or was she sort of, you know, chosen as she is going to be the one that's going to show up?

Lonnie: No, the people chose her. She wasn't chosen in that way ahead of time, that they were choosing just why she was on the show. But it wasn't until she started getting more fan mail than everybody else. And she also, for the time, you got to remember the fifties is a very different time then now. People forget that there were a lot of things going on then, the civil rights movement was just starting and things were different. We had black kids on Talent Round Up that wasn't usual. And, we had two Hispanic kids the first year, which is very unusual... Mary Espinosa and Dickie Dodd, although the Dickie Dodd was not related to Jimmy Dodd and we had some Jewish kids on and Doreen is Jewish. And Annie was very definitely ethnic as Italian and at that time that's not what was shown on TV. So, that was very innovative too.

Lou: And we'll talk about a number of ways that the show and Walt I mean, was an innovator even as something as simple as the opening animation. And you know, obviously it's the fifties, everything is shown in black and white and he has that shot in color in anticipation of what is to come.

Lonnie: I have that on my website, you click on it, you go to YouTube and you can see the whole thing in color.

Lou: Yeah.

Lonnie: And they have done some of their DVDs too.

Lou: Exactly, you can get the Walt Disney Treasures DVDs, but you know, you talked about its kind of being like school. And I think in a number of ways it sounds like it's kind of was because much like in school there's little groups and cliques and there's the varsity team and the junior varsity team. Tell us about, you know, the red team and the white team and the blue team.

Lonnie: Well, the way that broke down was, they simply had to find a way to work around things and this is the way it existed. At that time, kids could work six days a week instead of five, but on five of those days they had to have three hours of school and an hour for lunch, that's half your workday. So, they then would be able to work for us, so what they could do is have one team that would be rehearsing and one team would be in school and one team would be shooting. And that's how they got all of that product out there in time. And it wasn't easy, but once they got the hang of it was less of, you know, craziness on the second and third season. Because people weren't rushing around saying, get over there, shoot this, and learn this... And then you have to run back and have 15 minutes or half an hour to write an essay. And it was kind of hectic, but it was fun and it was an enjoyable thing to do. And it was just, unique, no question about it.

Lou: Yeah. Now you talked about the fact that it lasted four seasons and the shooting schedule. But something actually happened to you right before the third season, that kept you out of....

Lonnie: There was one team that did Roll Call. The only time everybody was a Mouseketeer and there were 24 then. We did Roll Call was at our first TV appearance at Disneyland, in 1955. But there were just some of us who did Roll Call, and our third year I am practicing doing a handstand. I fell down and I took this chunk out of my cheek, about the size of a silver dollar. It couldn't be covered by makeup. They had no idea the show going to be running, you know, 53 years later, they said, we can't have one kid who's got this thing on his face for every opening, which is the roll call and every closing where we saying the Alma Mater, "Now it's time to say goodbye..."

Lonnie: And, so they said, well, we can't have Lonnie in there. I did a lot of featured stuff on the third season, but I wasn't a Roll Call. That's why also the pictures for the VHS films the ten that came out in about '92. And a lot of the ones of those have been transmitted to DVD in the last few years, have pictures of nine kids, but they added Cheryl. There were six girls and three boys, I suppose, of the nine of us who lasted the entire filming, which was five girls and four boys. And that's why I wasn't in Roll Call the last year... Bobby said someplace recently that... Tommy replaced me and it was just silly that's not what happened. But we're all getting older so things like that creep in.

Lou: Right. And you start to, you know, it gets less important I guess maybe as time goes on but you know, we were talking about the teams and you're sort of being featured on the show. You obviously were recognized very much for your talent as a dancer.

Lonnie: That's the main one, yeah.

Lou: But really as an actor too, you are given, I guess some maybe leeway that other people weren't. You were actually given the ability to ad lib a little bit.

Lonnie: No, I've read that online too and it's not true. You don't ad lib in those situations unless you're Don Rickles or somebody who's a big star, otherwise you get fired. No, I never ad lib what I might do is continue on while we're shooting more than the other kids because I was a pro, you didn't stop until the director told you to stop. That gave me a bad situation once we were doing this number and what most people considered the three best dancers on the show were Sharon, Bobby and myself. And so when I was dancing, Sharon and I were in the front row and we did this Tyrolean thing where the guys are wearing these silly hats, big feathers which he didn't much care for it because they covered our hair... our pompadour and these lederhosen which are weird shorts but suspenders and have all these goo gahs all over them.

So, I wasn't too pleased anyway, but I was smiling and we started the shoot and right below the zipper of my pants, all the way up to the waistband and the rear just came open. I'm dancing with a part of my shorts exposed. But I continued when we finished the shot and then I went to tell the director a little what had happened that he felt it was sort of a personal front to him. And I said, well I couldn't help it, I didn't try to do that and I'm embarrassed because I'm you know, I was 13 and my shorts are showing in this shot, but they had to re shoot it. But those days have it and no I didn't, if something came up and there was a miscue on camera, the same as I would on stage, I would say something. And if they thought they liked it; they kept it. But that's the only way I would ad lib.

Lou: Right. And you know, you reminisce a little bit about the shorts thing, but looking back in, or do you have any single memory or couple of memories that really sort of stand out as something being the fondest or the funniest or the thing that you really carry with you today?

Lonnie: Yeah. Well, yeah, two things come to mind right away. The first one is this, in the first season there were twenty-four kids and I've heard that a female Mouseketeer repeat my story while I wasn't there recently. Things change with age, but I'm walking along the street and Walt was out there talking to another gentlemen. And on the way to the cafeteria, which is right on Dopey Drive there by the Animation building. And he had his pipe in his mouth and he's talking to Scott and I walked by and he says hello. I said, oh, hi Mr. Disney, good to see you. And then I went on to the cafeteria and I was thinking to myself, there's twenty-four kids here and Walt Disney knows I am. And that instant I realized I was wearing my shirt with huge letters, 'Lonnie'.

The other one is when we did the Mickey Mouse Club circus because we were there before the park opened. That means this, one, no lines, number two, we got to go on the rides, not every day but sometimes. And the guys liked, you know, the teacups because we could get four guys and one would go until we got tired and then we would get to go so fast, we were all dizzy and we hoped nobody would upchuck on anybody else. But the cars were great, you know, Utopia because I wanted to have a car long before sixteen and they had governors on them. At that time, they weren't on a rail or track and they had governors that kept them down to like five miles an hour, but they had the governors off in the morning, they had to warm them up. So, this saved the guys driving around for them these dopey little cars... but for the guys this was like having a car and you can get it to like ten and eleven miles an hour. That was really awesome. At that age it was very cool.

Lou: You mentioned Walt Disney and I have to ask you about Walt himself, you know, either, do you remember the first time you met him or just some of your interactions with him?

Lonnie: I remember my general reaction, not the first time I met him, I may have been too nervous, even though I was a pro. I mean Walt Disney was a legend even then and he was still alive. He was very avuncular like your uncle, you know, he was just very open and cordial and a lot of people now say that he wasn't around... and that's not true. He would be there occasionally and we shot a few things with him, like the fourth anniversary of Disneyland. They were going to make a movie out of Oz and we were trying to convince him on camera. So, we put that together and we did a number from the show and it never got made unfortunately. But he was just again, like your uncle, like he wasn't like this, you know, a standoff star or some big Orson Wells... Walt wasn't Hollywood at all... he was just a regular guy.

Lou: Did you ever see him you know, outside, you know, off the set?

Lonnie: No, I did not, one or two the other Mouseketeers like Bob ran into him once someplace where he was vacationing, but no I did not.

Lou: At the time, I mean, I'm sure nobody probably does, especially you because you're a kid and you're dating Annette Funicello. But did you realize at the time, or did anybody realize at the time that you were a part of something big, not just for the Disney company, but really for television and especially children's programming as a whole?

Lonnie: Oh, well, we did, again, you got to get history straight and realize that I'd heard about the screaming women for Frank

Sinatra, prior to my time. But you know the Beatles hadn't happened yet and then there was Elvis. But hearing while you're working that your show is a big hit and all that stuff and getting fan mail, it's all nice. But it didn't really hit us tangibly until we went on the road the first time and we flew into Oklahoma City and as we were landing, you're seeing all these thousands of people around. At first, I thought maybe something bad had happened or something, I didn't know what was going on. And they were all there to see us and they were singing our songs and saying our names as we got off the plane. And they put us on a bus and took us downtown to the TV station and the cops had on there the sirens and their lights leading us through. And it was just an amazing thing and then it was concrete for everybody. I mean, it was solid, he said, we're hits. It was really a big deal here.

Lou: But for you, I mean, as a kid, you're now you're idolized and you're envied. And probably to a certain degree, you're revered by millions of kids across the country. I mean, your name now isn't Lonnie, it's Mouseketeer Lonnie, you know, it's, look, it's tough enough, I guess growing up as a kid. But now you are a part of something else, you know, something so much larger.

Lonnie: That's bigger than you, sure. But again, unfortunately, having been in the business a long time, I could handle that. It wasn't a problem. I didn't act any differently than I did before. I didn't put on any ears; I was still the same Lonnie I was. And even after the show I was fortunate enough to be one of the ones that had my own fan clubs, like Annie, there were a lot of clubs for the whole club, even though they would have favorites, it was going to be for the Mickey Mouse Club as opposed to for Lonnie or a Annette or a Cheryl or whomever. But that did come about, on the other hand, I wrote a piece, I've written for a lot of magazines and newspapers as well as books and plays and poetry and some TV stuff.

And it bothered me after the show because I was trying to be you know, I was three years ahead in school that folds into the dating at nine. So, you've got to understand I was fourteen in my senior year of high school and I finished that after the last season that we filmed. And I went straight through a bachelor's and a master's and then some work on a doctorate. None of the other Mouseketeers had done that until Karen went back in her middle years to get a bachelor's degree and a graduate degree in her work, because she counsels women. But I wanted to be a young Cary Grant or Fred Astaire and for years it wasn't working for me, you know, so I dissociated myself from the show and I thought of it as a kid's show, but I was trying to be an adult.

Now, a lot of people go through that. But since I was three years ahead in school, I was hanging out with guys and girls who were three or four years older than me and dating girls at that age and I was fairly sophisticated. And it bothered me because it kept me a kid as opposed to an adult and I wasn't until 1980 when we all came together in a live show at Disneyland that was just four of us. And then we did the 25 years of Mouseketeers, which was a TV session with the twenty fifth anniversary.

I was going to work behind camera too as a second writer. But we were all hosts and I realized that people had not forgotten. On the contrary, they were just enthused, they went nuts seeing us and we even heard at a parade at Disneyland that here that we were chatted out. Somebody said, "God, they look great! I thought they were dead!" It was so long ago in their childhood, but it was a very great thing. And I started to realize the errors of my thinking about the show because it meant so much to people. It was just an amazing thing, one time and this is later or another occasion at Disneyland, we're signing autographs and I see this guy walking up and I figure I hope security is here because this looks really difficult.

He's like a biker, you know, tattoos all over and a big beard and he looked like he was going to be trouble. Instead he came up and he asked for my autograph and I'm signing and he says, you know, my life is going the wrong the way. And I listened to Jimmy Dodd's songs and I turned it around, it's real important to me. It just makes you say, oh my God, this is more than just entertaining people, you can really, a part of people's lives. And that kind of thing, just to be one part of the show makes you really feel good. Again, it's not like being a star, being an entertainer or being an actor. It's a whole different experience.

Lou: Right. And I mean, look, you're a career beyond the Mickey Mouse Club, you know, is worthy of clearly, you know, obviously the book that you wrote and I could talk to you for hours. I mean, you've worked and met people like Jimmy Stewart, Elvis Presley, Roy Rogers, Bob Hope, Sammy Davis, Danny Kaye, Jack Benny, Dean Martin...

Lonnie: Yep.

Lou: I mean, again, Sammy and Dean, I could talk to you about, you know, for hours.

Lonnie: I could tell you about Sammy, I can tell you what Sammy drank. Yeah, he liked bourbon and Coke in what's called a bucket glass. It's like a Mai Tai glass, and I can also tell you I worked with Sammy and Sweet Charity for Bob Fosse and Sharon Mclean. It was Bob's Fosse's first movie. But I thought it was doing the last play before he died... First Monday in October at the Kennedy Center. And I don't like crowds so it was right after the show, so I went to the farthest bar and there was nobody there. And this guy walks up and he's still wearing his costume... a full black robe as a Supreme Court judge. Yeah, I very wisely didn't say, "God, you were really good at that Mr Fonda..." and I made sure it was just none of that. So, he and I sat there for ten minutes and nobody else came over, I think because he was there and they said, well, we'd better not bother him.

But he did have a reputation and I find him very friendly and we sat there and talked about scotches. Now, I guess that was in my forties and we found that we both like a single malt called Dalwhinnie which is really great and doesn't have much peat. But we were talking about what they didn't have there and stuff, and it was just a very, very interesting situation. But I never worked with him, but it was an occasion that happened to be the same way. My second time to Europe, I was 20, I just finished my master's degree and I went to the Blue Angels to see Woody Allen, who at that time was a stand-up comedian. He had been a writer, but he had not made any of the films that made him famous and I being a brash young fellow at times, send a note back saying, I'd like to talk to you about comedy, you know, Lenny Bruce, things like that.

He came out and joined me, two of us at the table. I offered him a drink, he declined and he looked exactly like, he always looks here now, this disheveled kind of sweater thing and all that junk. And we sat there and talked about Shelley Berman and Mort Saul and Lenny, the kind of things that Lenny was doing as opposed to his problems with drugs and his problems with the police. But he was doing things that the great, late Georgia Carlin did later, but Lenny started all that stuff and we talked for like 15 minutes, just the two of us. He was very, you know, like a regular guy, no big deal. And I had no way of knowing he was going to be kind of a brilliant filmmaker.

Lou: Yeah. Again, I'm going to direct people when we're finished over to your website and definitely to check out your book where they can hear and read about it.

Lonnie: Thanks. Well, I would like to, excuse me, but I would like to clarify the book... you learn things about the Mickey Mouse

Club but you never knew like the day to day process we went through and all kinds of things and some of the friendships that were formed. For instance, Mouseketeer Sharon and Annette had been friends since the show and Cheryl and Doreen, the same thing. But the book is really about my life and not just about show business, there's a lot of show business in it because I've been doing it for 60 years, but I have five years before then. I actually start off where I start and I bring it to January of 2009 but it seems a lot of other things too. Some serious matters for one for instance, it's not because of my experience, I don't think kids should be in show business.

I think, if the children, as opposed to the parents really want to act or sing or dance, they should, perform. They should take classes and they should do it at school, they should do it in community theatre. But when money comes into it, it becomes a problem. And it's much worse now because compared to what we made, I mean, kids can make millions and I just don't think it's a good idea until they minimum finished high school or eighteen years old. Now, you wouldn't think that since I've never been in the tabloids or had problems or all that stuff. But it's something that I think parents have to think about instead of saying, "Wow, you know, Molly is so talented we've just got to get her out there."

Lou: Right.

Lonnie: I started by saying it is just an opinion, other people will tell you differently, but so there are substitutes matters. My search for God, I have Bible studies every week, you know, doing the ministry. I would say I changed my way about that, so the book is not just an anecdote here, anecdote there. It's a memoir, it's my life.

Lou: Well it seems very interesting and again, you know, from your acting career to directing and choreography and writing, there's so much more to learn. Fortunately, in many people's eyes, myself included, you will always be known as Mouseketeer Lonnie Burr. And that's actually the name of your website, it's MouseketeerLonnieBurr.com. There you can find *Confessions of an Accidental Mouseketeer*, I'll put all these links in the show notes. And again, Lonnie, thank you so very much.

Lonnie: Thank you so very much. Well, I've enjoyed it, I always enjoy talking about the show and about the people, about the times and it's great and I thank you for having me.

Lou: I appreciate you sharing that all with us.

Lonnie: You're welcome.

Lou: That was great.

Lonnie: I think so, I just wanted to…I know that people, because it's in the title and they're going to think it's just about being a Mouseketeer and it is about that, but it's not my whole life.

Lou: Right.

Lonnie: You know, there are Helen Hunts, there's Sally Fields and Ron Howard, but they are a minimum… so many kid actors have problems because of going through that experience, whereas if they really want to do it, let them be adults. It's difficult enough growing up with authority and this money.

Lou: Especially in this day and age… when certain things are so prevalent and the pressure is so high.

Lonnie: And the money is so high.

Lou: Right.

Lonnie: I mean, you know, we weren't making all that much, but doing okay for that time-frame. But nothing equivalent of what kids make now on TV series and films. I mean, you know, it's just silly.

Lou: Do you remember what you were making a week?

Lonnie: Sure, one eighty-five a week.

Lou: Okay. Which at the time...

Lonnie: We had seven year contracts and six months options guaranteed, twenty two paid weeks whether we worked or not, they always did find something for us to do... but twenty two out of twenty six and you got a perk, if you're option was picked up, a lot of the kids weren't. The majority, were just one season... But yeah that's the way it worked. At the end of the contract, you were making 500 bucks a week if you had lasted the whole seven years. And the only person that got it was Annie.

Lou: Now, forgive me, but putting it in context... one eighty-five a week... Was that standard, was that good?

Lonnie: That was a Screen Actors Guild minimum at that time. But you got to understand that a new car cost three or four grand.

Lou: Gotcha.

Lonnie: That's a Cadillac.

Lou: Right.

Lonnie: You got to understand that you can buy a house for ten thousand dollars.

Lou: Right.

Lonnie: And then you started thinking about that, you'd say, "Well... wait a second here." Oh, I see, it wasn't like a pittance, but it was the minimum to be a union allowed as opposed to some like Spin and Marty who made a lot more...they made more money right away. And the second version, they made almost what we would have made at the end of seven years, it was only a year later. I didn't find out until the fifties, but that's what it was.

Lou: And Annette was the only one who got up to that five hundred dollars pay scale.

Lonnie: Yeah, she, she tried to get out of the contract and failed because what would happen is that she would be loaned out for big money to then do a film, and then she only got what her contractual fee was, and then after that, after her first marriage, she was married to a very prominent agent who handled very prominent people like that. And she got out of her contract the second time because it wasn't fair, it would be the same thing. They used to do that in the studios, you know, with whether it's James Cagne or whatever... they sign you as a contract player. And then if you became a hit, you were still making that money and they were making a fortune and you couldn't get any of it. That's just the way that you know, the business works.

Lou: That was wonderful and so much fun. I really appreciate your time and sharing those stories with us.

Lonnie: That was great. Great interview, Lou. Really, really well done. You're very welcome.

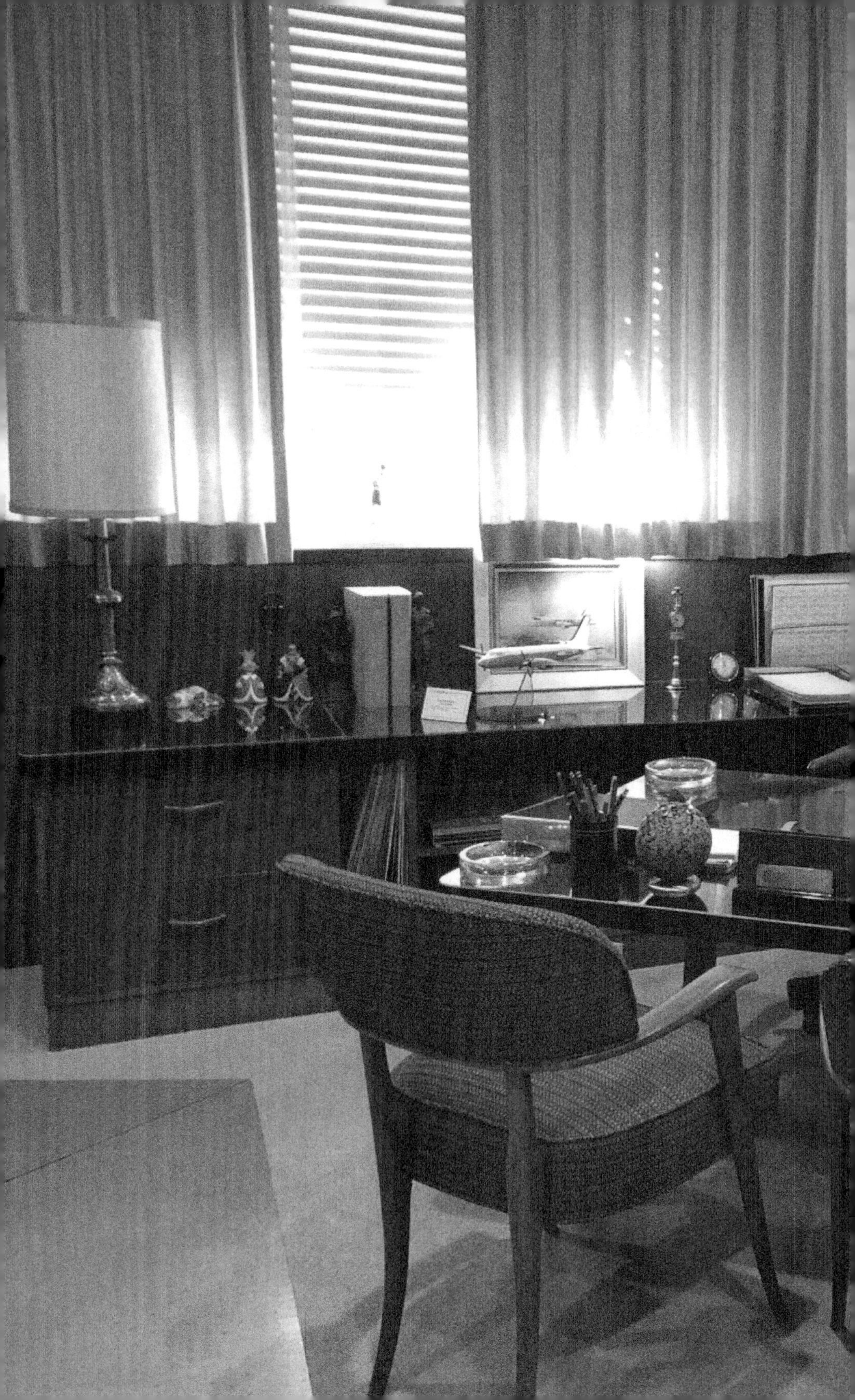

Walt Disney's Office

CONCLUSION

THANK YOU for sharing your time with me and my very special guests. I hope that these conversations give you deeper insight and understanding of the people who have done so much to bring us so much happiness on screen and in the Disney Parks.

When conducting an interview, and really for any segments on my WDW Radio podcast, I want you to not feel as though you are a passive reader or listener, but that you are sitting there with us, and are part of the conversation. I research and endeavor to ask questions that you, as a curious fan, would want to hear the answers to, while letting my guest share their stories and journey.

In addition to the interviews in this book, I have conducted dozens of other interviews with Disney, Marvel, and Star Wars celebrities, legends, executives, actors, Imagineers, and Cast Members including:

- **Alan Menken** (Composer and songwriter of scores and songs for Walt Disney Animation Studios films, including The Little Mermaid, Beauty and the Beast, Aladdin, Pocahontas, The Hunchback of Notre Dame, Enchanted, and Tangled) — WDWRadio.com/196

- **David Prowse** (The man behind the mask of Darth Vader in the original Star Wars trilogy) — WDWRadio.com/273

- **Ashley Eckstein** (The voice of Ahsoka Tano throughout the Star Wars franchise and founder of HerUniverse.com) — WDWRadio.com/523

- **Kevin Feige** (President of Marvel Studios) — WDWRadio.com/519

For these, and many more interviews, reviews, Top Tens, Disney Parks vacation planning advice, and much more, I invite you to please listen and subscribe to my WDW Radio podcast. It is available on a number of different (free) podcast apps, including:

- Apple Podcasts — WDWRadio.com/Podcast
- Spotify — WDWRadio.com/Spotify
- Stitcher — WDWRadio.com/Stitcher
- Google Podcasts — WDWRadio.com/GooglePodcasts

You can also listen right from your web browser, and find each episode's show notes at WDWRadio.com.

I sincerely appreciate you taking the time to read this book, and invite you to continue to be part of the conversation by listening to the show, and joining our community.

If there is anything I can do for you, please reach out to me via messaging on social media, or via email. Please note that I answer every email and message personally, but I promise to get back to you as soon as possible.

I appreciate you.

Lou

THERE'S MORE...

Subscribe to the WDW Radio podcast — it's FREE!

From the parks to the screens, and everything in between.

To listen to these and catch every new, weekly episode of WDW Radio, subscribe (it's FREE!) in Apple Podcasts (WDWRadio.com/Podcast)

Some episodes to help get you started:

Top Tens

1. Top Ten Smells in Walt Disney World (WDWRadio.com/75)
2. Top Ten Emotional Experiences in Walt Disney World (WDWRadio.com/514)
3. Top Ten Underrated Attractions in Walt Disney World (WDWRadio.com/378)
4. Top Ten Views in Walt Disney World (WDWRadio.com/455)
5. Top Ten Resorts in Walt Disney World (WDWRadio.com/577)
6. Top Ten Emotional Experiences in Walt Disney World (WDWRadio.com/514)
7. Top Ten Reasons To Go To Walt Disney World Solo (WDWRadio.com/453)
8. Top Ten Things in Walt Disney World Everyone Needs To Do at Least Once (WDWRadio.com/450)
9. Top Ten Buildings in Walt Disney World (WDWRadio.com/522)
10. Top Ten Things You Don't Have To Wait In Line For (WDWRadio.com/509)

Live Dining Reviews

- The Boathouse in Disney Springs (WDWRadio.com/448)
- The Best Theme Park Restaurant in Walt Disney World You've Probably Never Tried (WDWRadio.com/365)
- Jock Lindsey's Hangar Bar (WDWRadio.com/428)
- Afternoon Tea at Disney's Grand Floridian (WDWRadio.com/435)
- Nomad Lounge at Disney's Animal Kingdom (WDWRadio.com/510)

Other Episodes

- Moving to Disney (Part 1) and (Part 2) (WDWRadio.com/532 and WDWRadio.com/533)
- 10 Things You Didn't Know About Walt Disney (WDWRadio.com/501)
- History of Walt Disney's Carousel of Progress (WDWRadio.com/136)
- DSI: Disney Scene Investigation of Main Street, USA (WDWRadio.com/197)
- History of the Walt Disney World Railroad (WDWRadio.com/395)

To listen to these and catch every new, weekly episode of WDW Radio, subscribe (it's FREE!) in Apple Podcasts at WDWRadio.com/Podcast

Visit WDWRadio.com

For even more interviews, reviews, Top Tens, LIVE video, blog posts, videos, online and live events and so much more, please visit WDWRadio.com.

There you will find Disney, Marvel, and Star Wars news, Walt Disney World vacation planning, reviews, trivia, history, fun facts, contests, exclusive interviews with Disney Imagineers, executives, celebrities and more!

The unofficial "Walt Disney World Information Station," WDW Radio has been named Best Travel Podcast for nine consecutive years, and is also home to Lou's books, Audio Tours of Walt Disney World and much more!

Helpful Posts from the WDW Radio Blog (WDWRadio.com/Blog)

- Walt Disney World History 101 — "How to buy 27,000 acres of land and have no one notice"
- Practically Perfect Disney Techniques: Disney Themed Fonts 101
- The Top 10 Walt Disney World Parade Soundtracks
- Top 12 Best Walt Disney World Character Greetings — PART 1
- 100 Things to Do at Walt Disney World Before You Die
- 5 Things You Should Always Pack for Walt Disney World
- Practically Perfect Disney Crafting: DIY MagicBand Decor

Some of Our Favorite WDW Radio Videos (WDWRadio.com/Videos)

- Disney in a Minute — 20,000 Leagues Reference
- Live Show from the WDW Radio Cruise on the Disney Dream with Disney Legend Richard Sherman
- Five Snacks under $5 Epcot
- Disney Artist Robert Olszewski Interview
- Running Team And Make A Wish Meet-up

Watch, chat, call-in and more LIVE each week!

WDWRadioLIVE.com — Watch, chat and call-in Wednesdays 7:30pm ET for Disney, Marvel, and Star Wars news and updates, Top Five LIVE, contests, your calls and questions, and more!

Connect and Join The Community

Be part of the fun, welcoming, friendly community and conversation by joining our WDW Radio Box People group on Facebook at WDWRadio.com/Community.

There are other ways to connect, including:

- WDWRadio.com/Podcasts — Show notes, links and photos
- 407-900-9391 — Call the voicemail with a question, comment or "Hello!" from the parks
- WDWRadio.com/Events — Upcoming WDW Radio Disney meets, On the Road events, cruises, and more!

Let's Get Social!

- Twitter.com/LouMongello
- WDWRadio.com/Community
- Instagram.com/LouMongello
- Facebook.com/WDWRadio
- YouTube.com/WDWRadio
- Pinterest.com/LouMongello
- LinkedIn.com/in/LouMongello

Other Books, Audio Tours, Shirts, and more

- The Walt Disney World Trivia Books, Volume I and II
- 102 Ways to Save Money For and At Walt Disney World (WDWRadio.com/102Ways)
- 102 Things To Do at Walt Disney World at Least Once (FREE! — WDWRadio.com/Subscribe)
- Audio Walking Tours of Magic Kingdom in Walt Disney World (WDWRadio.com/AudioTours)
- WDW Radio logo gear, Disney, Marvel, and Star Wars shirts, mugs, stickers, and magnets (WDWRadio.com/shirts)

Get our FREE Newsletter delivered to your inbox!

Subscribe to our free, weekly email newsletter, and get the latest Disney information, news, exclusive content, special offers, exclusive info, and much more!

By signing up for the FREE WDW Radio newsletter, you get:

- Updates on the latest WDW Radio podcasts and blog posts
- Exclusive Contests
- Notice of upcoming events and live broadcasts
- Disney, Marvel, and Star Wars news
- Community updates, and much more!

The newsletter is completely FREE and we will never, EVER share or sell your email address or information.

Don't miss out on anything, and get a little bit of Disney magic delivered to you wherever you are!

Plus, when you subscribe, you will receive a FREE copy of my book, **102 Things to Do In Walt Disney World At Least Once!**

I have put together a guide of 102 activities or experiences which are relatively "Easy," "Medium," or "Hard" to do, but all of them are fun (and often quite delicious!)

Subscribe at WDWRadio.com/Subscribe

317

GET EVEN MORE!

Join the the WDW Radio Nation

WDWRadioNATION.com — Join the WDW Radio NATION to get monthly rewards, and help support the show.

Thanks to you, for more than 16 years, my goal has been to inform, entertain and invite to you join me virtually around the table as we simply discuss the things about Walt Disney World that make us happy through the WDW Radio Disney podcast, and other free content on the WDW Radio site, blog, videos, meets and more.

The friendship you have extended to me is incredible, and I want to say thank you, and share even more with you, my friends, and members of the new WDW Radio Nation.

You can now also help support the show by contributing however much you would like, and in return, I will bring you even more content, access, special events, opportunities, and products! Most of the content and items created for the WDW Radio Nation will NOT be available for sale to the general public *(e.g. the Scavenger Hunts, Magic Band covers, logo gear, etc.)*

You can set any amount you want, and change or cancel your pledge at any time. Think of it as a way for you to help show your support for WDW Radio. Also, a portion of the proceeds of your contributions will go to the Dream Team Project to benefit the Make-A-Wish Foundation of America. Together, we have raised more than $300,000.00 to send children with life-threatening illnesses to Walt Disney World.

Thanks to YOU, WDW Radio has changed my life in profound ways I never could have imagined when I started. I want to continue to share my love of Disney with you, and give you even more. You have inspired me in so many ways, and I only hope that what I have been able to offer to you for the past decade has brought you some happiness as well.

THANK YOU!!!

Lou Mongello

Let Me Help YOU!

Let me help you turn what you love into what you do with one-on-one mentoring, mastermind groups, and my Momentum Retreat and Momentum Weekend Workshop in Walt Disney World. I can also speak at your event, conference, business, or school. To learn more, visit LouMongello.com

I left my career as an attorney to pursue my passion, move with my family to Florida, and share my love for Disney with others through my podcast, books, audio tours, live video, social media, events, and community, allowing me to be recognized as one a leading authority on Disney, social and new media.

As a featured keynote speaker, coach, and consultant, I share with businesses, associations and schools the magic of Disney and/or the power of new and social media, entrepreneurship, brand-building, storytelling, podcasting, live video, and more.

More importantly, I want to help YOU turn your passion into your profession, and what you LOVE into what you DO.

I provide mentoring, consulting, and workshops to those looking to build their business and brand. There are many ways we can work together, including:

- **Coaching and Mentoring —**
Learn more at <u>LouMongello.com/Coaching</u>
    - One-on-One Coaching — With 1:1 mentoring, Lou works with you to create and execute ideas and solutions that are unique to you and your business. He specializes in content creation, marketing, podcasting, building a brand, social media, community, monetization, and more.
    - Mastermind Group — "The Hub" group coaching program (limited to 6 members) includes weekly live video group calls, 1:1 video coaching calls, accountability partner, online community, unlimited email support, resource sharing, and more.
- **Momentum Retreat —**
Learn more at <u>LouMongello.com/Retreat</u>
    - In this weekend-long, small mastermind event, 10 like-minded entrepreneurs will get together in a luxury vacation home in Orlando for a three-day Mastermind Retreat. Together, we will strategize, prioritize, and execute, as the retreat will give you not just a supportive environment in which to discuss your dreams (big and small), but will help you get "unstuck" and keep moving forward with confidence and more clarity. Join us for a weekend filled with business brainstorming and 1:1 coaching in a small, supportive group setting! To ensure you focus only on you and the event, I'll take care of all the details, including your room, meals, and materials!

- **Momentum Weekend Workshop —**
  Learn more at LouMongello.com/Momentum
  - Built on the 3 pillars of inspiration, education, and community, the Momentum Weekend Workshop is unlike any other conference created for entrepreneurs. Limited to just 50 incredible entrepreneurs, the Momentum Weekend Workshop is a two-day event (with optional Mastermind Monday) where a small group of dedicated, like-minded entrepreneurs come together in an intimate setting to learn, share, discuss, troubleshoot, and make REAL changes to their lives and businesses. Through collective brainstorming, sharing, education, accountability and ongoing support, there is opportunity for real growth and results. Whether you are a content creator, have a product, or brick-and-mortar business, Momentum will help you over the weekend and with ongoing support and accountability.

- 5 Reasons Why You Need to Attend Momentum:
    I. You will LEARN from speakers, peers, and attendees to improve your efforts and make real, positive change.
    II. You'll make CONNECTIONS with like-minded entrepreneurs, and speakers who are there to help you.
    III. You'll be INSPIRED by speakers who have "walked the walk," not only in an informal, conversational, and relatable way, but will work with you in small groups and one-on-one.
    IV. You will CREATE RELATIONSHIPS and network with other entrepreneurs, and stay connected and accountable even after the conference is over.
    V. You'll have FUN: Not only is the event conducted in a relaxed environment, but did I mention that it's also in Walt Disney World?!? Disney Springs is right next door, and the fun (and food) continues even after the day's sessions are over!

- **Speaking** — Learn more at LouMongello.com/Speaking
  - I am a passionate, motivational keynote speaker who delivers customized presentations tailored to your specific needs and audience at conferences, corporate events, and schools. Through my engaging, thought-provoking, and entertaining presentations, I provide real-world, actionable content and strategies for entrepreneurs, business owners, executives, employees, and students alike. Topics can be specifically crafted for your industry and company. Some examples include:

- ENTREPRENEURS & BUSINESSES
    I. The Disney Difference: Achieving The Ultimate Customer Experience
    II. Leadership Lessons Learned from Walt Disney
    III. What Your Business Can Learn and Implement from the Disney Parks

- PODCASTING, SOCIAL MEDIA, & TECHNOLOGY
    I. Social Media for Your Business
    II. Building Your Brand with LIVE Video
    III. The Power of Community: Building and Nurturing You Community, Online and Offline

- SCHOOLS, STUDENTS, AND FACULTY — I will bring the "Disney magic" onto your campus with engaging and entertaining assembly programs for students and teachers for your: new student orientation, career day, retreats, assemblies, and faculty in-service days. I can also help teach or speak to your class or assembly virtually! Topics include:

    I. If You Can Dream It, You Can Do It!
    II. Life-Lessons Learned from Walt Disney
    III. Smart Social Media Tips for Students

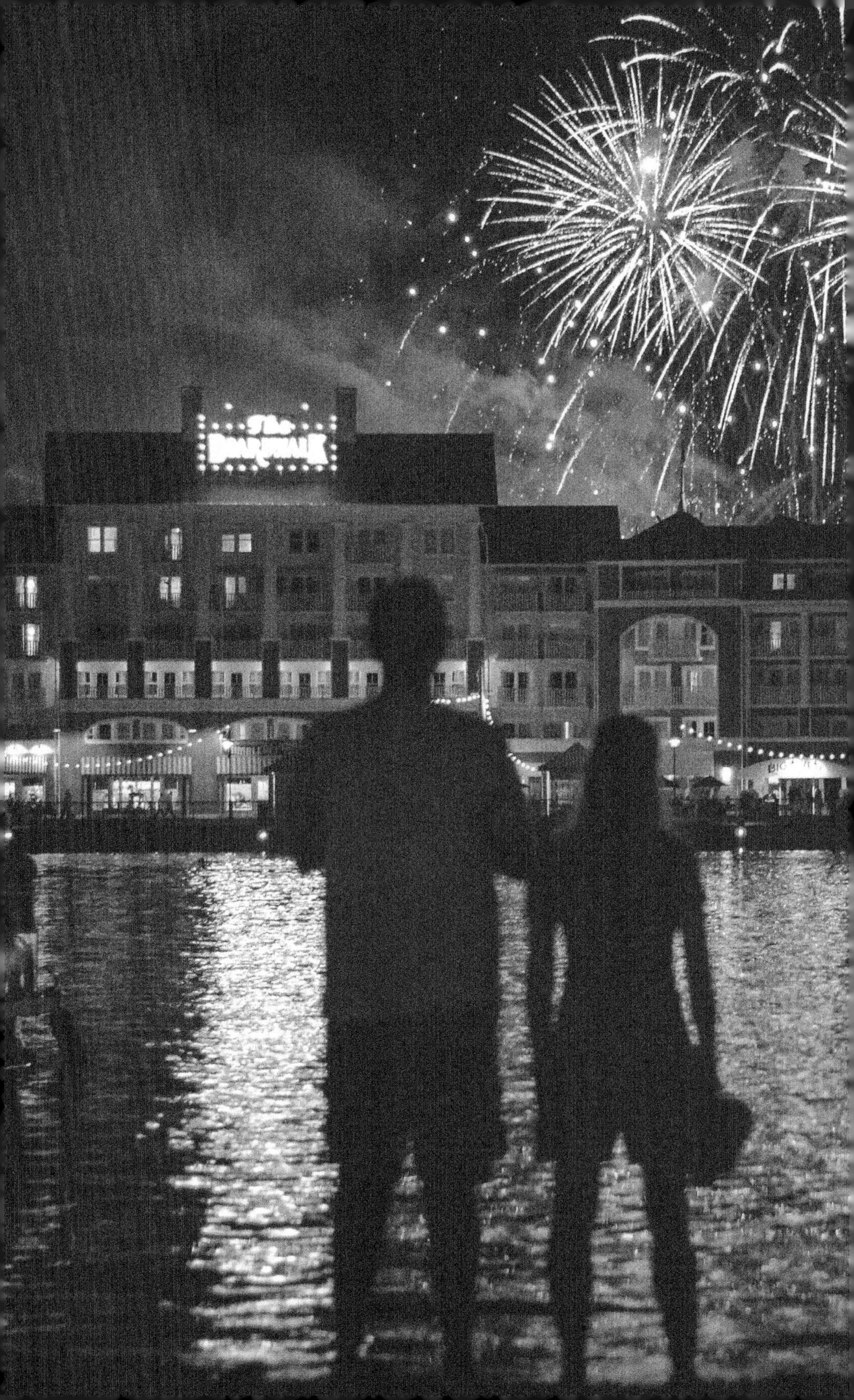
The
BOARDWALK

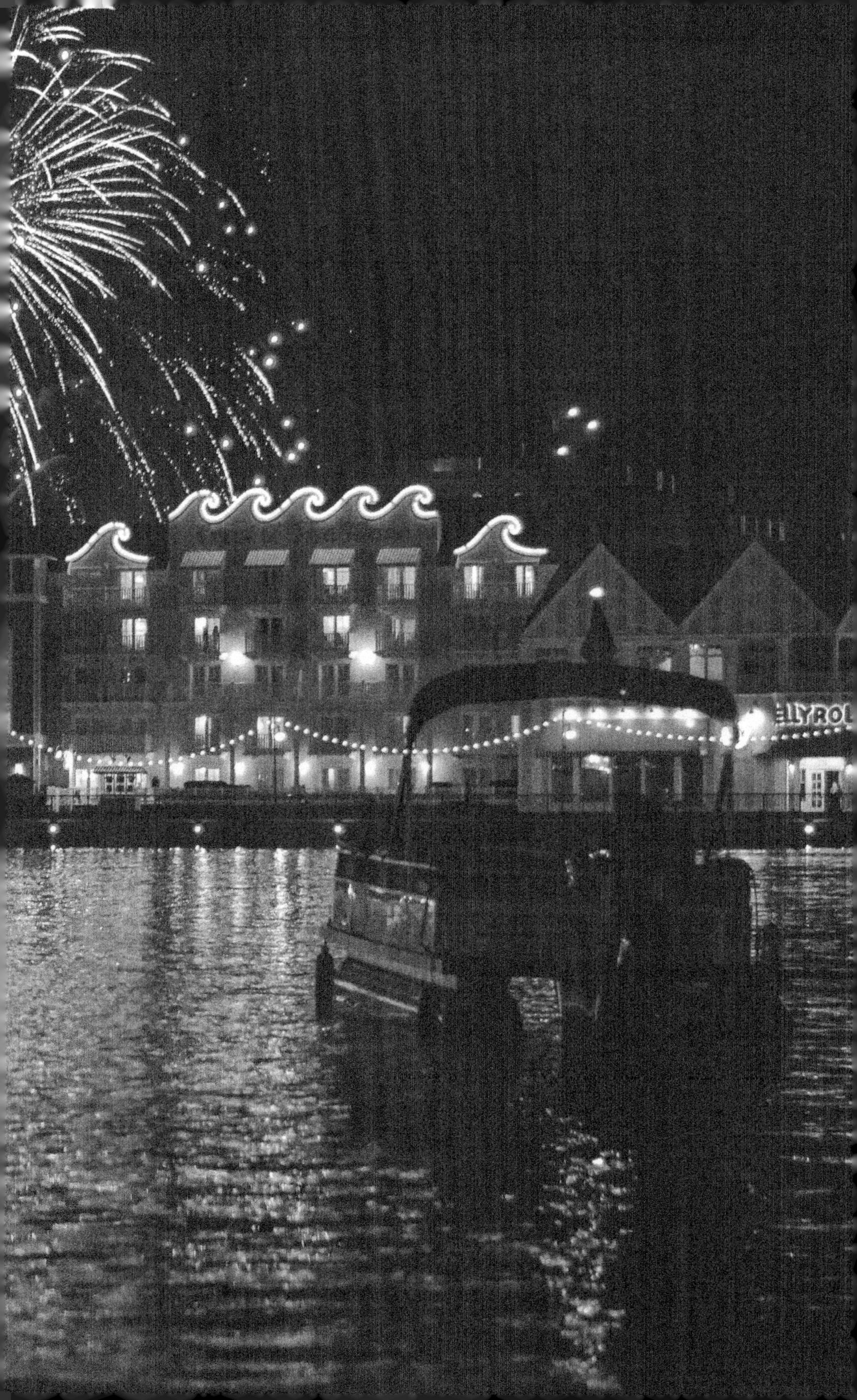

Printed in Great Britain
by Amazon